MW01484439

SAVING
YELLOWSTONE

To Sheryl —
For all your help on
all my projects!

Bob Hartley

Other Books by Robert E. Hartley

Charles H. Percy: A Political Perspective (1975)

Big Jim Thompson of Illinois (1979)

Paul Powell of Illinois: A Lifelong Democrat (1999)

Lewis and Clark in the Illinois Country: The Little-Told Story (2002)

An Uncertain Tradition: U.S. Senators from Illinois, 1818-2003, with David Kenney (2003)

Death Underground: The Centralia and West Frankfort Mine Disasters, with David Kenney (2006)

SAVING YELLOWSTONE

THE PRESIDENT ARTHUR
EXPEDITION OF 1883

ROBERT E. HARTLEY

Copyright © 2007 by Robert E. Hartley.

Library of Congress Control Number: 2007902717
ISBN: Hardcover   978-1-4257-7121-8
Softcover   978-1-4257-7117-1

Cover design by A. J. Hartley
Inside jacket photo by Pat C. Hartley

Cover: Chromolithograph of *The Castle Geyser, Upper Geyser Basin, Yellowstone National Park, 1875.* Artist: Thomas Moran (1837-1926); Louis Prang, publisher. Buffalo Bill Historical Center, Cody, Wyoming. Gift of Clara S. Peck. 18.71.3.

Map by David M. Carttar. Identification of campsites by F. Jay Haynes using landscape map prepared by the Office of Chief Engineer, Military Division of Missouri, © 1881.

Material reprinted by permission of the University of Nebraska Press:

Yellowstone and the Great West: Journals, Letters, and Images from the 1871 Hayden Expedition, edited by Marlene Deahl Merrill, © 1999.
The Discovery of Yellowstone Park: Journal of the Washburn Expedition to the Yellowstone and Firehole Rivers in the Year 1870, by Nathaniel Pitt Langford.
Journal of a Trapper: A Hunter's Rambles Among the Wilds of the Rocky Mountains, by Osborne Russell and edited by Aubrey Haines.
American Indian Leaders: Studies in Diversity, edited by R. David Edmunds, © 1980.

All rights reserved. No part of this book may be reproduced or transmitted in any form or by any means, electronic or mechanical, including photocopying, recording, or by any information storage and retrieval system, without permission in writing from the copyright owner.

This book was printed in the United States of America.

To order additional copies of this book, contact:
Sniktau Publications
2404 W. 107th Drive
Westminster, CO 80234-3160
Sniktau@aol.com
http://www.savingyellowstone.com

Xlibris Corporation
1-888-795-4274
www.Xlibris.com
Orders@Xlibris.com
37023

DEDICATION

To the memory of Arwin Grant

For Mary, partner for 50-plus years

Contents

Illustrations

Preface

MY FRIEND AND BEST MAN AT OUR WEDDING, ARWIN Grant, a longtime geography teacher and Orvis guide in Jackson Hole country, invited me to wet a line on selected nearby waters in August 1995.

Our first day's journey started from U.S. 26-89-191 outside of Jackson. We left the highway, heading east on blacktop that followed the Gros Ventre River and eventually became a dirt road on the north bank. The farther east we went, the more beautiful the river scenery and ranchland. Periodically, we turned to look westward at the looming Teton Mountains.

We finally stopped where creeks form headwaters of the Gros Ventre, looking ahead at slopes of the Wind River mountain range. As we worked the streams for cutthroat trout, Arwin began telling me about the August 1883 expedition to Yellowstone National Park by President Chester A. Arthur and his few friends. He described how they came over the mountain crest, down along the river to its confluence with the Snake River and continued on to the park. That was my introduction to the historic journey overland from Green River Station, Wyoming, through Jackson Hole and Yellowstone Park, and, finally, to a rail line in Montana.

A sometime student of the presidency, I was intrigued by a new story. That began my quest to gather information about a journey that is recognized in history books but is treated lightly. The only published version I could find was an article in a Montana history magazine. That gave me a start; and thanks to generous assistance from the Wyoming Historical Society, I accumulated published accounts of the expedition and launched a research quest that lasts to this day, 125 years or more after the event. Along the way, I wrote and read a history paper about the Arthur expedition at a symposium and had an expanded version published in a journal devoted to interests of geographers.

As the years passed, my wife and I returned to the Gros Ventre to drink in the sights, enhanced by an increased appreciation for the Arthur expedition as a stroke of history in a once distant and wild region. The more one understands the journey and knows the river, the more incredible the accomplishment becomes. Views of the Teton Range along the Gros Ventre are as memorable today as described by the expedition's reporter.

The death of Arwin Grant on July 10, 2001, tragic and premature as it was, only whetted my appetite for additional information about our shared interest. Further research and reading gradually placed my fascination with the expedition in a larger context of Yellowstone National Park's development.

When viewed for its own value, the 1883 trip offers much to digest. Arthur was the first president in office to visit the park and was the only president in American history to make a trip largely on horseback across Wyoming. One controversy that recurred throughout the journey was a ban on newspaper reporters by order of President Arthur. The consequences were predictable and lamentable. Such an order, of course, would be unthinkable today and was controversial then.

Having a military officer send daily "news" dispatches to the Associated Press (AP), as was done, is simply beyond belief for us. A president so far out of touch that he could be reached in case of emergency only by couriers on horseback from a distant telegraph office is another oddity. There is no way to compare and comprehend communications between 1883 and the twenty-first century. The fact that Arthur had no vice president in Washington to mind matters in his absence (Arthur became president when James Garfield was assassinated) makes the trip almost unimaginable by modern standards.

The story presented in these pages looks at the excursion as part of a full picture, not as a stand-alone event. The journey takes on meaning beyond curiosity when viewed as the centerpiece of a valiant effort to save Yellowstone National Park from neglect and excessive commercial development. Two of the main figures in that contest from 1882 to 1886, Gen. Philip H. Sheridan and Sen. George G. Vest, were involved in the Arthur expedition and were responsible in large part for Arthur making the trip. When surrounded by events occurring in Washington and in the park, the Arthur expedition becomes pivotal in understanding the campaign to elevate awareness of the park's splendors in the public mind and to bring pressure on public officials entrusted with the park's future.

The courageous efforts of Sheridan, Vest, and others, such as scientist and conservationist George Bird Grinnell, are explored in detail with much of the account taken from available correspondence and documents. As the quest to secure the park unfolds, there is a sense of high expectation and drama with no shortage of noble intent, scoundrels, and opportunists. If a novel were written, readers might clearly anticipate defined heroes and a crescendo climax. However, as the story plays out, reality is rarely as predictable as fiction.

The history of Yellowstone National Park has been written in many versions since the park was established in 1872. This book is not an attempt to revise history or repeat it in any major way. The work of past and current historians is evident and fully attributed in this snapshot account of park lore. The Arthur expedition is offered in detail and perspective not presented before and takes on meaning as more than a vacation trip to restore the president's health. Primarily, it serves to highlight the individual and concerted efforts to save the park.

Each book effort, I learn, carries with it an obligation and desire to mention those who helped with the project. It bears repeating that each book by this author is a joint effort, and I fully acknowledge my dependence.

I am especially indebted to Lee H. Whittlesey, Yellowstone National Park historian and author, for his comments on the manuscript and his encouragement. His positive reaction to the narrative offers readers assurance that this book adds appreciably to the literature of park history.

I pressed into service my good friend and coauthor on two books, retired professor David Kenney. He read the manuscript and offered advice and counsel. Others who read the draft included D. G. Schumacher and David Wetzel, a retired, longtime editor of publications for the Colorado Historical Society and frequent visitor to the area covered by the story. Mary Hartley always gets first crack at a manuscript and has considerable influence on the final product. I appreciate an important contribution from my friend Jerry Wallace, a former National Archives employee. Files of the archives and collections from the Library of Congress were critical elements. There is no adequate way to express appreciation for the extensive files and collections on Western history at the Denver Public Library. I am fortunate to live a short drive's distance from that institution.

Friends at the Abraham Lincoln Presidential Library and Museum in Springfield, Illinois, including the indispensable Cheryl Schnirring, provided access to the remarkable collection of photographs from the Arthur expedition taken by F. Jay Haynes, who, for many years, was the park's official photographer. The portfolio also contains reproduction of the precise reports sent to the Associated Press from the expedition. Only a few of the dozen portfolios published in 1883 are known to exist today. One belonged to Robert Todd Lincoln, a traveler on the Arthur expedition, and is now part of his collection at the library. Another is on file at the Library of Congress, where Kenneth Johnson provided assistance in access to Haynes's photographs. The Library of Congress also provided selections from the papers of Philip Sheridan. Adding to the flavor of the visual story are images made available by Bridgette Guild of the National Park Service at Yellowstone National Park.

Major contributions to this book came from A. J. Hartley, who did the cover design, and David Carttar, who produced the map that presents a reader-friendly view of the route followed by the expedition. This is my second book partnership with Xlibris Corporation, whose Cheryl Gratz helped keep the production on schedule.

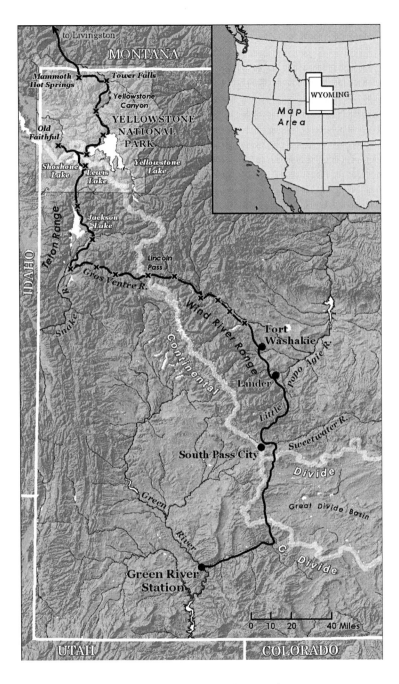

Overland route of 1883 Arthur expedition
based on 1881 map. X=campsites
identified by F. Jay Haynes.
Map by David M. Carttar

Introduction

A National Park Emerges, 1807-1880

SUPPORTERS AND DREAMERS ALIKE IMAGINED THE newly established Yellowstone National Park in 1872 as an idyllic wonderland, easily preserved and maintained—exploited too—for future generations. Despite their good intentions, the dream failed so miserably that the park's future was in doubt a decade later. The story of unfulfilled promise and neglect is a prelude to the actions of people who rose to the challenge of saving one of the truly unique locations on earth.

Until the first written reports of expeditions to the Upper Yellowstone River country and the appearance of nearby geyser fields in 1870, awareness of the region rested mostly on myth and word of mouth. Since those earliest accounts that led to a law establishing the park, Yellowstone history has continued to evolve into the twenty-first century. Primarily, historians have labored to separate fact from fiction about mysteries of the park, natural and human.

The Yellowstone story, until the end of civilian control in 1886, had a cast of characters that would warm the heart of a movie producer: an early visitor whose journeys are still shrouded in mystery; a quaint rustic guide and mountain man whose ramblings turned out to be accurate; opportunists who, from the beginning, could see the potential for profits; scientists hoping to make their reputation on surveys of the park; early visitors, artists, and photographers whose renditions of the wonderland made everyone swoon; a short-sighted congress; and visionaries who warned of a park in danger.

The role of each person and party helps answer the question: why did Yellowstone National Park nearly come to an inglorious end?

Native people knew the Yellowstone region well before the first white people "discovered" its freakish wonders and told others of them. John Colter, a Lewis and Clark expedition member and early trapper in the area that now includes Montana and Wyoming, is considered the first white person to experience the magic of the Upper Yellowstone River, although he wrote nothing about it and his story remains mostly unproven.[1] Colter's travels on the trails and waters date to the period immediately after

1806 when he left the Corps of Discovery on the Missouri River in Dakota country. He traveled extensively through the Yellowstone region and later provided information about it to William Clark, who was working on publication of the expedition's journals. Lewis and Clark skirted the park area on their epic journey and made no mention of it in the original journals.[2]

Tales of Yellowstone's curiosities increased from the early handful of trappers and mountain men who roamed the rivers and streams of Idaho, Wyoming, and Montana from the 1820s to 1840s in search of beaver skins. A few of the journals kept by trappers mentioned travels along the Snake and Yellowstone rivers and their tributaries, but the journals were not published until many years later. Historians believe some people visited the region every year after 1826.[3] As those wanderers and hunters gathered at rendezvous to swap beaver skins and goods, celebrate with Indians, and exchange wild tales of personal adventures, the stories grew in number and fanciful details. Eventually, word reached population centers and produced inevitable speculation and proposed expeditions. By the 1850s and 1860s, much of the United States had been explored; but the Upper Yellowstone River valley, the park known today, was a blank spot on the map and was still a mystery.

Organized efforts to probe the region began in 1860 with a military excursion to explore the West "from the Yellowstone to the south pass," headed by Capt. William F. Raynolds, a thirty-nine-year-old topographical engineer.[4] Raynolds's party included a link to the past of the park. Jim Bridger—scout, mountain man, and adventurer—served as guide.

Raynolds failed to make his way into the land of geysers, rivers, and canyons due to many problems, some of his own making. In his report, Raynolds explained the failure, "Bridger had said at the outset that this would be impossible . . . [and] remarked triumphantly and forcibly to me upon reaching this spot, 'I told you you could not go through. A bird can't fly over that without taking a supply of grub along.' I had no reply to offer, and mentally conceded the accuracy of the information of 'the old man of the mountains.'"[5]

Bridger was the source of many stories branded as rumors, and it is ironic that he could not direct Raynolds to places the guide had visited many times before. A verification of the wonders by Raynolds would have lifted Bridger's reputation from campfire storyteller to sage. As it was, Bridger could offer no written descriptions of what he saw or experienced because he was illiterate.

Proximity to the park region gave residents of Montana frequent opportunities to hear the rumors and speculate about the partially explained phenomena. As a result, explorations of the park in 1869 and 1870 resulted from efforts by Montanans. The first occurred in 1869 when three residents of the territory—David E. Folsom, Charles W. Cook, and William Peterson—decided to explore the Yellowstone region. Folsom, Cook, and Peterson worked for the same company in Diamond City, Montana Territory.[6] Originally, they planned to participate in a larger expedition, but prospective participants shied away after reports of Indian raids. So, beginning on September 6, the three went by themselves up the Yellowstone and Lamar rivers to the falls and the lake, west over the divide into the geyser basins, and back into Montana. Folsom proved prescient when he expressed thanks to have seen Yellowstone Lake "before its primeval solitude [would] be broken by the crowds of pleasure seekers which at no distant day will throng its shores."[7]

Cook and Folsom attempted to interest mass-circulation publications of the day in their account of the adventure but failed. The *Western Monthly* of Chicago, with a circulation of just nine thousand, published an abbreviated version of an article written by Folsom and Cook. It was the first published account of the Yellowstone wonderland. Writing of the journey, historian Aubrey L. Haines said, "The contributions of the Folsom party of 1869 to their definitive exploration of the Yellowstone region are these: a descriptive magazine article, a greatly improved map, a suggestion for reservation in the public interest, and the encouragement of the Washburn party of explorers."[8]

The following year, Montanans again stepped forward to continue exploration of the upper Yellowstone region. The expedition headed by Gen. Henry D. Washburn, Montana Territory surveyor general, provided primary impetus for a law establishing Yellowstone National Park and became history's most honored and applauded park exploration.[9] Accounts by members of the expedition provided enticing word descriptions of thermal explosions, a deep colorful canyon, a sprawling lake, pristine rivers, and countless species of game.

Thirty-eight-year-old Washburn, a commander during the Civil War, was brevetted—a temporary promotion usually based on valor—a major general at war's end and later served two terms as congressman from an Indiana district. He was appointed to the surveyor's position in Montana by his military and civilian commander, President Ulysses S. Grant. Given his experience, position, and location in Montana, he seemed the perfect man to lead the expedition. It was, however, the nonmilitary Nathaniel Pitt Langford, living in Helena, Montana, who had the connections to make the trip possible.

The idea of going south out of Montana to test the accuracy of rumors about natural wonders had occurred to Langford as early as 1866, and he had considered trips in 1867 and 1868 until Indian uprisings dampened enthusiasm.[10] An excursion received further encouragement in May 1870 when Lt. Gen. Philip H. Sheridan visited in Montana on a tour of military facilities. He talked with Cook, Folsom, and Peterson and promised a military escort if another trip was undertaken.[11]

Following his own conversations with Folsom, Cook, and Peterson, Langford met on June 4 near Philadelphia with Jay Cooke, financier and investor in the Northern Pacific Railroad (NP) who was looking to development of the northwest for future railroad riches.[12] Langford impressed Cooke with accounts of the 1869 Cook-Folsom-Peterson journey, and almost immediately, Cooke recognized the commercial potential for Northern Pacific by exploiting features of Yellowstone Country. It marked the beginning of the railroad's involvement in commercial development of the park that stretched far into the future.

With Cooke's financial pledge in his pocket, Langford and Washburn drew final plans by August 1. Gen. Winfield Scott Hancock followed through on Sheridan's promise;

and an armed military escort commanded by Lt. Gustavus Cheyney Doane, including four enlisted men, joined the expedition.[13] Doane had forcefully lobbied to accompany the party, believing in the threat of confrontations with Indians. He also was fascinated with the exploratory prospect.

On August 17, the assembled party that included nine civilians and the Doane escort departed from Washburn's office for the upper Yellowstone Valley. They took enough supplies for thirty days although expecting to be home sooner. On September 27, Langford returned to Helena, exhausted but elated at what he had seen and experienced. Others in the party felt the same way. Six wrote accounts of the journey, including a twenty-five thousand-word report by Lieutenant Doane.[14] Langford wrote articles that appeared in popular publications and undertook an extensive lecture tour—Montana, Philadelphia, Washington, and New York—during which he described the wonders of Yellowstone in elaborate detail and promoted the interests of the Northern Pacific Railroad.

Langford, later named first superintendent of the park, repaid Cooke many times over by connecting the splendors of Yellowstone with the railroad. For example, in an article written for *Scribner's* in June 1871, Langford said, "By means of the Northern Pacific Railroad, which will doubtless be completed within the next three years, the traveler will be able to make the trip to Montana from the Atlantic seaboard in three days, and thousands of tourists will be attracted to both Montana and Wyoming in order to behold with their own eyes the wonders here described."[15]

Langford's publicity effort caught the attention of Ferdinand V. Hayden, head of the U.S. Geological and Geographical Survey of the Territories and a Civil War veteran. In January 1871, he attended one of Langford's lectures in Washington and immediately began to develop a scientific survey for later in the year.[16] For funding, he went to work on personal connections in Congress, including Rep. James G. Blaine, speaker of the House, and Rep. Henry C. Dawes of Massachusetts. In the background again were Cooke and the Northern Pacific Railroad, who had sponsored Langford's lecture tour. The effort resulted in an appropriation by March 1871 of $40,000 for Hayden, who put together a forty-man party of scientists, artists, and photographers.[17] Among the latter were photographer William Henry Jackson and artist Thomas Moran, whose patron, Cooke, saw that he accompanied the expedition.

Hayden's survey projected him into the primary role for scientific study of the Yellowstone Valley and nearby mountain regions. He made return visits in 1872, 1877, and 1878. The importance of the first survey is that the government financed it. The decision also placed the role of scientific study in the hands of the U.S. Geological and Geographical Survey and not in the hands of the army as General Sheridan would have preferred. Instead, the Hayden decision forced Sheridan into a defensive position to maintain an army-exploration presence in Yellowstone by sending small military reconnaissances.

Hayden assembled his team at Ogden, Utah, and prepared to head north by horseback through western Idaho to Montana. At Ogden, he learned in a telegram from Capt. John Barlow that Sheridan had ordered a small army escort commanded by the chief engineer of the U.S. Army's Division of the Missouri—including the topographer, photographer, and draftsman, Capt. David Heap.[18] The military group joined Hayden at Fort Ellis, bringing the total number in the party to eighty-three.[19]

While it may appear that Sheridan assigned the escort primarily to guard against Indian attack (the West was under siege in 1870 with troops and Indians in constant conflict), he had other intentions. Sheridan wanted Barlow and Heap to keep a watch on Hayden's work and look for opportunities to conduct independent scientific study that did not duplicate or compete with Hayden. The two parties worked together on the same or nearby routes most of the way.

Hayden's survey was eventful from scientific and strategic standpoints. In his book *The Yellowstone National Park*, Hiram Chittenden, who supervised the building of much of the park's road system, described one of the major discoveries by Hayden: "At the very outset of their journey they branched off from the Washburn route at the mouth of the Gardiner River, and, by ascending this stream, discovered the wonderful formations now known as Mammoth Hot Springs."[20] From that point, they traveled east to the Yellowstone River, south along the west shore to Mount Washburn, to the canyon and falls, and to the northwest corner of the lake. They turned due west to the Lower Geyser Basin, to the Upper Geyser Basin, and back eastward to the West Thumb of the lake. As described by Hayden, "The Lake lay before us, a vast sheet of quiet water, of a most delicate ultramarine hue, one of the most beautiful scenes I have ever beheld."[21] The party followed the southern shore of the lake and then north to the Lamar River, then called the east fork of the Yellowstone, and its confluence with the Yellowstone. They returned to Mammoth Hot Springs and left the park.

True to his commander's wishes, Barlow occasionally separated from the Hayden party to make his own discoveries. Those included Heart Lake and Fairy Falls. He named a mountain near the lake for General Sheridan. The map of the entire region by Barlow and Heap was the most accurate to date. A special supplement containing portions of Barlow's report appeared in Chicago's *Evening Journal* on January 13, 1872, and the final report was published as a Senate document in the spring.

Returning to Washington late in the summer, Hayden began participation in a new venture proposed by Northern Pacific Railroad interests as outlined in a letter to Hayden from A. B. Nettleton, an associate of Jay Cooke's. It said in part, "Judge Kelley [William D. "Pig Iron" Kelley, of Philadelphia] has made a suggestion which strikes me as being an excellent one, viz.: Let Congress pass a bill reserving the Great Geyser Basin as a public park forever—just as it has reserved that far inferior wonder the Yosemite valley and big trees. If you approve this would such a recommendation be appropriate in your official report?"[22] Hayden agreed to the suggestion, prompting Cooke to begin a vigorous campaign for a law.

Who originated the idea of a national park has been debated for decades, with any number of claims made. Historian Haines wrote that the first suggestions for a park surfaced in 1865, 1869, and 1870—before people started taking credit for the idea. Hayden announced that he had the idea first, although no one took him seriously.

Langford, in his journal, attempted to credit journalist Cornelius Hedges, a companion on the Washburn expedition. According to the author, members of the party sat around a campfire the evening of September 19, 1870, discussing how the region, or parts of it, might be preserved. After several suggestions for individual purchases of land in the public domain that included the wonders they had just seen, Hedges spoke. Langford wrote, "Mr. Hedges then said that he did not approve of any of these plans—that there ought to be no private ownership of any portion of that region, but that the whole of it ought to be set apart as a great National Park, and that each one of us ought to make an effort to have this accomplished." Historians who studied the Langford version and other claims have concluded that the Hedges story is a myth. In other words, it is not true. Regardless of that judgment, National Park Service officials prefer to leave the story in official accounts because it is a part of Yellowstone lore.[23]

However the idea evolved, members of Congress supported it, having been convinced by Hayden with photographs by Jackson and drawings by Moran to introduce a bill for Yellowstone National Park in December 1871. Montana Delegate to Congress William H. Clagett offered the bill in the House, and Samuel Clarke Pomeroy of Kansas submitted the same bill in the Senate.[24] A wave of promotion and hustle for passage began. Hayden sent copies of Jackson's most dramatic photos and Moran's watercolors to each member of Congress and set up exhibits of specimens at the Capitol Rotunda and Smithsonian Institution. He recruited Dawes to guide the bill in the House and had four hundred copies of Langford's *Scribner's* articles printed and distributed in Congress.[25]

In almost record time for Congress, the bills moved through each chamber and were approved. The measure passed the Senate on January 30, 1872, and in the House on February 27 by a vote of 115 to 65, with sixty not voting. On March 1, President Grant signed the bill.[26] The United States had its first national park, even if government officials were unsure what that meant or how to make it succeed.

As approved, it read,

> Be it enacted by the Senate and House of Representatives of the United States of America in Congress assembled, That the tract of land in the Territories of Montana and Wyoming lying near the headwaters of the Yellowstone River, and described as follows, to wit: commencing at the junction of Gardiner's River with the Yellowstone River, and running east to the meridian passage ten miles to the eastward of the most eastern point of Yellowstone Lake; thence south along said meridian to the parallel of latitude passing ten miles south of the most southern point of Yellowstone lake; thence west along said parallel to the meridian passing fifteen miles west of the most western point of Madison Lake; thence north along said meridian to the latitude of the junction of the Yellowstone; and Gardiner's River; thence east to the place of beginning, is hereby reserved and withdrawn from settlement, occupancy, or sale under the laws of the United States, and dedicated and set apart as a public park of pleasuring-ground for the benefit and enjoyment of the people;

and all persons who shall locate, or settle upon or occupy the same, or any part thereof, except as hereinafter provided, shall be considered trespassers, and removed therefrom.

Sec. 2. That said public park shall be under the exclusive control of the Secretary of the Interior, whose duty it shall be as soon as practicable, to make and publish such rules and regulations as he may deem necessary or proper for the care and management of the same. Such regulations shall provide for the preservation from injury or spoliation of all timber, mineral deposits, natural curiosities, or wonders within said park, and their retention in their natural condition.

The Secretary may, in his discretion, grant leases for building purposes, for terms not exceeding ten years, of small parcels of ground, at such places in said park as shall require the erection of buildings for the accommodation of visitors; all of the proceeds of said leases, and all other revenues that may be derived from any source connected with said park, to be expended under his direction in the management of the same, and the construction of roads and bridle-paths therein. He shall provide against the wanton destruction of the fish and game found within said park, and against their capture or destruction for the purposes of merchandise or profit. He shall also cause all persons trespassing upon the same after passage of this act to be removed therefrom, and generally shall be authorized to take all such measures as shall be necessary or proper to fully carry out the objects and purposes of this act.[27]

The act began a national legacy of national parks and monuments, but the nonspecific language failed to anticipate the issues of administering a park and created a mountain of problems that plagued operations for at least fifteen years. The euphoria of establishing a grand experiment soon passed. In many respects, it was forgotten, along with the park and the promises of promoters.

Official abdication began almost immediately after the act passed. Congress refused to appropriate a dime for administration of the park until it agreed to spend $10,000 in 1878.[28] During those years, Congress did not pay a salary for the park superintendent. As a consequence, the position was mostly honorary and carried no influence in Washington. Until 1883, superintendents lived outside the park and rarely visited there.

Langford, whose efforts contributed greatly to publicizing the park and passage of the law, received his "payment" with appointment as the first of five park superintendents who served into 1886. Without salary or expenses, he needed other full-time employment to earn a living and had little time for park affairs. In 1872, he was appointed as a federal bank examiner for the territories and Pacific Coast states and held the position until April 1877.[29]

As personally committed to Yellowstone National Park as anyone, Langford failed in the role of creator of federal public policy to confront problems and pursue solutions. He returned to the park in 1872 with the second Hayden survey and submitted an annual report, the only one of his tenure. He requested an appropriation of $15,000 for roads, stating that a single amount in one year could be stretched over several, but the recommendation got little attention. When President Rutherford B. Hayes won the presidency in 1876, Langford's time had run out. Hayes appointed Philetus Norris as superintendent.

From 1872 to 1886, six men served as secretary of the interior with full powers and responsibilities by law for protecting and improving the park. Superintendents and secretaries had differing attitudes toward granting leases for park concessions, leading to confusion from the top down. Without consistent policies and regulations or sufficient law enforcement, people mostly did as they pleased in the park.

Meanwhile, the numbers of wild game in the park had diminished dramatically after the Washburn expedition. Poachers had increased their activity, slaughtering thousands of animals and clearing timber as they wished. The steady increase in number of visitors brought more damage to the precious resources.

The promised surge of tourists traveling to the park on rails of the Northern Pacific did not materialize in the early years. The national recession and financial panic of 1873 nearly ended NP's drive westward by cutting its monetary lifeline. During the recession, Cooke's financial business folded, leaving the railroad without cash flow.[30] Later in the decade, the railroad slowly regained its economic standing and found new leadership. It progressed across Minnesota, the Dakotas, and into Montana by the end of the 1870s and was heavily involved in plans for commercial development of the park.

While stagnation appeared to be the descriptive word for the park after passage of the act and Hayden's 1872 survey, Sheridan continued to direct military expeditions to Yellowstone. They often had the stated purpose of tracking hostile Indian activities, but the process of exploration and science also moved forward. The first of these ventures, an expedition led by Capt. William A. Jones in August 1873, had long-term significance in demonstrating that access to the park from the south could be accomplished.[31]

Jones and a party that included experts on botany, geology, entomology, and thermal waters found a passage through the Absaroka mountain range and entered the park due east of the northern shore of Yellowstone Lake and north of today's Sylvan Pass. He wrote in a report about the thrill of seeing the lake after an arduous journey: "Perhaps there was something that moved us in the broad and startling contrast between the dreary deserts, the sage-brush plains, the awful and majestic mountains, and that broad expanse of fresh, hazy and sensuous beauty that looked up so invitingly at us from below; but there was also the proud feeling that we had crossed the 'impassable' mountains."[32]

After touring the park and gathering scientific information, the party returned to the southern portion and located Two Ocean Pass—just beyond the southeast corner of the park where waters formed the Yellowstone and Snake rivers, which made their way to the Atlantic and Pacific oceans. On Jones's path out of the park, an Indian guide named Togwotee showed the party a pass to the Wind River from the Snake River drainage.[33] Today, this route takes travelers on U.S. highways 287 and 26 over Togwotee Pass, in and out of Jackson Hole.

In 1875, two military groups, with contrasting participants and approaches, made summer tours of the park, adding to growing concern over conditions. Secretary of War, Henry Belknap, led a contingent that included four general officers from Washington and Chicago.[34] They were met in the park by a general, a colonel, and Lieutenant Doane of the Washburn expedition. The objective of the fifty-three-day journey, taken by rail and military wagons, seemed mostly to have a good time, according to reports of alcohol consumption and fishing scores. However, one of the generals, William E. Strong, wrote a published account that received attention for its candid remarks about deteriorating conditions in the park. Strong was appalled at the wholesale slaughter of deer and elk, mostly for commercial purposes.

While the party enjoyed the government-paid excursion, Belknap's report launched a campaign for military involvement in the park. In the 1870s, it was no secret in Washington that high-ranking military officers believed the Department of War should handle matters such as relationships with Indian tribes and management of the park. Confronting this conflict, Belknap called for greater cooperation between the war and interior departments in surveying and improving the park. He suggested placing the engineers in charge of building roads and stationing a contingent of soldiers to provide law enforcement.[35]

Also, that summer of 1875, military officials ordered a reconnaissance of Montana areas where Indian activities had been reported and, if time permitted, suggested a brief excursion into the park from Fort Ellis. Heading the group of eleven soldiers and civilians was Capt. William Ludlow, an engineer stationed in the West since 1872.[36] This was Ludlow's second Western reconnaissance under the overall command of Sheridan. He had accompanied Gen. George Armstrong Custer on an 1874 expedition to the Black Hills. For the summer of 1875, Ludlow was authorized to include a geologist and three other scientists for the journey. Ludlow chose George Bird Grinnell as the geologist, whom he had met on the Custer expedition. After completing the mission in Montana, Ludlow's group entered the park on August 14. The small group spent just ten days observing, much of it along the Yellowstone River where accurate measurements of the falls were made.

Ludlow's report reflected the awe with which he viewed the wonders of Yellowstone, and his shock at depredations by tourists and poachers. He addressed the park's failings, offering suggestions for making the area a national park in more than name. Acknowledging the lack of administration and supervision, he called for a temporary military presence that could be relaxed if civilian authorities later lived in the park. The Department of the Interior, generally not favorable toward military intervention, waited a decade before accepting the advice of Belknap and Ludlow.[37]

As an engineer, Ludlow saw the need for improving roads and trails. He called for assigning an engineer officer to the park with an annual appropriation of $8,000 to $10,000 for transportation work and surveys. The first engineer assigned to such duty entered the park in 1883. Eventually, most of Ludlow's recommendations came to pass.

Another impact of the Ludlow expedition involved Grinnell, who completed a report on zoological and geological observations. He joined Ludlow in condemning the rampant killing of game and calling for a military presence. Moved by the experience, Grinnell committed his life and work to conservation projects and, four years later, became editor of *Forest and Stream* magazine that provided critical leadership in efforts to save the park.[38]

With encounters between army forces and Indians mostly concluded by 1880, Sheridan decided to conduct his own expeditions to the park, beginning a personal and professional interest that inspired others to fight for survival of Yellowstone. To those who cherished the park but decried its neglect, prospects were not encouraging.

1

Phil Sheridan to the Rescue

PHILIP H. SHERIDAN'S FINGERPRINTS HAD BEEN ON explorations of Yellowstone National Park from 1870 until 1880. In terms of individuals involved continuously with the park, few other persons, military or civilian, could make that claim. He preferred to stay in the background while scientists, artists, politicians, and other civilians gained headlines, made speeches, and showed photographs and paintings to Congress. As they came and went, Sheridan stayed involved, and in 1881, his interest turned toward personal journeys to Yellowstone.

Sheridan made his reputation as a general in the Union army during the Civil War, especially battles in the Shenandoah. When the war ended, he was one of the Big Three generals who continued in high command of the army: Ulysses S. Grant, William T. Sherman, and Sheridan, who then was thirty-four. Until 1868 when Grant was elected president, Sherman and Sheridan shared responsibilities for military operations in the West, mostly futile attempts to bring peace with Indians. When Grant moved to the White House, Sherman became commanding general of the army. Sheridan, then promoted to lieutenant general, took command of the Division of the Missouri, which included army troops from Chicago to the western areas of New Mexico, Idaho, Montana, and Wyoming territories.[1]

In this role as number 2 commander in the army, Sheridan, beginning in 1868, dispatched officers and enlisted men to fight Indian tribes as white settlement pressures mounted. Sheridan made occasional appearances at military outposts in those years, but he maintained offices and a home for his family in Chicago. When not occupied with military matters, Sheridan made friends with the business and political leadership of the city. Those connections were useful in his later campaign to save the park.

Sheridan had a hand in encouraging the 1870 Washburn expedition, and that set a pattern for his involvement through the 1870s. He approved four military expeditions to northwest Wyoming and the park during the decade. (They were discussed in detail in the Introduction.) The first in 1871 coincided with the Hayden survey and was led by Capt. John W. Barlow and Capt. David P. Heap. One achievement by Barlow-Heap was the naming of 10,308-foot Mount Sheridan overlooking Heart Lake.

Capt. William A. Jones commanded a group that surveyed a route from southern Wyoming to the park in 1873. Jones mapped two passes through the Absaroka Range, east of the park: Two Ocean Pass and Togwotee Pass. In August 1875, Sheridan dispatched a small group of soldiers and scientists commanded by Capt. William Ludlow to conduct a reconnaissance. A year later, Sheridan sent Lieutenant Doane, who accompanied the Washburn-Langford expedition in 1870, into the park with orders to explore origins of the Snake River.

Sheridan also assigned several military parties to explore the Yellowstone River region in Montana for strategic purposes associated with efforts to maintain peace among the Sioux Indian tribes in the Dakota, Montana, and Wyoming territories. In the fledgling years of Yellowstone Park, U.S. army units and Indian tribes fought some of the nation's most publicized and deadly conflicts at places such as Piegan Indian lands in Montana, the Little Bighorn, and the Rosebud River, where the 1876 Battle of the Rosebud took place. Also during that time, the great Sioux chiefs and warriors who created havoc among army units were tracked, captured, and imprisoned.

By 1880, stability had been reached across the West in relationships with Indian tribes, freeing Sheridan to think more seriously about a personal involvement in affairs of Yellowstone Park. Sheridan's growing concerns about protecting wildlife, controlling commercial development, and stopping vandalism had been whetted in reports by his commanders who saw for themselves the deteriorating conditions in the park and its lack of adequate administration. While the small military parties that had been to the park served a purpose in advancing knowledge, only the commanding general could create an expedition large enough to produce results that would catch the attention of the nation's civilian and military leadership.

In 1881, Sheridan began plans for the first of three consecutive annual expeditions to the park.[2] While each of the excursions was military in nature and ostensibly to survey new areas for civilian settlement, Sheridan included a small number of civilians and military friends. These numbered seven in 1881: Gen. Delos B. Sackett, army inspector general; retired Gen. M. D. Hardin; retired General Strong; Samuel Johnson and E. N. Sheldon, both of Chicago; and Dr. W. P. Wesselhoft and his son, William, of Boston. Each of the guests provided an important link to political and business interests.

Vital to Sheridan's travels were his aides, the general's brother Lt. Col. Michael V. Sheridan, Lt. Col. James F. Gregory, Capt. S. C. Kellogg, and surgeon W. H. Forwood. The supporting cast of military units, pack animals and packmasters, cooks, scouts, interpreters, and assorted helpers numbered more than 110, along with eighty-three horses and 183 mules.[3]

A number of Sheridan's friends and former colleagues also appeared on the expeditions in 1882 and 1883. Two from the 1881 journey, Generals Sackett and Strong, joined later excursions. Sackett wrote about his experiences as part of the congressional campaign to save the park. Strong already had spoken to the issues in his book about the 1875 Belknap expedition. Among support personnel, many of the same officers and enlisted men made two or all three of the journeys. Forwood wrote botanical reports after the trips in 1881 and 1882 and provided medical aid for the 1883 party.

The group of military officials and civilian guests left Chicago by train on July 27, 1881, arriving two days later at Rock Creek Station, Wyoming Territory, in the vicinity of Rock Creek, and the Medicine Bow River, about fifty miles northwest of Laramie. They took military spring wagons, a somewhat comfortable alternative to horseback, eighty-five miles north to Fort Fetterman, near today's Douglas; and the following day, they traveled ninety miles to the Powder River. Writing in his report, Sheridan commented on the rolling country, sandy soil, sagebrush, and scarcity of water.[4] He observed large herds of cattle and a number of ranches.

Traveling ahead of Sheridan and friends by almost two weeks was Lieutenant Colonel Gregory who had the mission to establish a camp on the Tongue River and wait for the commander to arrive. An escort and four packtrains headed by Thomas Moore reported to Gregory at Fort McKinney and proceeded to the Tongue River location on July 31.[5] On that day, a scout from Fort Custer with five Crow Indian scouts arrived.

The spring wagons carrying Sheridan and the special travelers met Gregory's assemblage on August 2. They had traveled 288 miles in four days, crossed numerous streams, and witnessed settlements of "thrifty farmers" growing wheat, oats, and barley. The entire party headed toward Yellowstone on a route that took them west through the Crow Indian reservation and the Yellowstone River valley.[6] They camped on the Bighorn River and made their way along Clark's Fork. Elk were plentiful, but Sheridan had decreed that only game enough for consumption by the party could be killed.

The most frequent route into the park was from the north through Montana Territory and down to Mammoth Hot Springs. Sheridan chose a trail farther east following the Yellowstone River that brought the party into the park at Tower Falls. At a point where the Lamar and Yellowstone rivers meet, they crossed on Baronett's Bridge, a toll station run by Collins Jack [John H.] Baronett. Gregory described Baronett as "the most famous guide and hunter of the country."[7] In his account of the 1875 expedition to Yellowstone, General Strong described Baronett as "a celebrated character in this country, and, although famous as an Indian fighter and hunter, he is still more celebrated as a guide."[8] Baronett had spent two decades in Montana, Wyoming, and Yellowstone Park as scout, fighter, guide, and businessman and had known Sheridan from those experiences, although his military service was with the Confederacy. At the general's request, Baronett accompanied the party to the geyser basins along an old Indian trail.

The party moved south, following the Yellowstone River. The lengthy train of humans, pack animals, and goods ascended Mount Washburn, reaching the summit on a cold and windy day. Gregory described what they found at the top of the mountain. "In a cairn of stones on the summit we found a tin box containing the names of many distinguished people who have been there. We carefully replaced the box, inclosing in it also the names of the members of our party, including those of our Crow scouts, Bad Belly and Bob-tail-crow, much to their delight."[9] The party camped at the falls of the

Yellowstone River, and then headed westward a day later at Yellowstone Lake to the Upper Geyser Basin and Old Faithful.

The written record and descriptions of Old Faithful from the earliest days of human observation would fill volumes. However, Gregory provided descriptions in his report of the Upper Geyser Basin, a horseback trip to some of the grandest sights of the immediate area, and geyser eruptions—some of which, in the twenty-first century, are unknown because of the changes beneath the surface.

He wrote on August 26:

> We have seen play all of the large geysers of the group except the Giant and Giantess. Today we visited them on horseback, and were rewarded by seeing many of them play. Yesterday the Grand played twice, but we were half a mile away, so today we went over to it at 3 p.m., and sat around on the rocks and under the trees until 5:45 p.m., when our patience was rewarded by a grand display. There were eight distinct eruptions, the later ones higher but of briefer duration than the earlier ones, and the total time of eruption was 22 minutes . . . . Yesterday and today we have seen eruptions of the following named geysers, some of them more than once and Old Faithful, a great many times: Fountain, Old Faithful, Beehive, Lion, Lioness, Castle and Splendid.[10]

Members of the expedition may have been in awe of the geysers and other splendors of the park, but Sheridan, realized the limited knowledge of the wonders in places of importance, such as Washington. In his report, Sheridan lamented, "Our only regret is in the indifference shown by the government, probably from want of appreciation of the wonders of this interesting country . . . ."[11] As his later actions would demonstrate, Sheridan intended to correct that situation.

Sheridan and others saw at firsthand the mindless vandalism of the geyser basins, and their outrage was captured in government reports. Gregory's journal included this passage describing in detail the damage committed by visitors:

> Mr. [Philetus W.] Norris, the superintendent of the Park, is doing a good work in making wagon roads to the principal points of interest and trails to the less important ones. If in addition, some means could be devised to stop and prevent the vandalism which seems to pervade the average American citizen and restrain his or her, especially *her*, propensities to hammer and chip off rocks to break down and destroy every growing thing, and to fill up with trees, sticks, and etc., the wonderful craters, a great indebtedness would be felt by every person appreciative of these greatest natural wonders of the world. The beauty of Old Faithful's crater as well as that of the other geysers has been greatly marred in this way, and the work of destruction is rapidly going on. We saw persons with hatchets who were hammering and cracking

the beautiful tracery around the geysers, without even the poor excuse of obtaining specimens, as they did not take away what they broke off. They destroyed for the pleasure they had in their work.[12]

While members of the Sheridan party apparently did not deface any of the geyser landmarks, there was a moment or two of frivolity that, in the eyes of Gregory and others, did not constitute disreputable behavior. However, in modern times, the episode described by Gregory would be considered disgraceful. He wrote, "Our men made Old Faithful useful as well as ornamental by throwing their soiled clothes into the crater during the period of quiescence. With the eruption, which occurs every sixty-five or sixty-seven minutes, the clothes are thrown high in the air, two hundred or more feet, and when picked up are found to be perfectly washed. Cotton and linen clothes were not injured, but woolen shirts and pants were usually torn to shreds."[13]

Sheridan made observations of his own regarding supervision in the park and the condition of roads and trails. The annual congressional appropriation of $15,000 covered two salaries and incidental expenses for officials in the park: the superintendent and gamekeeper. Sheridan said the amount was too small to make any improvements in the park. Consequently, "the work done in the summer has to be so temporary that it is washed out by the winter rain. These two men cannot take care of the extensive park. A large appropriation should be given by Congress . . . ."[14]

Sheridan's party moved westward from the geyser basins and left the park after joining the Madison River. They continued over a pass into Idaho and made their way to Camas station on the Utah and Northern Railroad that ran from Utah north to Montana. Sheridan took the train to its connection with the Union Pacific (UP) and headed back east. He left the group at Cheyenne and returned to Chicago by way of Denver and Pueblo, Colorado. Meanwhile, Kellogg and Company I of the Fifth Cavalry, which had provided an escort for Sheridan, took an overland route that would benefit Sheridan's trips in 1882 and 1883.

Company I traveled into the Teton River Basin of Idaho, across Teton Pass and down into Jackson Hole and the Snake River valleys. Of the valley, Kellogg wrote, "Jackson's Hole appears to be as little known as is the Teton Basin, except perhaps for a small number of trappers or Indians."[15] At the confluence of the Snake and the Gros Ventre rivers, directly east of the majestic Teton Mountains, the soldiers headed up the Gros Ventre toward the crest of the Wind River mountain range. Of the Gros Ventre, Kellogg stated, "[It is] a considerable stream with a very wide bed and heavily timbered banks, which the trail crosses and follows along the north shore." On the journey over the pass and across Jackson Hole, the company apparently did not encounter any other people or signs of people. At least none was mentioned in Kellogg's report. Most of the traffic through the region consisted of hunters, trappers, and survey teams. Settlers did not arrive until later in the 1880s.[16]

After several miles following the river, Kellogg took his company on a jog southward where they crossed the Wind River's crest at Union Pass and continued to the river, along much of the route Sheridan would take in 1882 and 1883. They descended to Fort Washakie at the foot of the mountains where the Shoshone and Arapaho Indians lived on a reservation. The Shoshones had a long history of friendship and nonviolence with white settlers and army personnel, thanks mostly to the work of Chief Washakie. Company I moved to the east and to Fort Laramie.

Sheridan's Yellowstone expedition of 1881 did nothing to calm the general's fears about conditions in the park or to satisfy his curiosity about the region that included the park and areas just outside the boundaries. He soon began planning a journey to Yellowstone in 1882 that would explore more of Jackson Hole, providing further opportunities for ways to save the park.

Sheridan always said the 1882 journey was Robert Todd Lincoln's expedition, although it had every handprint Sheridan could put on it.[17] Lincoln—the only surviving child of President Abraham Lincoln and his wife, Mary—was appointed secretary of war by President James Garfield, who was elected in 1880. After the assassination of Garfield a few months into his term during 1881, Chester A. Arthur, elected vice president with Garfield, assumed the presidency and immediately began appointing his own cabinet members. The one exception was Lincoln, whom he continued in office. Lincoln was Sheridan's civilian boss and an important ally in any political battles the general planned to fight in protecting Yellowstone. The two also had developed a social friendship during their time in Chicago when Lincoln was practicing law and Sheridan had his command headquarters.

A look at the invitation list for special guests on the trip indicates Sheridan probably chose them although Lincoln may have nodded in assent. Repeat travelers from the 1881 excursion included General Sackett and retired General Strong, vice president and superintendent of Western Union Company, a close personal friend of Sheridan's who had supported Lincoln's appointment to the Garfield/Arthur cabinets. Strong was making his third guided tour of Yellowstone. Others with either military or Chicago connections included Sheridan's friend retired Gen. Anson Stager, C. D. Rhodes, and John McCullough. The remaining VIP was H. R. Bishop of New York.[18]

Heading up Sheridan's staff were repeat travelers Lieutenant Colonel Sheridan and Lieutenant Colonel Gregory and a new addition, Capt. William Philo Clark, who had established an enviable record in the Indian Wars. He joined the staff of Gen. George Crook during the Great Sioux War of 1876-77, and commanded a force of three hundred Indian scouts.[19] He also served under Gen. Nelson Miles in Northwest campaigns and personally accepted the surrender of Crazy Horse and Little Wolf. He conducted the final action against Sitting Bull in 1879. Sheridan asked Clark, a student of Indian culture, to prepare a study of Indian sign language, with remarks on cultural habits. Clark died in 1884, but his book *The Indian Sign Language* was published in 1885.

All of these guests and key staff members were part of a huge party numbering 129 individuals, accompanied by eighty-three horses and 157 mules that spread across the countryside en route to Yellowstone. To handle the horses and mules, Sheridan again brought along Thomas Moore, Crook's highly praised packmaster.

Sheridan, guests, and the main body of support troops left Chicago on August 1, headed for Green River Station, Wyoming Territory, via the Rock Island and Pacific and the Union Pacific railroads. One member of Sheridan's staff was not aboard the train to Green River. Sheridan gave Gregory a special assignment, and the officer left Chicago by train on July 10 for Rawlins, Wyoming Territory.[20]

At Rawlins, Gregory was joined by soldiers and four army wagons for a reconnaissance journey to Fort Washakie at the foot of the Wind River mountain range where he was to meet Sheridan. He reported the trip covered 141 miles by way of Lander, or twelve miles shorter than the journey Sheridan and others took from Green River Station to Fort Washakie. Gregory wrote in his report that the Rawlins road was "much better" than the road from Green River.[21]

Sheridan's party left Green River Station, traveling across the Wyoming countryside in military wagons, and took a route to Fort Washakie that headed north along the Green River valley to the Big Sandy and through Lander City. After he paid respects to Shoshone Indian chief, Washakie, and assisted by Indian guides, Sheridan led his expedition along the Wind River, toward the mountain range summit. This was similar to the area descended in 1881 by Kellogg and his cavalry company as they departed Jackson Hole and headed to Fort Washakie. Sheridan named each campsite along the way for guest members in the party, and friends and associates who did not make the trip.[22]

Near the summit, the party made camp at an altitude Sheridan estimated as 9,200 feet above sea level. They had traveled fifteen miles on the timbered mountain slopes that day. Sheridan wrote, "This pass was unknown to white men, and seemed to have been used in the past only by Indians. It is much better than the Union Pass to the south of it [traveled by Captain Kellogg in 1881], or the pass to the north of it [Togwotee]. It was named Lincoln Pass, after honorable Robert T. Lincoln, secretary of war, whose expedition this really was, but the adjournment of Congress and official duties prevented him, at the last moment, from being its head."[23] The general gave the location his blessing: "It is by far the best pass I have ever seen over the Continental Divide."

On August 13, almost two weeks after leaving Chicago, the party dropped down from the summit of Lincoln Pass into the Gros Ventre River Valley and joined the trail that Kellogg took over Union Pass the year before. Sheridan's expedition followed the footsteps of Kellogg along the north side of the river, stopping to camp and enjoy the impressive valley scenery and the bounty of wildlife. Upon the first view of the towering Teton Mountains, Sheridan exclaimed, "The view was the grandest and most impressive I have ever seen."[24] They encountered antelope, elk, bear, and deer and caught scores of trout from one to three pounds each. Sheridan issued an order similar to one in 1881 that they were to kill only enough game to be consumed on the march.

Upon reaching the confluence of the Gros Ventre with the Snake River, Sheridan had covered the known trail into Jackson Hole. At that point, the party turned north in search of a trail that would provide a useful southern entrance to Yellowstone National Park. They entered the park on August 17, following the Snake to the Lewis River, then called Lewis Fork, and Lewis Lake and continued to the West Thumb of Yellowstone

Lake. Until 1895, when a road was built on this route into and out of the park, it was the main traffic way and was called the Sheridan Trail. Today it follows highways U.S. 191-89-287 into the park. Gregory summarized the importance of the southern approach to Yellowstone in his report. He wrote, "The exploration has proved the practicality of the route into the National Park from the forks of Wind River by way of Lincoln Pass, the valleys of the Gros Ventre and Snake rivers and of Lewis's Lake or Lake Fork of the Snake River."[25]

At the Thumb, the party turned west along Lewis Lake and Shoshone Lake to the Upper Geyser Basin and Old Faithful. Gregory described the scene as the party left the lake: "After feasting our eyes on this beautiful lake, which was so deep that the color of the water was as blue as indigo, we turned from it and crossed the Continental Divide, going over to the headwaters of Fire Hole River and down it to the Upper Geyser Basin."[26] They pitched tents about two hundred yards from Old Faithful, which, in those days, erupted approximately every hour.

Sheridan commented in his report on the status of the Upper Geyser Basin and specific conditions that revealed the force of nature. He said, "The geysers in the National Park presented nearly the same conditions as in the previous year, but there seemed to be greater action on the part of some of them. Old Faithful, the Bee-Hive, and the Grand showing a marked increase in their efforts . . . . Quite a large section of the crater next to the Fire Hole River has been torn out and on each eruption an immense volume of water is emptied into that river. The bed of the river contains many large blocks of stone, thrown out by the violent action which has taken place."[27]

Sheridan and guests met with park officials and staff and talked with visitors. They learned that the conditions found and described in reports during and after the 1881 expedition remained a concern. If anything, in Sheridan's mind, matters were worse. The slaughter of game and encroachment of commercial interests alarmed the general, and he wrote,

> I regretted exceedingly that the National Park had been rented out to private parties. The place is worthy of being a National Park, geyser phenomena and the Yellowstone Canon having no parallel in any nation. The improvements in the park should be national, the control in the hands of an officer of the government, and small appropriations be made and expended each year for the improvement of roads and trails. It has been now placed in the hands of private parties for money-making purposes, from which claims and conditions will arise that may be hard for the government and the courts to shake off. The game is being killed off rapidly, especially in the winter.[28]

Sheridan was told that more than four thousand elk, which he called grand animals, had been killed in one winter, primarily for their hides. He cited a report that as many as two thousand elk were killed "around the edges of the park." That did not include the slaughter of mountain sheep, antelope, deer, and other game. He had noted in 1881 that the small park staff was ill equipped by training or background to protect the park from poachers. Vandalism of the park's features, especially the geysers, continued unabated. This prompted Sheridan to offer a means for protection of the park to members of Congress. "I will engage to keep out skin hunters and all other hunters by use of troops from Fort Washakie on the south, Custer on the east, and Ellis on the north, and, if necessary, I can keep sufficient troops in the park to accomplish this object, and give a place of refuge and safety for our noble game."[29]

His call to arms also included a proposal to expand the park on the east by forty miles and on the south by ten miles, extending to the 44th parallel. Originally, the park contained 3,300 square miles, and Sheridan's plan would have increased the size by 3,000 square miles. He wrote, "[This] would make a preserve for the large game of the West, now so rapidly decreasing. This extension would not be taking anything away from the people, as the territory thus annexed to the park can never be settled upon. It is rough, mountain country, with an altitude too high for cultivation or winter grazing for cattle." Sheridan addressed the need for action in his report, saying, "I respectfully make an appeal to all sportsmen of this country, and to the different sportsmen's clubs, to assist in getting Congress to make the extension I describe, thus securing a refuge for our wild game."[30]

After leaving the geyser basins, Sheridan's expedition returned to Yellowstone Lake and followed the Grand Canyon of the Yellowstone to the northeast corner of the park. The party's guide for that portion of the trip was Jack Baronett. The general had intended to follow the Clark's Fork trail northward to the Yellowstone River, a route used by Sheridan in 1881, and to continue along the river to Billings. However, forest fires in the region forced them to consider passage over the Beartooth Plateau, "hitherto regarded as impossible."[31]

Helping to convince Sheridan that the expedition could make the difficult trip was a guide referred to in the reports as Mr. Geer, who owned a ranch on the Yellowstone River near the mouth of Clark's Fork and who was familiar with passage through the Beartooths. Not everyone associated with the venture agreed with Sheridan's decision to employ Geer. Gregory wrote that the guide was engaged "somewhat against the judgment of older guides." To avoid the forest fires, Gregory wrote, "We passed down the mountain with much difficulty, the fire extending across our line of march. The journey this day was through high mountain peaks covered on top with perpetual snow." The trail taken by Sheridan later became the U.S. highway 212, or the Cooke City route to and from the park.

It took the party four days to reach Billings, crossing some of the most rugged territory bordering the park. At Billings, participants departed on a special Northern Pacific train for Chicago. They arrived in the city on September 3, five weeks after leaving.

While catching the train in Montana, Sheridan learned that a group of investors working to gain a monopoly for commercial development of the park had succeeded in obtaining a contract agreement with Secretary of the Interior, Henry Moore Teller. This news escalated efforts in Congress, at Sheridan's office, and among interested civilian conservation groups to save the park from intrusive commerce.

2

A Picture of the Park in 1883

FINDING THE WAY INTO AND THROUGH
Yellowstone National Park in 1883 was an ordeal. It might have been easier than in the
1830s when the trappers and hunters arrived, but it was a far sight from today's luxurious
and manicured park. People, vehicles, walkways at the geyser basins, commercial ventures,
viewpoints of the canyon, and hard-surfaced roads today enhance the experience and
make a visit available to nearly everyone. On the other hand, the park, in all its scenic
glory, has remained essentially the same—with some natural changes.

As trapper Osborne Russell struggled through downed timber, swamps, and crusty
geyser lands of the park in 1834, he came upon a place he later called the Secluded Valley.
Aubrey Haines, who edited Russell's journal, identified the location as the valley of the
Lamar River, in the northeastern portion of the park.[1] On one of his visits to the valley,
Russell left generations of Yellowstone visitors with a statement that countless tourists
to the park must have experienced over the decades. At one point, he wrote:

> There is something in the wild romantic scenery of this valley which I cannot
> nor will I, attempt to describe but the impressions made upon my mind while
> gazing from a high eminence on the surrounding landscape one evening as the
> sun was gently gliding behind the western mountain and casting its gigantic
> shadows across the vale were such as time can never efface from my memory
> but as I am neither Poet Painter or Romance writer I must content myself to
> be what I am, a humble journalist and leave this beautiful Vale in obscurity
> until visited by some more skillful admirer of the beauties of nature who may
> chance to stroll this way at some future period.[2]

In July 1883, just weeks before General Sheridan led a third consecutive expedition
to Yellowstone, Abraham S. Wiley and his son, Howard B. Wiley, toured the park as
visitors with horses and wagon, keeping a journal as they went. It is believed Abraham

contributed the most to the journal, providing readers of his account with careful details of camping, hunting, meeting fellow travelers, and identifying the spectacular sights.[3] They rose one morning along the Yellowstone River, south of Hayden Valley. Abraham described the scene around the camp: "Snow covered peaks are all around us and not far off, the sound of the rushing stream, the wind through the cottonwoods and the occasional rumble of a passing team are soothing accompaniments as we sit under shade of the tent."[4] The journal keeper spoke in plain language with no attempt to be eloquent but, in a few words, caught the same awe that Russell wrote about almost fifty years earlier.

In different ways during the eleven years after the park was established, artists, photographers, and writers brought their descriptions to the people of the United States, still mostly settled east of the hundredth meridian and along the California coast. Thomas Moran painted the splendors while William Henry Jackson set up his box camera and captured in black and white the spectacles we have come to know by memory and sight. Also, Ferdinand Hayden and others created word pictures at great length for national and congressional audiences. Because the federal government had not found the rhythm of caring for a national park, events were leading to 1883 as a crossroads in the life of Yellowstone.

The park was in place. The wonders within beckoned. The number of visitors had increased every year although they found everything still in a primitive state. The curious people from places in the East and Midwest needed a means of getting close to the park and the wherewithal and constitution to endure the discomforts of travel and lack of accommodations.

From 1834 to 1843 when Osborne Russell trapped for beaver with associates, he made at least four passes through the Upper Yellowstone River region, to and from fertile waters nearby.[5] The Yellowstone River, Madison River, and Clark's Fork were favorites of trappers on the northern side of the park. Trappers in Idaho country had favorite locations, especially Henry's Fork, the Snake River, and the Teton River. An often-taken route from the south through portions of the region began with access from Teton Pass and continued through Jackson Hole to the Yellowstone Valley. Trappers followed old wildlife runs and Indian trails in order to avoid downed trees and impassable water routes. By 1883, not much had changed. Tourists, commercial interests, expeditions, and poachers of game used these same ancient trails and paths. The visitors, past and current, had one thing in common: they clamored for relief from routes made impassable by rain and snow.

Fifty years after Russell, access to Yellowstone favored routes from the north and west. Although hunters and trappers had traipsed through Jackson Hole, the Snake River, and Gros Ventre River areas on the south, and rivers and creeks on the east for decades, few people came to the park from those directions in 1883. The common belief by many was that those routes were impassable and could not provide convenient access.[6] It wasn't until Sheridan brought his expedition along the Snake and Lewis rivers in 1882, now the main highway route from the south, that a good trail was established. When settlers came to Jackson Hole in the late 1880s and 1890s, this became a much more popular route to the park, especially to Yellowstone Lake and the geyser basins.

Eastern access was rarely used in 1883 even by hunters and others bent on escaping with timber and animal skins because it required crossing the rugged forests and mountains of the Absaroka and Beartooth ranges. Visitors today enter from Cody over Sylvan Pass and from Cooke City through the extreme northeast corner of the park. The Milwaukee Road railroad eventually brought passengers to the Gallatin Gateway on the northeast in 1926, and the Burlington (CB&Q) provided service to Cody and the eastern gateway beginning in 1901.

Travel into the park from the west received a boost in the 1870s when extension of the Utah and Northern Railway from the Union Pacific line at Soda Springs, Idaho Territory, shortened the route by wagons and horses. The only rail route of 1883 was on the north, through the Dakotas and Montana via the Northern Pacific. The railroad company was a miracle in its own right—having survived bankruptcies, recessions, nasty winters, conflicts with Indians, and difficulty with the unpredictable personalities of the Missouri River. The irony of it all, after finally arriving at the gateway to the park, was that the NP remained unpopular with those fighting to protect Yellowstone. The railroad was the hated symbol of progress and growth.

The Northern Pacific began its life on July 2, 1864, with a grant of forty-seven million acres of government land in exchange for building a railroad to an undeveloped territory in the northwest, much of it along the route followed by Meriwether Lewis and William Clark in 1804-06.[7] Because of such a large land grant, the company received no federal financial assistance. With Josiah Perham as its president, the railroad struggled for financing from the beginning and did not break ground until 1870 when it pushed west from Minnesota. At the same time, NP began work in Washington Territory northward from Kalama toward Tacoma. By that time, most of the financing came from the efforts of Jay Cooke, who began his financial career in Ohio and took it to New York. In behalf of NP, Cooke reached the pockets of wealthy investors who trusted him although they knew little about the difficulties of building a railroad in hostile territory.

On February 15, 1870, near Duluth, Minnesota, ground was broken for the railway, the same year as the Washburn expedition. Methodically, NP pushed westward to the Minnesota-Dakota Territory border and began surveying Dakota land. The army sent six hundred soldiers under command of Gen. Winfield Scott Hancock to protect workers from raids by Indians. In June 1872, the NP reached Fargo and, a year later, sat at the Missouri River in Bismarck. Although competitors were fast on NP's heels, it appeared Cooke was winning the race. However, financial disaster struck Cooke and the United States in 1873, when a deep recession hit the nation. The huge debt of financing NP expansion proved too much for Cooke and the railroad. This double blow left the railroad stymied in Dakota Territory and facing the huge expense of crossing the Missouri. Few people expected NP to survive. Frederick Billings, namesake of the Montana city, reorganized the railroad in 1876, but little progress was made on construction.[8]

Fortunately for NP, there was another financial wizard with deep pockets and backers available. He was Henry Villard, who was Northern Pacific's primary competitor in the Northwest. Villard decided the way to beat NP was to obtain financial control, and he did in 1880 although legal disagreements with Billings slowed progress. Under Villard's leadership, $60 million was raised to breathe life into the railroad.[9] With money again being no obstacle, Villard took over as company president, began pushing NP westward, and made it possible to build a bridge over the Missouri at Bismarck. No more did NP ferry passengers and freight travel across the Missouri in the summer and put rails on the ice in winter. In 1881 and 1882, the line entered Montana; and on January 15, 1883, the first train reached Livingston, which became a town in November 1882.

During this time, Villard and other officials at NP reached the conclusion that the line must get close to Yellowstone National Park to meet increased passenger and tourist demand. Wealthy people could travel as far as Livingston, a growing rail center of two thousand people in 1883, and then hire wagons, guides, and drivers for the fifty-six-mile trek to Yellowstone. Many others could not. The railroad's main line from Livingston ran north of the park entrance by some distance.

Those with less available cash needed rail service nearer the park. Villard realized NP had to push even closer, or other railroads would meet the building demand. With visions of passenger traffic to the park, NP built the Park Branch Line from Livingston along the Yellowstone River, through a passage called Yankee Jim Canyon, to a small settlement known as Cinnabar.[10] NP built the branchline in just six months, showing how anxious the company was to get passengers closer to the park. Until 1903, this was the terminus of the NP line, only a short distance from Mammoth Hot Springs and the location of a fancy new hotel under construction early in 1883.

The north entrance near Gardiner and at Mammoth Hot Springs bustled with activity during 1883, with tourists arriving by rail and wagon and with work under way on the hotel. Crews hired by the builder, Yellowstone Park Improvement Company (YPIC), cut timber as fast as possible and hauled it to sawmills erected near the hotel site. In hopes of having the hotel ready for tourists in the summer season of 1883, the company raced to overcome delays in the work schedule caused by weather and opposition of a few park protectionists.

Simply being close to the park was not enough for Villard. He wanted to build a line into the park and to control the building and operation of hotel facilities. This outreach to commercial development of the park led NP to an alliance with the improvement company and, eventually, to conflict with organizations formed to protect the park. While NP never built rail lines inside the park, it was not for lack of trying. Although it took more than a decade, opponents fought the effort successfully in spite of support within Congress.

Abraham Wiley and son, Howard, came into the park in July 1883 from the north, following a route from Livingston up the Yellowstone River. Their visit to Yellowstone was fairly typical of curious civilians who did their own laundry, cooked meals, fished, shot game, and traveled on horseback over ancient trails and virtually nonexistent roads. Historians consider Abraham's journal to be an accurate and detailed account of life in the park for visitors a dozen years or more after the first organized explorations.[11]

It took the Wileys five days to make the journey to Yellowstone, passing through Yankee Jim Canyon and entering from Gardiner, the NP route. No part of the excursion to the park and back was without some calamity for the Wileys. Before reaching the park while the two were temporarily away from camp one day, stray cows created chaos. Abraham wrote, "[They] knocked our salt-bag about and licked it until it was all wet, ate up most of our potatoes, trod on our knives and forks, breaking several, tramped on our lemons and half upset our camp."[12] The travelers seemed to take it in stride.

En route to the park, Wiley complained about bad roads and poor results in fishing the Yellowstone. Instead of fresh fish for one dinner, they ate tomatoes, corn and bread, and washed it down with tea. Later, still unable to catch fish for a meal, they sat down for a breakfast of fried bacon, potatoes, coffee, and fresh bread. Periodically, they did catch fish, shot ducks and a goose, providing meals that Abraham pronounced "splendid."[13] Fine dining was not part of the park fare, but expectations were modest.

Personal hygiene received attention when conditions warranted. Upon reaching Mammoth Hot Springs, they felt the need to wash off a week's grime, and headed to nearby Bath Lake. Named in the 1880s, it was at one time a popular bathing site for Fort Yellowstone soldiers.[14] Although bathing and swimming in the park's thermal features has long been outlawed, in 1883, it was perfectly acceptable to sample the offerings of Bath Lake and other such soaking places in the name of personal cleanliness.

Father and son moved southward in the park from Mammoth Hot Springs down the Gibbon River to the falls, which Abraham declared as "the most beautiful Fall I ever saw."[15] They worked their way through fallen timber and over rocks to the paint pots and stopped briefly at Norris Geyser Basin, where Abraham estimated the number of geysers and hot springs at more than one thousand, a number that was probably high. During this stretch, they recorded little other human activity, except for a few people near houses along the Gibbon. That situation changed as they arrived at the Upper Geyser Basin and approached Old Faithful.

In 1883, the gathering place at the Upper Geyser Basin was Marshall's Hotel, a modest two-story log facility—some were less charitable in describing the structure—with a few outbuildings on the Firehole River. On July 10, the Wileys stopped at the hotel where they met several people they knew and some who knew their friends. They did not stay at the hotel, but camped close to about twenty people. In need of clean clothes and a bath, Abraham and Howard, went to the Queen's Laundry Bath House located near the western end of Sentinel Meadows in the Lower Geyser Basin. Abraham explained that water flowed from a hot spring through a trough to the bathtub and was cooled by river water. The log structure used as the bathhouse was constructed in 1881.[16] After that visit, the Wileys returned to the hotel and played cards with guests. Wiley summed up the evening in his journal by declaring, "It was a glorious bath and was followed by a good sleep."

The table at Marshall's Hotel featured a tasty selection of the park's game, according to Wiley. On one occasion, "we had for breakfast, fried grayling and elk steak." The travelers heard the elk at night and saw their tracks but were unable to find elk of their own for shooting. Disappointed, the Wileys bought elk meat from Marshall's for the return trip to Livingston.[17]

As with most people—civilians, soldiers, journalists, public officials, foreigners—the natural wonders of the geyser basins brought out the journal writer's best work and fearful moments. After an eruption of Fountain Geyser, Abraham wrote, "The water was thrown up some 20 or 30 feet in immense quantities boiling hot. The whole hill was steaming so that it was, to us, a hot vapor bath. The ground rumbled and shook beneath our feet in a terrible manner. I would not advise a timid person ever to try to witness this sight."[18] Recovering from his fright, he stated in the journal, "I was never so deeply impressed with awe by anything I have ever seen yet. The littleness and feebleness of man is forced home upon one in the most impressive manner. I do not envy that man who can stand unmoved in this terrible presence."

While in the vicinity of geysers for several days, Wiley and son proved that almost everyone could be tempted to deface the grounds and try stunts that today would be held in contempt, not to mention unlawful. Abraham found names written years before at the bottom of pools, preserved by transparent deposits and "still distinct." So inspired, Abraham and Howard wrote Detroit Safe Co. in one and described another casual act: "We threw a tomato can into the Old Faithful just before its eruption it was thrown up 75 to 100 feet in the air. We recovered it later to find it scratched and battered by the rocks in its exit. We threw others after the geyser had subsided and heard them tumbling, tumbling down for a long time."[19] In the twenty-first century, Yellowstone employees still must contend with people who throw rocks and other debris into the geysers and hot springs.

As the two men moved from the geyser basins to Yellowstone Lake and the Upper and Lower falls, Abraham commented on game in the park, "The hills around us abound with elk and deer. We see their tracks all around . . . . There must be thousands upon thousands of them. Bear are also very plentiful, black, cinnamon, and grizzly." The natural instinct of men on their own and making do on available meat sources led them to an assault on game, regardless of regulations. At one point, Abraham acknowledged legal limits on hunting in the park, saying, "It is against the law to shoot anything but bears in the park."[20] Nevertheless, they chased wolves and foxes and shot at owls but failed to hit the prey.

Two weeks after they began the trek to Yellowstone, Abraham and Howard were outside the park on the way home to Livingston where they looked forward to sitting down at a table to eat a home-cooked meal and to the comfort of a well-kept bed.

Beyond the natural wonders described in detail by promoters such as the NP Railroad, the general U.S. public had little knowledge of living conditions in the park. Even when magazine articles discussed controversies such as expansion of commercial interests, few specifics were mentioned. Plans to build a new hotel at Mammoth Hot

Springs received attention because of a national controversy over granting a lease. Occasionally, visitors to the park sent letters to officials and family after returning home with highlights included, and a few wrote articles for hometown newspapers. In that category was J. W. Weimer, an early settler of southern Kansas, a Civil War veteran, a farmer, and a former member of the Kansas House of Representatives.[21]

Weimer was, however, more than a tourist who wandered through the park in 1883. He was one of ten assistant superintendents appointed by Secretary of the Interior Teller.[22] Earlier that year, Congress appropriated funds to pay $900 a year to an assistant, providing he lived and worked in the park. Weimer entered the park in July 1883 and stayed until 1886. From the fall of 1883 to the spring of 1884, he wrote occasional articles for the *Winfield Courier* in which he described life in an unsettled world while carefully avoiding controversial political statements.[23] Weimer had a strong command of the language, and his entertaining descriptions of the landscape provide another view of the park at a critical time.

Weimer, an Indian "scout," and his two colleagues started their journey, as did many, from Mammoth Hot Springs on the north.[24] While he rode a horse, Weimer passed along his observations about more expensive means of touring. "A large number of the tourists, or sight-seeing pilgrims, go in wagons provided for that purpose, and at great expense, being entirely at the mercy of the hotel and stage company, who, as might be expected, are here for the money there is in it, and their scruples for charging have developed in like proportions. This mode of traveling not only prevents access to many objects of interest, but shortens the time on account of excessive expense."[25]

In an article entitled "The National Park: A Visit in the National Playground, or the Wonderland of America" dated October 16 and published in the paper on November 1, he described another more primitive method of travel, which happened to apply to his small group of travelers.

> Others more daring, as well as wiser and more curious, avail themselves with aboriginal methods of traveling in the mountains. If any of you are ever fortunate enough to take a trip of this kind in a country where side-hill grades are only wide enough for a donkey to trail, and steep enough to require his ears to be pried back to keep the bridle off, you will never wonder why Indians ride single file, even back in the states where roads are roomy and smooth.

Much activity was occurring at Mammoth Hot Springs, even if other parts of the park remained less traveled and occupied. Work continued on the large hotel, built by the Yellowstone National Park Improvement Company, and the location was headquarters for the park superintendent and his assistants. A fairly constant stream of visitors passed by. Weimer described the building where Supt. Patrick H. Conger resided and worked as "a log building one and a half stories high with shed rooms on three sides and a dome-like fixing of octagon shape on top, on each side of which is a post-hole, intended for sentinels and self defense in Indian times; on top of this is a flag pole ornamented with a large brass ball." The building faced "the great formation of springs," and to the right nearby was "a more imposing steaming mountain."[26]

He presented the sights at Mammoth Hot Springs in considerable detail, including the temperatures of springs (100 to 175 degrees). Of the springs, he wrote, "They hold in solution a great amount of substance and are very transparent. The colors vary according to the substance held in solution, giving to each spring, basin, pool or bowl, as you may wish to call them, a different color." Among the curiosities, Weimer mentioned Bath Lake, "used for bathing, and large enough to accommodate five hundred at one time, of swimming depth, and temperature to suit your own idea of comfort or health by approaching or receding from the heating source."[27]

After a brief period of adjustment at park headquarters, Weimer and associates spent nearly two weeks "in the mountains," which meant the less-traveled areas of the park. Weimer wrote several times of difficulties on the trail, including one incident early in the exploration. The horses and riders climbed to the highest point on the trail, leaving Mammoth, then began a "small descent" when the packhorse lost its footing, "sending his burden in loose parcels in every direction over the side of the mountain, plunging still-legged, head-long over rocks and logs, taking with him our faithful scout who was leading him at the time." Weimer caught the flavor of the accident with this description of the accident site: "Cooking utensils, fresh bread, canned fruit, bacon, and blankets well seasoned with baking powder . . . was the pony, scout, and the side of the mountain." The scout and horses survived.

Another letter from Weimer published by the *Courier* placed him near the geyser basins early in September, which he said was "decidedly the best time in the year to visit the park."[28] He wrote, "After the 20th of this month [September] it is unsafe to cross these mountains with any degree of pleasure, on account of snow storms, especially for eastern or southern people (known here as 'tender feet' or 'pilgrims')." He advised readers to avoid earlier or later travels because of "bad roads, cold nights, and mosquitoes and flies in the spring, and snow storms in the fall."

The party reached the Lower Geyser Basin where they discovered a storehouse maintained by the government "for the keeping of supplies for the use of the men employed in improving roads and bridges, also a blacksmith shop, for the same purpose and for the accommodation of the traveling public." To the west, Weimer saw steam rising from the Queen's Laundry, "appropriately named, as it is frequently used for cleaning garments, by throwing them in, and after being held in agitation in its seething caldron a few hours, they are taken out perfectly cleaned."[29]

Much of a lengthy letter was used to describe specific geysers, many in the Upper Basin, and the environment, which Weimer appeared to enjoy. With large accumulations of snow in the vicinity, he wrote, "The weather is all that the charms of winter could afford. Where the snow is not drifted it is 6 feet deep . . . . Mercury planning at zero, sometimes a little below, and as high as 32 above. It is said by Montana papers the winter is unprecedented for mildness. Bands of elk in sight every day and graze within rifle shot of our quarters, and eat of our hay."[30]

He concluded days at the basins with this almost poetic summary of the sounds of Geyser Country: "Thus day and night the scenes with the accompanying music go on, some lashing the air in angry fury with boiling water while others fill the air with groans of monster spirits writhing in agony on account of close confinement. On a clear bright morning the basin looks like a great manufacturing city, only instead of the dirty, black smoke, there are white clouds of steam and in most places the surroundings are exquisitely clean."[31]

Fresh from his sojourn away from Mammoth headquarters, Weimer provided readers with a perspective on development and facilities. "Lest your readers get the idea that this is an old place and considerably improved, let me say that such is not the case. The National Hotel [Mammoth Hot Springs Hotel], partially completed, and the superintendent's quarters are the only improvements worth speaking of; a few cabins and dugouts complete the amount. Other improvements are tents and teepees, and it is not uncommon for bears to come to the back door to molest the quiet slumber of tenderfeet and pilgrims."[32]

Weimer said that discomforts and indignities aside, Yellowstone National Park made everything worthwhile. "No other district of the same size in the world can afford the same amount of natural scenery of a different nature." After serving in the park, Weimer and his family settled in Indiana.[33]

A notable omission from Weimer's letters was the existence of Marshall's Hotel at the Firehole River. Operating in the publicity shadow of the new hotel at Mammoth Hot Springs in 1883, Marshall's remained the best-kept secret of the internal workings of the park from the human standpoint.

George Washington Marshall, born on March 24, 1846 in Illinois, found work and business interests throughout the West at a time when opportunities to make a living often related to providing forms of transportation and sources of food. He went to California in 1860, driving horses all the way, and stopped for twelve years in Sacramento and San Francisco where he continued to work with horses and a livery business.[34]

Marshall bounced around in Nevada and Utah during the 1870s, running a stage station, driving horses, and buying cattle. Such entrepreneurial ventures brought Marshall to Montana, where he ran a freight line from Eagle Rock to Butte City, Montana, the terminus of the Utah and Western Railroad that ran north from Ogden. That lasted until late 1878. The federal government signed a contract with him to provide mail service from Virginia City, Montana Territory, to Mammoth Hot Springs; but after a year, the government canceled the contract.[35]

Marshall made good use of the time under contract to scout for business opportunities. He noticed a need for hotels to accommodate an increasing number of visitors, official and unofficial, who spent their days camped in the woods as they were left without alternatives. Marshall decided to fill the void at the Upper Geyser Basin along the Firehole River. He moved his wife and children to that vicinity where he built a cabin. The idea of a hotel advanced beyond plans after an encounter in 1880 during the tour of Secretary of the Interior Carl Schurz and a party of friends and VIPs. In a biographical statement dictated in 1885, Marshall described the meeting with Schurz:

> Carl Shurz [sic], Sec. of Interior was out visiting the Park in 80 and had to sleep out under the trees near my cabin one night it rained He told me next morning I would have given twenty dollars ($20) to have got into a house last night and suggested that I should prepare to keep travelers said that he would see that I got a permit from the Government and when they got their leeses [sic] filed would see that I got a leese. I remained on a permit till last year [1884] when Sec of Interior granted me a lease for 10 yrs. My first year here I did not make anything, second year came out $180 dollars in debt.[36]

Marshall formed a partnership with John B. Goff to build a hotel along the river. Little is known about Goff, who soon after the arrangement moved to Montana where he became a guide. The two-story building was a hotel in name only, but it was better than no hotel, and it served visitors to that portion of the park for eleven years beginning in 1883. The facility was described as "a fine shingle roofed mail station and hotel" with a barn and outbuildings, all costing about $1,000.[37] After constructing the hotel, Marshall and Goff organized a transportation service in the park, using a wagon they owned.

During construction, which required two good-weather seasons in 1881 and 1882, a number of special guests signed the hotel register along with many of lesser fame. For example, in 1881, guests included U.S. Sen. Benjamin Harrison of Indiana, who served a term as president of the United States from 1889-1895. Another was John W. Hoyt, governor of Montana Territory.

The Marshalls were the only people who did not leave the park during winter. As such, George; his wife, Sarah; and four children became the first people to remain among the geysers in the coldest of times. In a letter to friends, Marshall wrote the following about one of the winters:

> Although many have contended that it would be impossible to live here in winter in such close proximity to the vast volumes of steam of geysers and springs, we have thus far found it . . . a delightful experience . . . the healthiest climate we have ever lived in . . . . The colder the mornings the grander the view. The thousands of columns of steam ascending heavenward present a picture words will never describe, and the myriads of brilliant ice pendants and diamond-like atoms of frost upon the forests [provide] one vast mass of glittering gems . . . . Even in the heart of winter, Old Faithful and the balance of the geysers were just as regular in their displays as in summer.[38]

Living in the park during the 1880s exposed the Marshalls to more than snow and cold. In the spring of 1881, George was gone from the park for thirty days on business, leaving Sarah and the children alone before summer guests began arriving. George had been gone only a short while when Sarah discovered two bears trying to gain entry to the storehouse of food near the hotel. She grabbed a rifle and shot one of the bears. Instead of leaving, the wounded bruin charged Sarah and nearly reached her before she slammed the storehouse door. The bear soon left, but Sarah was not done. She tracked the animal some distance into the woods and finished the job with a final shot.[39]

Marshall and another partner, G. G. Henderson, built a second hotel building near the first as business thrived. Nonetheless, by 1885, Marshall had tired of the hotel routine. At the age of thirty-nine, he sold out to Henderson; decided to "retire" in Bozeman, Montana; and started new businesses.[40]

Yellowstone National Park seemed primed for change in 1883. To accommodate more visitors, it needed new facilities, better roads, and convenient transportation. Competing for attention with these demands were the conservation interests that seemed ready to mount a strengthened effort, beginning with pressure for new Yellowstone laws and expanded boundaries.

3

The Developing Storm

THE YELLOWSTONE PARK PROTECTION AND survival movement, which gathered momentum with Sheridan's reconnaissance missions and published reports in 1881 and 1882, brought together a handful of individuals determined to save Wonderland from disgrace and perhaps from oblivion.

Those who saw the needs and accepted the leadership challenges for action included Sheridan, Sen. George Graham Vest of Missouri, and magazine editor George Bird Grinnell. They reached out to military, congressional, and conservation constituencies that identified and publicized the park's needs and battled with influential business interests. This coalition worked toward changes in laws and park administration and pressed for military assistance that eventually altered the course of Yellowstone and, hence, national parks' histories. The three enabled dozens more in supporting roles who contributed to successes and shared in the occasional triumphs.

Reform ventures often are launched from events that galvanize forces. In the case of Yellowstone Park, that motivating episode occurred prior to and during Sheridan's 1882 expedition when investors began to see an opportunity for profits in the park. Acting on his initiative, Secretary of the Interior Teller responded to a request from men loosely associated with the Northern Pacific Railroad for a lease of land in the park to develop hotels and string telegraph lines and to provide other conveniences. At the same time, the Northern Pacific was approaching the northern boundary of the park, and company officials wanted to extend rails into the park as well as build facilities for visitors. By 1882, it was clear that tourism in the park was going to be big business. The secretary's role would be pivotal.

The law creating Yellowstone passed by Congress and signed by President Ulysses Grant in 1872 specified responsibilities of the secretary of the interior as related to operations of the park. In effect, the secretary had full authority for operations and development. He could publish regulations and rules without constraint as long as they broadly protected the park and its environment, and the power to appoint park officials rested entirely with the secretary. This same department official could determine what constituted preservation of the park's timber, natural curiosities, and attractions.

Importantly, the secretary had broad authority to grant leases for buildings and commercial ventures. A few restrictions were spelled out in the law. He could not sign leases for more than ten years, and only "small parcels of ground" could be used for buildings to accommodate visitors. The fact was, however, that the secretary was dictator of the park and could do almost as he pleased. In many instances, secretaries chose not to do much. Occasionally, one decided to test the limits.

Based on his interpretation, Teller thought he had full authority to negotiate a lease with commercial interests. That conclusion eventually got him in trouble but not before he tried to go it alone. Ultimately, Teller's errors included the assumption that his authority was unilateral, and he did not need to inform Congress about his intent and the conditions of the lease. He may also have decided his action would not be controversial, although that would have required an enormous amount of naiveté.

The general apathy of Congress toward Yellowstone also might have led Teller to believe he could take charge without consultation. Documents and correspondence point to a conclusion by Teller that his action was the only practical course for orderly development of the park. In the end, he arrogantly overstepped the imaginary boundary of authority and got caught. His attempt to approve a lease in relative secrecy backfired.

After his appointment early in 1882, Teller received a number of written requests for leases, reflecting a change of administrations in Washington and also a change in secretary. Secretary Schurz, who served under President Hayes until 1881, had declared he would not grant a monopoly lease for park development. That order died with the Hayes administration. After the assassination of Garfield, the ascension to the presidency of Arthur, and the appointment of Teller, all within a few months, investors and developers may have sensed new opportunity. In the absence of a declaration against monopolies by Teller, it appeared the administration was open for business.

Most of the requests for leases were not tempting, but that changed with submission of a request in April from ten men, many with connections to the park. Headed by E. M. Russell and E. S. Topping, the group of investors asked for leases of ground and other privileges to build tourist facilities.[1] Teller wrote to the park's Supt. Patrick Conger, appointed to the position on April 1, 1882, asking him to inquire "into the responsibility of the applicants named, and if assured of their ability to carry out the projects they suggest, make such recommendations as in your judgment may seem advisable . . . ."[2]

In that same letter, Teller spelled out the specifications of a lease. He said that no lease could be longer than ten years, and no lease could cover lands "containing any of the natural curiosities or mineral springs within the park, or that will in any way prevent free access to such curiosities or springs." One of the issues raised in subsequent considerations by Congress was maintaining full public access to the sights.

In keeping with the Yellowstone law that limited the secretary's authority in issuing a lease, Teller said no agreement would grant more than twenty acres in any one tract. He mentioned these absolute terms:

- For tracts not exceeding five acres, $10 a year.
- For tracts exceeding five acres and not more than twenty acres, $1 additional for each acre over five.
- Yearly payments in advance will be required, and failure to pay within ninety days of the approval of the lease would be regarded as grounds for cancellation.

In addition to Russell and Topping, names on the application included S. J. Hoyt, Ed Parker, William T. Kirkwood, James Gourley, R. H. Rowland, George W. Marshall, R. R. Odell, and George W. Monroe.

Topping had operated boats unsuccessfully on Yellowstone Lake in 1874 to 1876. He headed to the Black Hills of Dakota Territory when it was opened for gold prospecting. Gourley prospected for gold in Montana—particularly in the Cooke City area—and also in Mammoth, Gardiner, and Bear Creek areas, all inside the park or just outside. In 1884, he became recorder for Gallatin County, Montana, and had other business interests.

Marshall came to Montana Territory from Elko, Nevada, and opened a stage line to carry mail between Butte City, terminus of the Utah and Northern Railway, and Eagle Rock. He built a hotel near Old Faithful in 1878. His daughter, Rose Park, was the first white child born in the park in 1881.

For some unexplained reason, the Russell-Topping application stalled and died. No documents exist to explain the inaction. Meanwhile, in the following months, Teller corresponded with Gen. James S. Brisbin, who wished to build and operate a tourist steamer on Yellowstone Lake for ten years. In just two weeks' time, without engaging Brisbin regarding details of the steamer plan or other requirements for the lease, Teller wrote the applicant on July 27, "The privilege of putting a steam vessel for carrying passengers on the Yellowstone Lake in the Yellowstone National Park, requested by you in your letter of the 12th instant [July], is hereby granted."[3] Teller then sent a letter to Conger telling him of the decision. Later, Brisbin relinquished his permit after much correspondence and dissatisfaction with the department.

Although Teller seriously considered two different groups of investors for a lease to build hotels, they did not overlap. From the outset that meant Teller was dealing in a noncompetitive situation, or monopoly. With Russell-Topping apparently out of contention, the door was open again. On July 31, Teller received a letter from U.S. Sen. William Windom of Minnesota, accompanying a letter containing a proposed lease from Carroll T. Hobart and H. F. Douglas.[4] There may have been earlier contact or a notice of some kind to Teller, but there is no record. Hobart of Fargo was a Northern Pacific Railroad superintendent in Dakota Territory, and Douglas had served as a post trader at Fort Yates in Dakota Territory. He was credited with having political connections in Washington. As representatives of an investor group, the two men proposed:

First. The erection of a first-class hotel costing not less than $100,000, with such additional hotels as the wants of the public may require.

Second. The construction and operation of one or more steamboats on the Yellowstone Lake.

Third. The establishment of stage lines and livery accommodation for the conveyance of passengers from all railroads and other highways reaching the Park to all points of interest within the Park.

Fourth. To supply guides and other facilities necessary to enable visitors to see the wonders of the Yellowstone Park.

Fifth. All employees of the company to be uniformed and render strict discipline; all charges of every kind to be scheduled, published, and approved by the Secretary of the Interior, and all extra charges and fees strictly prohibited.[5]

They requested all rights and privileges to execute the plan, including extracting materials from the park for construction of buildings and steamboats and using worthless timber for fuel. They expected to begin operations sixty days after the approval by the secretary.

While documents peg the arrangement between Teller and the Hobart-Douglas group to July, the first known word of an organization bent on gaining approval to develop commercial interests in the park appeared on January 15, 1882, in the *New York Times*.[6] Ultimately, some of the information used in the article turned out to be wrong, but the intent of the investor group was made clear and provided some indication that the secretary probably knew of the effort long before July. Here is what the *Times* published:

A syndicate has been formed of wealthy gentlemen, more or less intimately connected with the Northern Pacific, to build a branch tourists' line from some point on the line, probably Bozeman, Montana, to the heart of the Yellowstone National Park, and erect there a large hotel for the accommodation of visitors. Among those embarked on this enterprise are Senator Windom, State Senator J. B. Gilfillan, of Minneapolis; E. H. Bly of Bismarck, proprietor of the Little Missouri Coal Mines; and Superintendent Hobart of the Northern Pacific. The road will be 80 miles long, half outside of the park and half within, and will cost $20,000 per mile. The syndicate is to raise $60,000 and the Northern Pacific is to lend the rest of the capital, which is to be guaranteed at 7 per cent interest. The syndicate has exclusive hotel privileges for the park, and will invest $150,000 in a hotel of 500 rooms, to be ready for occupancy when the road is open. There were some 3,600 visitors to the park last year, though several hundred miles of staging are now necessary to reach it. It is thought the new line will pass from Bozeman up the West Gallatin Valley and thus reach Geyser Basin by the easiest route. The hotel will probably be at some central point near Geyser Lake and the Falls of the Yellowstone.

A hint of the political force behind the request was signaled by Windom's involvement. He had served briefly as secretary of the treasury in the Garfield administration and had political connections throughout Congress and the White House.[7] Windom's letter to Teller said he had "no doubt of their [Hobart's and Douglas's] ability to carry out their propositions to the entire satisfaction of the department." He closed the letter, saying he would be in touch with Teller "within a day or two."

As might be expected, the applicants wanted a tight lease, keeping competitors at bay and providing as close to a monopoly as possible. As learned later, the applicants hoped to receive a lease granting control over seven tracts of land covering the entire geyser basins: six of them with 640 acres to the tract, and the seventh tract with 600 acres. Together, the grants would have included 4,400 acres, and all were of the most desirable tracts. In addition to the geyser basins, the deal included Mammoth Hot Springs, Old Faithful, Yellowstone Lake, and the Grand Canyon of the Yellowstone. The rights covered all arable land, retail development, and the use of timber and coal as needed. The rent to be paid was about $2 an acre or less.

That was the news Sheridan learned upon completing his journey through the park in August. Afterward, knowledge of the presumed lease spread through the ranks of park protectors, including members of Congress. When Sheridan finished writing his report on the excursion, he sent a copy to Senator Vest of Missouri along with a map showing the general's proposed new boundary lines. Sheridan asked the senator to champion the park's cause, support his expansion plan, and establish a wildlife refuge. He added, "The suggestions made in my report are the only things left for us to do to save this noble game."[8]

Vest, elected to the Senate in 1878, was a Democrat member of the Committee on Territories. With no particular public record on the subject of Yellowstone, he nevertheless took an immediate interest in park preservation and eventually became Yellowstone's most stalwart supporter in the Senate.[9] The alliance of Vest and Sheridan is intriguing in one sense because of their pasts related to the Civil War. Sheridan's record as a Union officer and hero is well-known. Vest served as a representative in the Confederate Congress from 1862 to 1865 and was appointed a senator in the Confederate Congress in 1865. His service to the Confederacy ended when the Union prevailed, and he resumed law practice in Missouri. Whatever drove the attitudes and intentions of the two men twenty-seven years earlier did not get in the way of their cooperation about Yellowstone.

Historian Richard A. Bartlett recounts a story to explain how Vest became interested in preserving the park.[10] In the fall of 1882, Vest happened to be staying in a hotel near tracks of the Northern Pacific Railroad. He adjourned to a restaurant by himself for dinner and "sought a dark corner where he could dine without attracting attention." From that location, he overheard conversation among what appeared to be several businessmen. They were celebrating having persuaded the Department of the Interior to grant them a lease for hotel facilities throughout the park. This was allegedly Vest's first knowledge of what became the landgrab. The senator returned to Washington and began his mission to save the park.

Before Vest's fateful experience and receipt of Sheridan's report, Department of the Interior's machinery moved forward. On August 10, 1882, with the secretary out of the office (some said conveniently so), M. L. Joslyn, acting secretary, sent a brief letter to Conger, saying, "I enclose herewith a copy of an application of Messrs. C. T. Hobart and H. F. Douglas for hotel and other privileges in the Yellowstone National Park. Also a copy of a letter from Hon. [Senator] William Windom, favorable to the application, and will thank you to report, as early as practicable, your views as to the propriety of granting to said parties the privileges asked."[11] None of the correspondence, beginning with the Hobart-Douglas application, was made available to members of Congress at the time.

Vest learned later that Hobart and Douglas, with the aid of wealthy New York investor and political operator Rufus Hatch, had assembled a list of directors or investors with capital of $800,000 to begin construction of hotel facilities in the park. These names were provided later by Teller and were entered in the Senate record as being directors:

Robert S. Green, Elizabeth, New Jersey[12]
C. E. Haupt, St. Paul, Minnesota
C. A. Roberts, Fargo, Dakota
J. B. Gilfillan, Minneapolis, Minnesota
P. H. Kelly, St. Paul, Minnesota
C. M. Loring, Minneapolis, Minnesota
H. F. Douglas, Fort Yates, Dakota Territory
Sen. Roscoe Conkling, New York, New York (a long time political associate of Arthur's)
A. J. Vanderpool, New York, New York
Rufus Hatch, New York, New York
Charles L. Quincey, New York, New York
Gen. J. A. Williamson, Boston, Massachusetts
John B. Lyon, Chicago, Illinois
J. B. Houston, New York, New York
John Clay, Jr., Chicago, Illinois, and Branford, Ontario
Hon. R. T. Merrick, Washington, DC
Elijah Smith, Boston, Massachusetts
Carroll T. Hobart, Fargo, Dakota
Hugh J. Hastings, New York, New York
Hon. John R. Brady, New York, New York
Samuel W. Allerton, Chicago, Illinois
Frederic E. Church, New York, New York
John C. Wyman, Valley Falls, Rhode Island
Albert J. Hatch, Stamford, Connecticut (brother of Rufus)
George Ely, Lyme, Connecticut
A. V. H. Carpenter, Milwaukee, Wisconsin
Web. M. Samuel, St. Louis, Missouri

U. S. Senator George Vest
U. S. Senate Historical Office

U. S. Senator William Windom
U. S. Senate Historical Office

Secretary of the Interior Henry M. Teller
Courtesy Colorado Historical Society, Teller collection, F1472/10037120

"Desecration of Our National Parks"
Library of Congress/Harper's Weekly

William Fullerton, New York, New York
D. W. Marratta, Pittsburgh, Pennsylvania
E. H. Goodman, Philadelphia, Pennsylvania
J. R. Barrett, Sedalia, Missouri
John N. Abbott, New York, New York

When the list of investors was submitted to Teller, Hobart and Douglas called them "representative and responsible men, who will give the enterprise a national character."

While it might have seemed appropriate to wait for Conger's opinion about the Hobart-Douglas group, the superintendent did not have a voice in the decision. Joslyn, and presumably his boss, Teller, signed a contract with the investor group on September 1, at the request of Hobart and Douglas as incentive for investors to commit funds to a hotel project.[13] A contract was the first step in granting a lease. Adding to pressure on the department was a telegram on August 24 from Senator Windom, stating, "Hobart and associates propose reaching Washington next Thursday morning. Can Contract for park privileges be prepared and executed by that time answer."[14] There is no answer in the record. Windom may have envisioned being an investor in the scheme, but the eventual department agreement with Hobart and Douglas prohibited members or delegates to Congress from sharing in the agreement with the Department of the Interior.

Conger wrote an assessment of the application, received by Joslyn for Teller, from Mammoth Hot Springs on September 20, 1882. If Teller expected Conger to roll over and tacitly recommend a lease, he must have been surprised at the letter's content.[15] Here is what Conger said:

> In reply to your letter of August 10, directing me to report as early as practicable my views as to the propriety of granting the application of Messrs. C. T. Hobart and H. F. Douglas for hotel and other privileges in the Yellowstone National Park, I beg to say that their application to you lies before me. I have considered the same as well as I am able, and notwithstanding the high endorsement the gentlemen have received from Senator Windom [of Minnesota], and their undoubted respectability and financial ability, yet it is my judgment that they ask to cover entirely too much ground. The National Park is a great territory, and the day is not distant, in my opinion, when the franchise they ask will be worth a very large sum of money. Besides, I believe the public would be restive were all of these privileges granted to a single party or corporation.

This letter also was not made available to parties outside the department until Vest and the Senate asked for and received copies of all correspondence and lease discussions during 1882. Meanwhile, at Mammoth Hot Springs, Hobart and Douglas assumed they had approval to begin work on a hotel and other facilities. They wanted to be ready for the expected increase in visitors to the park in the summer of 1883. In November,

Teller received a letter from Hobart, Douglas, and Hatch, then acting as attorney for the group, spelling out their intentions and making specific requests of the secretary and Congress.[16]

They referred to "an outlay of several hundred thousand dollars" for improvements of the park according to the contract awarded by Teller and mentioned the target date for hotel operations as June 1, 1883. The letter contained two comments on conditions in the park and requested means of remedy. First, they accused tourists and U.S. soldiers of "extraordinary vandalism," including burning of thousands of acres of timber, destruction or mutilation of geyser cones, and "the wanton slaughtering of black-tail deer and other choice game, apparently as objects of marksmanship merely, heaps of as many as five carcasses behind left on the ground to rot."

The men sought passage of laws by Congress prohibiting destruction of all or any objects within the park, animate or inanimate, "together with the fixing of penalties for violations of such laws or regulations and the establishment of judicial authority" with power to administer the laws.

The other complaint dealt with the condition of roads and trails and was the first of several letters of criticism over the months ahead. Stating that it was the responsibility of government to do something about road conditions, they mentioned, "mere wagon trails unfit for our ambulance and tourists' coaches." The letter requested a congressional appropriation of $500,000 for roadwork compared to the requested amount by the department of $75,000. They stated, "There are now not over 84 miles of acceptable road in the entire Park, whereas there should be 300 miles, or in round figures 200 miles additional."

To underscore their demands, the letter reminded Teller of the financial risks undertaken by investors and their intention to build facilities that would attract tourists from throughout the nation. They also noted that the government was not in any position to undertake such expenditures and provide management expertise. The letter announced that Hobart was in charge of work in the park and would be the primary contact for Teller and the department. Meanwhile, Hobart hired work crews, began cutting timber in the park for the hotel structure, and erected sawmills. By mid-December, shacks and stables were built for workmen, horses, and oxen. The scope of timber cutting is revealed in the first annual report of Hatch for the improvement company to Teller, in which he said the total amount of timber cut up to September 1, 1883, was 1,686,482 board feet.[17]

With rumors flying and little information forthcoming from Teller, Vest began a study of the situation, asked Teller for copies of correspondence and leases, and prepared a report to the Senate as a precursor to the proposed legislation. Teller provided the documents, and Vest discovered that the Russell-Topping lease application had not been approved and that another request essentially backed by railroad interests had been proposed. The secretary's process remained in motion as the fall progressed, and Vest had a lot of ground to make up to get congressional control of matters.

In a letter of December 6, Douglas and Hobart informed Teller they had formed Yellowstone National Park Improvement Company with Rufus Hatch as financier and legal counsel regarding all matters of agreements with the government.[18] Hatch, also affectionately known as Uncle Rufus, was a native of Maine who left the family farm and headed west to make his fortune. He worked at odd jobs before settling in Rockford, Illinois. He entered the grain commission business in Chicago in 1854, later joined the firm of Armstrong and Company, and earned his first fortune. Two years later, he lost it when the Armstrong firm failed. In 1862, Hatch moved to New York, where he lived the rest of his life. He opened a stock brokerage on Wall Street and immediately plunged into speculative investments.

Hatch survived the 1873 national recession although he lost three quarters of his fortune. A few years later, he guessed wrong on several investments and, again, was out of money. He bounced back, however, utilizing his vast investor connections and relationships with powerful New York and national politicians. In the early 1880s, he invested heavily in stock of Northern Pacific Railroad, which led him to involvement with the Yellowstone National Park Improvement Company. Hatch later said officials of the Northern Pacific invited him to meet Hobart and asked the New Yorker to take charge of raising money for the lease on a national basis. Late in 1883, financial failure struck Hatch again when the Northern Pacific stock tumbled in price. A short while later, nearly broke, he retreated to New York and lived quietly until his death on February 24, 1893.

Hatch took great pride in having paid off his debts from the first two financial failures. That credibility with business people left his reputation intact and allowed him to regain his fiscal balance. However, he did not have the funds to pay off all of his debts from the third failure, and that is one reason why he did not again work in the speculative markets. The *New York Times*, writing upon his death, called him a plunger, adding, "Mr. Hatch was a man of big ideas. Anything that he went into he went into with all his heart."[19]

While Hatch may have been in the background of deliberations by Hobart and Douglas, he never acknowledged being involved until a meeting after the contract was approved by the Department of the Interior in September 1882. Hatch wrote, "I took a trip West, at the invitation of Mr. [Frederick H.] Billings and other officers of the Northern Pacific Road, and at Fargo was met by C. T. Hobart who presented me with a letter of introduction . . . setting forth that Hobart had a contract with the Government for developing the wonders of the Park, and asking that I take hold of the affair with Hobart, and try to make it a national undertaking."[20] If there was any question about the Northern Pacific being in the background of this effort, Hatch put that to rest. Hobart and Douglas simply did not have the personal wherewithal or connections to raise money for major development plans, and Hatch and the railroad came into play.

On September 19, Hobart and Douglas provided Hatch with 35 percent equity in the project. Hatch said, "On that basis I organized a Company with the best men I could think of as Directors, trying to secure about an equal number of Democrats and Republicans, Eastern and Western men." Reflecting his political instincts, Hatch corralled Senator Conkling, perhaps the single most powerful political operator in New York State, and he was powerful in Washington too. Others assembled by Hatch included an ex-judge and New Jersey congressman. Hatch and his friends committed to $112,000, "hard cash" for a hotel at Mammoth Hot Springs, and guaranteed about $30,000 more.

During the fall, Vest's investigation of Department of the Interior's involvements with Hobart, Douglas, and Hatch convinced the senator that immediate action was required to stop the secretary's intention to issue a monopoly lease for park development. The Senate approved a resolution introduced by Vest on December 12, calling for a report from the Committee on Territories on the Yellowstone matter. This caused Teller to put the lease on hold until attempts at legislation were resolved. Vest's committee issued a report to the Senate, dated January 5, 1883.[21] The senator intended for the report to set the stage for approval by the Senate and House of a resolution calling for the appointment of five senators to examine and report on the present condition of the park and action taken by the Department of the Interior on management and leases.[22]

Vest also planned legislation to correct what he viewed as excesses of the secretary. The resolution, introduced on February 17, called for legislation to "protect the timber, game or objects of curiosity and interest in said park, and to establish a system of police, and to secure the proper administration of justice." Furthermore, it called upon the secretary to withhold any action on leases or contracts. Vest also rolled into the resolution a request that the secretary call upon military authorities "for whatever force is necessary to protect game and the park's attractions." The Senate never voted on the resolution.

Vest's committee report included statements from a report by Lieutenant Colonel Gregory of the 1881 trip to Yellowstone and a lengthy portion of Sheridan's report on the 1882 expedition, both focusing on problems in the park and potential solutions. Additionally, Vest included communications to the committee from John Schuyler Crosby, governor of Montana Territory, and Gen. D. B. Sackett, inspector general of the United States. Crosby was a former aide to General Sheridan, and Sackett served on both the 1881 and 1882 expeditions led by Sheridan into Yellowstone. Both men provided strong support among various constituencies in behalf of protection for the park and Sheridan's ideas.

Crosby encountered Sheridan during the Civil War when he served as an aide to the general. Crosby attained the rank of colonel and, after the conflict, was the U.S. consul in Florence, Italy. He served as Montana territorial governor from 1882 to 1884. When asked by Vest to comment on Yellowstone issues, Crosby accepted the challenge immediately and wrote a letter dated December 29, 1882.[23]

As might be expected, given his background with Sheridan, Crosby voiced strong support for the remedies outlined by the general's 1882 report with emphasis on the protection of game. "The report of General Sheridan presents evidence of a lamentable deficiency in the means or power of enforcement" of protection for large game in the park, Crosby observed. He repeated the elk kill numbers advanced by Sheridan and quoted from the general's report. In regard to protecting game, Crosby urged Congress to enact Sheridan's proposal for extension of park boundaries. "Insomuch as I am informed, by officers and others who have been over the country of the Shoshone ranges of mountains between 44 and 45 north latitude, adjoining and east of the Yellowstone Park, that the altitude and general roughness of this region are such that it can never be utilized by settlers, while it is the natural habitat of the game to be preserved," Crosby wrote.

Crosby suggested assigning an engineer officer of the army to work in the office of the secretary of the interior, with powers granted to design and build roads and make the necessary improvements. He jumped on the military bandwagon by supporting the granting of authority "to call upon the military stationed in the neighborhood for such details of troops as may be needed for emergencies." He said if new laws are passed in this regard, the park superintendent should be in a position to enforce them, "which now is impossible."

Crosby continued his efforts on behalf of Sheridan's plan for the park in a message to the Montana Territorial Legislature on January 25, 1883. He appealed for legislators to cooperate with the federal government to convert Yellowstone into "an asylum for the great game of the Northwest."[24]

Sackett chose to present a case for less commercial development of the park and voiced disagreement with plans to allow commercial control by a single company. He said, "This last summer I saw a number of these happy parties encamped within two hundred yards of 'Old Faithful.' Should this lease for 640 acres of land around 'Old Faithful' be made, I fear these good people will find no spot near this grandest of geysers on which they will be permitted to pitch their tents, nor will they be able to find a place for the purpose of wherever within the Upper Geyser Basin, as the 640 acre grant would cover every foot of ground in the basin."[25]

He called for competition to provide modest accommodations for visitors. "[A]ll that is really needed at this time, or that will be required for some time to come, are a few comfortable lodging and eating houses at three or four of the more important points. Let there be an opportunity for competition, and there soon will be ample conveniences at the various points of interest for the comfortable accommodation of all those who may visit the Yellowstone Park," he added.

Sackett joined others in calling for a military presence to prevent vandalism and poaching; only his proposal was on a scale less than proposed by others. He stated, "A single troop of cavalry sent to the Park for two and a half months each summer would afford all the protection needed for the extinguishment of forest fires, and for the protection of the cones of the geysers, and this could be done with little expense to the War Department, and certainly with none to the Department of the Interior." He recommended assignment of five or six men to assist the park superintendent with patrols of the Upper Geyser Basin, adding, "The deposits and formations in this basin constitute about all that requires any special protection; no one can injure or carry off the Yellowstone Falls or the lake."

The committee's report began with the assertion that Teller overreached his authority as granted by the Yellowstone law of 1872. Vest wrote, "It seems evident to the committee, from the entire scope and terms of the act of March 1, 1872, that Congress did not intend that the Secretary of the Interior should, under the provision giving him discretion to grant leases for building purposes of small parcels of ground, place under the exclusive control of private parties 4,400 acres of the Park, embracing all the objects and points of interest which make the Park valuable for the purpose to which it is dedicated . . . . The virtual and real effect of the contract and lease is to put the entire Park, containing 3,300 square miles, under the control of the lessees for a term of ten years at a nominal yearly rent of a few thousand dollars."[26]

Further attacking the creation of a commercial monopoly, Vest went to the heart of Teller's defense. "It is urged in defense of the monopoly, that it must be created in order to induce persons of capital and enterprise to furnish proper and sufficient accommodations to the public. The assumption is false and unfounded. If the public wish to visit the Park, enterprise and capital will very soon discover the fact, and be ready to meet the demand." Vest wanted to retain Interior's jurisdiction over the park, but with reduced authority for the secretary. "The monopoly feature in the contract and lease should be stricken out," he demanded, "and no contract should be executed by the department which does not reserve the right to permit other hotels to be erected within the Park, if, in the judgment of the Secretary, the interests of the public so require."

Making another point about agreements with commercial interests, Vest cited the secretary's approval of an agreement with Brisbin to operate a tourist steamship on Yellowstone Lake. Vest contended Teller did not place any restrictions on Brisbin "either as to the capacity of the vessel, the accommodations furnished, or the rates charged." He said any agreement for operating on the lake should "insure the comfort of visitors and the absence of extortion." Vest made his point by adding, "Nothing but absolute necessity, however, should permit the great National Park to be used for money making by private persons, and in our judgment no such necessity exists."

Picking up on recommendations from Sheridan, Gregory, Crosby, and Sackett, all quoted at length in the report, Vest added the committee's voice to expanding the east and south boundaries of the park and to providing two companies of cavalry or mounted police to patrol the park. These would provide a "secure retreat" for game and would "exclude the mercenary wretches who slaughter these noble animals for profit," the report stated.[27]

The report also said that the small congressional appropriation of $15,000 a year "does not furnish the superintendent with a sufficient number of men to police the Park and prevent destruction of the game or natural objects of interest." Vest called for "liberal appropriations" annually for construction of bridges and improvement of park roads. Finally, the report required placing the park within the criminal jurisdiction of the territorial courts of Montana regarding crimes against life or private property. Vest and committee incorporated these proposals and others in a bill submitted to the Senate on January 5, 1883.[28]

The committee report served to Congress a menu of significant changes for Yellowstone Park; and it applied political pressure on Teller. No matter what legislation Congress might pass, there were immediate expectations for the department to take certain measures within the authority of the secretary. In an order dated January 15,

1883, Teller responded to Vest's pressure and concerns by others over poaching in the park with instructions to Superintendent Conger.[29] Teller told Conger to inform all persons coming into the park of regulations against vandalism and wanton killing of game. Conger was told that the Department of the Interior absolutely prohibited the killing, wounding, or capturing of any buffalo, bison, moose, elk, mountain sheep, and other game. Teller placed prohibitions on fishing in the park and outlawed "all cutting of timber in the Park, except upon special permission from the Department of the Interior." While Teller was responsive to congressional threats, the fact remained that Conger had no more money or people with which to enforce the declaration. Teller, politically astute, knew he had to show sensitivity to congressional concern or he would pay a price, and details such as enforcement would have to wait.

Following Vest's report and proposals to Congress, Teller began to play ball in the open with Congress. By granting time for Congress to act until the session ended in March, Teller gave Vest and protectionists of Yellowstone a slightly open window for action. Having been a U.S. senator before appointment as secretary, he knew the deliberations for major legislation by his former colleagues probably could not be concluded satisfactorily in that time frame.

In defense of Teller's actions during 1882, biographer Duane A. Smith surmised that Teller realized "adequate visitor facilities—such as roads, hotels, liveries and restrooms—desperately needed to be provided."[30] Smith said that small underfinanced businessmen did not have sufficient capital to provide facilities for the large crowds of visitors that soon would descend on the park. "Concessionaires and a concessionaire policy were hit-and-miss propositions in the first decade of the park's existence," Smith observed.

With that reality, Smith wrote that Teller believed that an "association of persons" with substantial capital could provide fine accommodations. That is why Teller proceeded to sign a contract with representatives of the railroad to build hotels and run stages to "principle points in the park." Smith concludes that the deal was a "pragmatic solution." Correctly, Smith noted that no thought had been given to the Department of the Interior providing funds for facilities or managing them. "That left only a well-financed business monopoly as the logical answer," Smith wrote. Logical or not, pragmatic or not, the concept of a monopoly operation in the park raised hackles across the nation. The word "landgrab," then being used by interested parties, called for different tactics and explanations with the expectation of congressional study and debate.

By the end of 1882, the campaign to protect Yellowstone Park was in full swing. Sheridan's reconnaissance reports for 1881 and 1882 had aroused friends and supporters and prompted a rally of military associates. He became a one-man public relations whirlwind. The general's contact with Vest had been highly productive, resulting in immediate political pressure on the secretary of the Interior and a report that laid out plans for legislation. The American Forestry Association signed up to preserve timber in the park. Sheridan's network of former associates turned up William "Buffalo Bill" Cody, once a scout for Sheridan during the Indian Wars of the late 1860s. Cody wrote a letter in support of Sheridan's plan.[31]

In an attempt to gain support in Congress for a contract and lease with the improvement company, Assistant Secretary Joslyn prepared a document for the Senate Committee on Territories that modified the September 1, 1882, contract.[32] According to Joslyn, a new contract would not grant a monopoly for park development. A newspaper account said, "They are to be granted the use of one section of land at the great geyser [Old Faithful], and a half section at six other springs, making four sections in all, for which they are to pay a rent not to exceed $2 per acre . . . . The chief feature of the new contract is that the control of the park is still kept in the hands of the Secretary of the Interior and no one is given exclusive privileges." Joslyn said officials of the improvement company agreed to the modification.

Upon reading the newspaper article in St. Paul, Minnesota, former park superintendent Langford responded with a strongly worded letter to Vest in opposition to the original contract and the modification. Langford condemned the idea of allowing a monopoly development interest. He said during his tenure as superintendent that he operated on the concept that no person or company should lease more than ten acres, and "no contiguous pieces of land should be leased . . . ." He concluded, "I think it will be a great mistake to lease more than 10 acres; and no lease holder should be permitted to exclude any visitor who does not choose to patronize his hotel."[33]

Outreach to interested and concerned civilians fell to George Bird Grinnell, editor of the weekly *Forest and Stream* magazine, published in New York. The magazine was devoted primarily to hunting, fishing, and preservation of lands for sporting purposes although the editor periodically championed campaigns to limit commercial growth. Grinnell had been editor since 1876, devoting his attention to conservation issues across the nation but primarily in the Northeast. Grinnell enlisted in the campaign after hearing Sheridan's appeal "to all sportsmen's clubs" to lobby Congress. As noted earlier, Grinnell and Sheridan had a connection dating to Custer's 1874 excursion to the Black Hills. As a member of the Ludlow expedition in 1875, Grinnell had been to Yellowstone in his capacity as a scientist.

Grinnell was at the beginning of a career that would bring him accolades as a student of American Indians, especially the Cheyenne tribe.[34] He lived among many tribes in an effort to learn their cultures and wrote about them in articles and books. His work to conserve lands in Montana, spurred by extensive personal exploration, eventually led to the creation of Glacier National Park. On a national scale, he received lasting attention for starting the Audubon Society. All of these adventures began after his work in behalf of Yellowstone Park. Through all his advocacy, Grinnell maintained residence and worked in his native New York. Until Grinnell stepped down as editor of the magazine in 1911, it provided a regular outlet for his editorial comments, crusades, articles on conservation, and reprints of works by others in the field.

Grinnell joined the outcry against the proposed lease to Hobart and Douglas from the Department of the Interior with an editorial in the December 21, 1882, issue entitled "Leasing the National Park."[35] He characterized the process as "a very charming scheme to railroad through a temporary land grab, which will, if successful put more money into the pockets of its projectors than any single set of individuals have lately made out of this government." Grinnell was especially angry at the small amount of rent or fees to be paid for use of parkland. He called $2 an acre per year "nothing or a mere song." Although he mentioned Hobart and Douglas as perpetrators of the scheme, he had especially harsh words for Hatch, whom Grinnell credited with most of the manipulative efforts behind the scenes.

Grinnell took a cautious position on the role of Teller. The editor noted that Teller "has hitherto kept in the background of the matter." Grinnell expressed hope the secretary would join with senators in an effort to change the most egregious provisions of the lease. "We must say that we fail to see why the Interior Department should give away a privilege of such great value," Grinnell wrote. The editor added, "Have Messrs. Hobart, Douglas, Windom and Hatch done anything to deserve so well of their country that the people's pleasure ground should be turned over to them, in order that they may make handsome fortunes out of the public?"

On a more pragmatic level, Grinnell stopped short of saying that the entire park should not be leased to private parties. "There is certain work to be done there which cannot well be undertaken by the government," he said. However, Grinnell insisted that the department should protect the rights of the public and the government "in every possible way." Grinnell pulled no punches in expressing his disdain for the investors, saying, "There appears to be good reason to believe that this project is neither more nor less than a barefaced attempt to use this government reservation for the purpose of enriching a few speculators at the expense of the people at large."

Grinnell mentioned briefly that a lease along lines of the one approved in contract form for the Yellowstone National Park Improvement Company (he often put "improvement company" in quotation marks) had support from a strong lobby. In later commentaries, Grinnell expanded on this notion with revelations about tactics to influence the press.

Two weeks later, with Vest and his committee prepared to release findings in a report to the Senate but little in the way of an offense under way, Grinnell wrote on "The Park Grab" with a sharpened pen. He had become the primary public spokesperson outside the government in a continuing campaign against interests associated with the improvement company. In that context, Grinnell focused on what he believed to be an untruthful public campaign and the backroom maneuverings of Hatch.[36]

Grinnell said early pronouncements indicated the company was "working solely and simply for the interests of the people of this country. They related with tears in their eyes most heartrending stories of the slaughter of game, and told about the destruction of geysers and other natural wonders." He said the comments were nothing new and were known to anyone who had kept informed about conditions in the park. Grinnell referred to plans by the company to develop a cattle business in the park. He added, "Truly, the modesty of these monopolists is startling, but not more so than the meekness with which the people endure this monstrous invasion of their rights."

Grinnell described the lobbying effort for the lease as a major factor in the creation of support for the company among citizens and press. He stated that Washington correspondents of the nation's major newspapers had been captured "at a very moderate cost." Grinnell related how an unnamed private secretary to Hatch had furnished a lavish dinner for members of the press as a means of influencing their attitudes about the park lease. Grinnell explained further, "The occasion was a delightful one; the company was good, the viands delicious; wine flowed freely; the schemes of the Yellowstone Park Improvement Company were discussed and applauded, and from this time the dispatches to the newspapers through the country took a different tone . . . . Just think of muzzling the press of the whole country by means of a good dinner, at a cost of only a few hundred dollars."

Grinnell did find one newspaper reporter who viewed the company's efforts with suspicion. The unnamed reporter writing in the *New York Herald* quoted someone who had been in the park recently about ongoing efforts of Hatch and associates to cut timber in the park for proposed hotels. The visitor said several sawmills were in operation just outside the park preparing materials for the hotels at seven sites. The writer, referring to intentions of the company to have a large-scale cattle operation, said, "It is believed that the contract, which appears to relate chiefly to hotels, includes the right to use all the grazing land in the Park, and that under this cover the most successful stock ranches can be conducted." Right or wrong, gossip or not, Grinnell was using his editorial page to denigrate the company's intentions and bolster opposition to a lease.

In a later editorial, during which he praised Montana Governor Crosby's letter to Vest's Senate committee, Grinnell spelled out precisely his idea of the right and wrong parties in the battle.

> The issues involved in this Yellowstone Park matter have been clearly defined, and are now well understood. On one side is corporate greed; on the other are the present and future interests of the people . . . . Public interest has been aroused. The people will carefully watch the course pursued by their representatives in Congress.[37]

The center of the Yellowstone debate had moved to the halls of Congress and especially to the Senate where Vest's advocacy was in full bloom. Over the first two months of 1883, the arcane process of legislating played out with intriguing debates and countermeasures. With attention focused on Washington, Sheridan and Vest did not rest. They already began talks about the next expedition to Yellowstone National Park, and Grinnell kept up a running commentary to keep his constituency aroused.

4

Washington Wars

SEN. GEORGE VEST MIGHT HAVE ANTICIPATED A clear and wide legislative road to correcting the ailments of administering Yellowstone National Park. After all, protectors of the park had a head of steam, specific proposals, and vocal supporters. However, time was short, and obstacles were many.

There could have been any number of reasons for inaction by Congress. Members often preferred to deliberate endlessly without regard for the importance of legislation. They took personal privilege and position seriously and could be easily offended when pressured to act quickly. Members could get exercised about outside influence too, and plenty of that had developed during the fall and early winter as park issues flared. In 1883, members had small staffs and few resources to dig deeply into last-minute legislative proposals. Finally, it was near the end of a regular session of Congress, and there was always anxiety to get appropriations done and to hand off controversial subjects to another session. All or none of those factors could have been at work, adding to the potential for delay of Vest's plan for the park.

Vest seemed determined to defy the calendar and the odds as Congress began deliberations in January. In effect, Vest and supporters had fewer than two months to stop momentum of the Yellowstone National Park Improvement Company and its backers in the Department of the Interior. The senator's plan was to push a resolution and a bill as far as he could in the time remaining.

Vest also was angered by reports that the company had unilaterally begun construction of a hotel at Mammoth Hot Springs, apparently without approval of Teller and without permission of Congress. Vest said, "In the face of the action of the Committee on Territories, in the face of the action of the [Interior] Department, a party of speculators—Rufus Hatch and others—have gone into this park and commenced the erection of a hotel, have cut down timber and are proceeding to treat the park as if it were their property exclusively, regardless of the rights of the United States."[1] Surely, Vest hoped, this example of arrogance would arouse his colleagues.

Vest also had to show senators that Teller had promised not to issue a lease, pending consideration of legislation by Congress. In a letter of December 12, 1882, Teller had told Vest a contract had been issued and had indicated a lease might be made later that would give a monopoly to the improvement company. The details were unchanged from an earlier statement by the Department of the Interior about proposed acreage in a lease—640 acres around each of the geysers and exclusive use of 4,400 acres of land in the park for a nominal rent of $2 per acre. Vest reported publicly, "I received from him the assurance that he had made no lease, that he did not propose to make any lease and no contract for any lease."

Confusing the matter by January were reports from Washington that the company and the department had reached an agreement on total park acreage smaller than the original contract because of complaints about the larger number. Vest needed to quash that report before senators overreacted. Vest went to the secretary for further assurances. To show fellow senators the truth of Teller's statements, Vest put a letter from Teller, written on January 18, on the record. It said:

> I have Mr. [Nathaniel Pitt] Langford's letter addressed to you and by you referred to me concerning the Yellowstone Park. I have determined not to take any action in the matter of the lease to Messrs. Hatch & Co. until Congress shall take action on your bill; at least not until the close of the session. If no action should be taken on the bill I shall feel inclined to execute to them a lease in strict accordance with the views expressed by your committee in the report made to the Senate. I have issued an order prohibiting the cutting of timber without special authority from the Secretary, and prohibiting the killing of game within the park. I trust you will procure the early passage of the bill, so that it may pass the House.[2]

Vest sent a copy of the letter to Sheridan. Supporters of park protection such as the *New York Times* applauded, saying, "The Yellowstone Park is likely to remain tolerably free to all visitors for several months to come, if the assurances of Secretary Teller are good . . . ." That is where the matter stood. Teller had issued a deadline. Vest and supporters on his committee had submitted a legislative proposal early in January, and a resolution he had introduced earlier was also on the table.

The senator wanted either the resolution or a law if he couldn't have both. Each put forward the specifics of changes for Yellowstone, reflecting concerns over treatment of wildlife, damage to geysers, wanton cutting of timber, and lackadaisical administration. He also proposed expanding the land area of the park as Sheridan and others had recommended.

With the congressional picture unclear early in February and time running out, the Department of the Interior mounted an offensive to minimize the influence of lobbying against a monopoly lease for the improvement company. Carrying the charge for the department was Assistant Secretary Joslyn while Teller kept his distance from any controversy. In the wake of legislative action in Minnesota and Illinois opposing the lease, a news dispatch from Washington to the *St. Paul Pioneer Press* dated February 10 carried Joslyn's rebuttal.[3] He declared the legislatures had acted without knowing the facts. The article stated, "He said that if they had taken the trouble to post themselves as to the exact terms of the contract they would have found that the company was powerless to do anything until the leases had been executed."

According to the paper, Joslyn also characterized parties opposed to the contract as being motivated by the fear of losing business opportunities if the improvement company received a monopoly. The article said, "He attributes the writing of the letter by Governor [John S.] Crosby to the pressure of certain parties he declined to name, who were instrumental in getting Crosby his appointment [as territorial governor], intimating that these gentlemen were interested in having the contract set aside."[4] The paper named Brisbin, who received permission for a steamboat on Yellowstone Lake, as an opponent of the contract. It also hinted that an "army ring," probably Sheridan and military associates, wanted to control the park.

The newspaper, obviously a proponent of putting most of the park's development in the hands of the improvement company, argued public interests would be served by the proposed arrangement. "The contract affords the most ample protection to the public against extortion as the schedule of rates is entirely under the control of the Secretary of the Interior. It is believed that it would be much better for the Park and visitors if the matter would be left in the hands of responsible parties, and not divided between all classes of vendors and adventurers," the newspaper stated.

On the eastern side of the nation, the *New York Times* joined the contest between Congress and the department, thanks to someone in Congress who provided the documents. On page 1 of the January 20 issue, the *Times* published information that unveiled how the improvement company obtained favored treatment by the department and received a contract on September 1, 1882.[5] Aside from revealing the transactions, the paper was most interested in the contradictions between Teller's statement in April as to how many acres would be allowed for development and what ended up in the contract with the company.

After reviewing the specifics of Teller's document to Conger and the contract signed in September, the paper said:

> It appears from the correspondence that Secretary Teller positively instructed Mr. Conger that no lease should cover more than 20 acres in any one tract, and that no lease tracts should include any of the mineral springs or natural curiosities. It also appears that Assistant Secretary Joslyn afterward agreed to lease to Hobart, Douglas & Hatch seven tracts of land, each containing 640 acres and including the springs and great natural curiosities.

The *Times* continued pounding on the issue with an editorial three days later in which it pointed out the evils of a proposed monopoly. The editorial said, "To pretend to reserve the Yellowstone region for the benefit of the people, and to lease it to a gang of speculators, is only to offer a premium for private greed and extortion."[6]

While Vest wrestled with procedures in his chamber, members of the U.S. House in sympathy with the senator's efforts also did significant work. One major piece of legislation regarding expenditures awaited action late in February: the Sundry Civil Bill, a catchall that wrapped up the remaining money proposals for the session. Debate on the bill containing this clause opened in the House on February 23:

> That the Secretary of the Interior in his discretion, may grant leases for terms not exceeding ten years of small parcels of ground within said park, but no more ground shall be so leased than is necessary for the hotels and storehouses necessary to the accommodation of grazing land in connection with said hotels; but no exclusive privileges or monopoly of any kind shall be granted to any person or company or corporation for any purpose within said park; nor shall any lease or contract be made which in any degree or manner interferes with or prevents the free and unrestricted access of the public to all portions of the park.[7]

As House members prepared to act on the proposed language, they'd had access to more than a month of frequent news stories and editorials regarding documents released by the Interior secretary. One of those, an editorial from the *Times*, reaffirmed the paper's concern for single-company development in the park. The paper attacked monopoly interests, surely aimed at the improvement company, and exposed the hypocrisy of their soothing words about saving the park from negative influences. The editorial said:

> It is not unreasonable that it should be proposed to build hotels for the accommodation of visitors. But when it is proposed to give to the hotel proprietors the better part of the National Park, it is simply a proposed surrender of the whole ground for the alleged reason that the United States Government cannot take care of it. The speculators will be the guardians of the park provided they are given all that makes that pleasure-ground desirable for visitors and travelers. On no other terms will they prepare hotels for tourists . . . . It would be a humiliating confession of weakness, if, unable to defend the park, Congress should decide to let the Interior Department lease the domain to sharpers, speculators, and land-grabbers.[8]

Later that day, the House was ready to vote on Sundry bill language. Rep. Anson G. McCook, Republican of New York, proposed to strike the original language and substitute the following:

> And the Secretary of the Interior is hereby prohibited from leasing any portion of the Yellowstone National Park to any person, company, or corporation

for any purpose whatever; and all leases, agreements, exclusive privileges, or monopolies granted or entered into are hereby declared to be of no force and effect. And the Secretary of War is hereby authorized and directed to make necessary details of troops to prevent trespassers or intruders entering the park with the object of destroying the game therein or for any other purpose prohibited by law.[9]

In effect, the proposed wording prohibited leasing to any person, company, or corporation, virtually nullifying the secretary's authority under the original act and called for a military takeover. McCook explained that his proposal would in effect freeze the situation with Teller and the improvement company until a comprehensive bill could be considered in the Senate and House. He deferred to Vest to initiate the legislation. In support of the proposal, McCook quoted from Sheridan's report on his 1882 excursion to the park and Vest's report to the Senate. McCook received widespread support, and the addition to the sundry bill was approved on a voice vote.[10] The bill also included an appropriation of $15,000 for salaries and expenses in the park. Now Vest had something to work with if neither his bill nor the resolution could pass in the Senate.

A day after action in the House, the *New York Times* again joined the fray in support of protectors, applauding the action of McCook and calling the bill "a tolerably clean sweep of the rubbish that has encumbered the Yellowstone National Park."[11] The *Times* took special notice of the call for troops to "prevent its [the park's] destruction or defacement and the unnecessary killing of game." On the larger question of the park's future, the editorial said, "What will be the result with the larger experiment of the Yellowstone National Park is difficult to say. The area embraced within the boundaries of the reservation is too vast to be properly policed." The editorial's final statement took aim directly at Congress, saying, "Those of us who hate jobbery [dishonesty] and distrust the policy of granting exclusive privileges to corporations will heartily approve the adoption by both houses of Congress of the provision excluding speculators from the Yellowstone National Park."

During debate on the Senate floor three days later, more than a month after submission of proposed legislation, Vest said he had been informed by Senate officials that his bill could not be passed during the current session.[12] A potential delay until later in 1883 alarmed Vest because he knew Teller was prepared to sign a lease for monopoly development in the park if Congress did nothing by March. He offered no lament to his fellow senators but pushed harder for consideration and passage of the resolution.

Sen. James B. Beck of Kentucky, a member of the Appropriations Committee, and two other senators—William B. Allison of Iowa and Frederick Hale of Maine—constituted a subcommittee considering the Sundry Civil Appropriations Bill, which included Yellowstone Park language. While the wording inserted in the House did not cover all the subjects on Vest's agenda, at least it advanced some of the subjects. It read:

> For the protection and improvement of the Yellowstone National Park: For every purpose and object necessary for the protection, preservation, and improvement of the Yellowstone National Park including compensation of superintendent and employees, $15,000; and the Secretary of the Interior is herby prohibited from leasing any portion of the Yellowstone National Park to any person, company, or corporation for any purpose whatever; and all leases agreements, exclusive privileges, or monopolies granted or entered into are hereby declared to be of no force and effect; and the Secretary of War is hereby authorized and directed to make necessary details of troops to prevent trespassers or intruders entering the park with the object of destroying game therein, or for any other purpose prohibited by law.[13]

In an earlier conversation between Vest and Beck, there was some concern about this statement being beyond the authority of an appropriations bill. Vest had concluded it probably would not appear in the final draft. But Beck said on the floor, "There are so many things in the sundry civil bill which are more or less legislative that I rather think we shall be compelled to recognize much of what the House has done."[14] Vest applauded the subcommittee's position and said he welcomed the language.

Senator Dawes of Massachusetts, one of the primary backers of the Yellowstone law, noted that the language said "don't" on several subjects but provided no guide to the secretary about what he ought to do in the park in the future. Dawes called for passage of the resolution in addition to the appropriations language. Dawes said the park "has lain there without attracting any notice from visitors or anybody else for ten years since the act was adopted, and now it has come to the point, railroads going through there, that there must be a disposition of the care of the park; as it shall set out this year what its fate will be. It will be either a permanent park, reserved according to the original idea, or it will waste away and disappear among public lands."

Quick to embrace the support of other senators, Vest said there was no conflict between the resolution and the Sundry Civil Bill language and "they can stand together." He added that unless something was done, the original purposes of the park would be nullified. "It will become to all intents and purposes private property." If Congress waited to act until the hotel was built, he feared the hotel investors would "come here with a bill for damages or remuneration, and we shall be told that a case of vandalism in that park has been perpetrated unless the money of the people is taken to recompense them for what they have lost."

The congressional session was scheduled to end on March 3. Vest had little time to craft something that would accomplish the goals he had worked toward since the fall of 1882. On March 1, the Senate again took up the park matter as part of the sundry bill. The time had come for senators to move quickly through the bill, approving or defeating amendments and making compromises in quick order so as not to delay spending bills. The original draft amount for Yellowstone expenses was $15,000. Vest, urged by his supporters to do something about the lack of adequate supervision in the park, wanted to ensure that superintendent and assistants resided in the park.

Vest offered an amendment to the sundry bill that altered the administrative arrangement. He proposed a $40,000 appropriation, with $2,000 paid to the park superintendent and $900 each to ten assistants.[15] All assistants would be appointed by the secretary and reside in the park. Their specific duties would include protecting the game, timber, and other resources. The balance of the appropriation would be spent for construction and improvement of roads, under the supervision and direction of an engineer assigned by the secretary of war.

Vest said the amendment would correct the deficiency of having a nonresident superintendent. He claimed that all current problems with vandalism and poaching game and timber could be reduced or eliminated with a superintendent and assistants on the scene. He might have mentioned that the superintendents were paid nothing until 1878. Vest concluded, "I say to the Senate that unless some provision of this kind is put into this bill we might as well deliver that park up; let the whole dedication go for nothing, and just say to the people who had gone in there, 'You can take and destroy just as much as you please.'"[16] After a few comments from senators, the amendment was approved.

Another amendment limited the secretary's authority in signing agreements for commercial use of parklands. It reflected concern for the amount of acreage that could be controlled by investors, full public access to the park's special features, and making sure that no work on a hotel could commence without a lease executed by the secretary. Perhaps the most reactionary phrase dealt with decisions already made. It stated, "[A]nd all contracts, agreements, or exclusive privileges heretofore made or given in regard to said park, or any part thereof, are hereby declared to be invalid, nor shall the Secretary of the Interior, in any lease which he may make and execute, grant any exclusive privileges within said park, except upon the ground leased."[17] In other words, everything done with the improvement company to that point would be null and void, and the secretary would not be able to turn over all commercial activity to a single investor or group of investors.

While that amendment certainly carried plenty of material for lengthy debate, senators seemed most concerned about the exact amount of acreage on which hotels and outbuildings could be built. The original draft called for limiting the amount to eighty acres. Vest called for an amendment to the amendment (the Senate did this frequently), reducing the number to twenty acres. This compared favorably with a statement by Teller regarding negotiations with improvement company representatives that tracts would not exceed twenty acres. That prompted a discussion of what constituted appropriate acreage for a hotel and outbuildings.

Vest began the discussion, saying, "Eighty acres is a small farm. With a hotel put in an eligible locality so as to command the entire view, as I have said eighty acres would constitute an absolute monopoly not only in terms but in fact. On the other hand, if twenty acres are given it would be ample for all purposes. There is very little arable land in the [canyons] . . . . To argue that any more is necessary is simply ridiculous; it is a travesty upon the conception of a hotel building and hotel grounds."

Senator Harrison of Indiana, who as president in 1891 set aside permanent forest preserves adjacent to the park, requested a change in the acreage to ten, adding, "Twenty acres is too much; ten acres is abundant in any of those places." Vest quickly agreed to ten acres. Harrison had visited Yellowstone in 1881 and used examples from that trip to bolster his argument.

As consensus began to build for ten acres, one senator reminded colleagues that other aspects of the amendment deserved their attention. Hale of Maine captured that sentiment with this comment: "The general principle is laid down in this amendment, which is for the purpose of restricting and controlling the privileges, that everything valuable to the general public shall not be leased. No Secretary of the Interior, under this provision, will ever venture to lease a geyser or any object of natural curiosity, or to let a hotel be put anywhere where it will in any way interfere with the enjoyment of the public."[18] Hale added that the exact acreage was immaterial if the essential points remained in the amendment.

When the Senate voted on the amendment to strike eighty acres and substitute ten acres, twenty-five voted for the change, and twenty voted against. Thirty-one senators were absent.[19]

One final amendment remained for action. Vest wanted to soften the House language regarding use of military in the park. Vest disagreed with taking the decision to use soldiers in the park away from the secretary. He preferred to maintain the secretary's authority as specified in the original act. Vest proposed this language:

> The Secretary of War, upon the request of the Secretary of the Interior, is hereby authorized and directed to make the necessary details of troops to prevent trespassers or intruders from entering the park for the purpose of destroying the game or objects of curiosity therein, or for any other purpose prohibited by law, and remove such persons from the park if found therein.[20]

On March 3, the Senate approved the sundry appropriations bill, containing specific language to protect the park, which erased the McCook amendment. Bowing to Vest and the Senate on the park question, the House approved the changes. Although Vest's proposed law and his resolution were not considered by Congress, the appropriations bill contained many of the proposals. The first portion dealt with use of a $40,000 budget:

> For every purpose and object necessary for the protection, preservation, and improvement of the Yellowstone National Park, including compensation of superintendent and employees, forty thousand dollars, two thousand dollars of said amount to be paid annually to a superintendent of said park and not exceeding nine hundred dollars annually to each of ten assistants, all of whom shall be appointed by the Secretary of the Interior, and reside continuously in the park and whose duty it shall be to protect the game, timber, and objects of interest therein; the balance of the sum appropriated to be expended in the construction and improvement of suitable roads and bridges within said park, under the supervision and direction of an engineer officer detailed by the Secretary of War for that purpose.

The second part of the Yellowstone language dealt with restrictions of the authority of the secretary in approving leases and, more significantly, disallowed any previous agreements and spoke to the issue of a monopoly.

> The Secretary of the Interior may lease small portions of ground in the park, not exceeding ten acres in extent for each tract, on which may be erected hotels and the necessary outbuildings, and for a period not exceeding ten years; but such lease shall not include any of the geysers or other objects of curiosity or interest in said park, or exclude the public from the free and convenient approach thereto; or include any ground within one quarter of a mile of any of the geysers, or the Yellowstone Falls, nor shall there be leased more than ten acres to any one person or corporation; nor shall any hotel or other buildings be erected within the park until such lease shall be executed by the Secretary of the Interior, and all contracts, agreements, or exclusive privileges heretofore made or given in regard to said park of any part thereof, are hereby declared to be invalid; nor shall the Secretary of the Interior, in any lease which he may make or execute, grant any exclusive privileges within said park, except upon the ground leased.[21]

The final clause introduced military involvement and included the precise language introduced by Vest earlier.

In summary, Vest and park enthusiasts got most of what they had proposed in other forms. They stopped the monopoly, reduced the acreage, and kept the park open to the public. However, the law did not include expansion of the east and south park boundaries as proposed by Sheridan.

George Bird Grinnell wrote at length about provisions of the new law in an editorial titled "Mr. Vest's Victory," appearing a week after passage.[22] He began by stating the park was protected "from the greed of the body of men who have so earnestly striven to wrest it from the people of this country and turn it into a speculation with which to line their own pockets."

The editor saw in the provisions an assurance that commercial interests received a major setback, notwithstanding a major effort to prevent Congress from taking action. Grinnell said, "If they did not succeed in accomplishing their object it was not for want of energy, shrewdness, money, nor powerful backing. Some of the sharpest intellects, some of the best business ability in the country worked for them; they had unlimited money with which to influence legislation; they had an enormous political power behind them." He noted the press across the nation supported the improvement company. He claimed newspapers became "the willing tools of the ring."

Grinnell was effusive in his praise of Vest, observing, "They failed because Senator George G. Vest, of Missouri, occupies a seat in the Senate of these United States. Therefore every citizen owes to this gentleman warm thanks . . . . Only the people were on his side. He persevered, and in the face of every opposition succeeded in carrying through the measures . . . . We congratulate the senator on his victory." At the end of the editorial, he thanked Vest for saving the nation from the monopolists.

Nevertheless, Grinnell was disappointed that the park expansion idea died. "It is a matter of regret that the bill which provided for the extension of the limits of the Park could not have been passed during the present session of Congress, but we trust that as the next steps may be taken, in time, to set aside from settlement a considerable additional tract of territory on the south and east of the present Park." The editor picked up on comments during debate in the Senate about increased expenses if the park was expanded, saying, "The time will come, even if it is not already here, when the Yellowstone Park will be cheap to this nation at a million dollars a year. The picayune policy of saving a few dollars now, and by that means losing in the future something that it will be then wholly out of our power to regain, cannot be too strongly condemned."

One aspect of the Sundry Civil Bill provision was implemented by June. At that time, Teller appointed ten assistant park superintendents who were to be paid $900 each annually. They paid their own transportation to the park and subsistence while living there. The good intentions of Congress in expanding oversight on a continuous basis in the park still left something to be desired in execution. All of the assistants were political hires from the East and Midwest.

Most had no concept of the park, no experience in living and surviving in the West, and no special training. The assistants were ridiculed by trespassers in the park, and because they had no authority to make arrests, little could be accomplished in confronting vandals and poachers.

Meanwhile, such animosity existed between Superintendent Conger and officials of the improvement company that an internal quarrel flared, with the YPIC launching a campaign to oust Conger and get someone in the superintendent's position more amenable to commercial interests.

In spite of congressional action, park activists did not consider the issues of protection resolved. Vest knew his victory was insufficient for the long term. In spite of authorization to bring military forces into the park, the secretary showed no interest in making such a move. Sheridan wanted his primary goal of park expansion, and officials still had no legal authority to make arrests or prosecute violators of the law. Nor was it clear what laws applied. Participants in the campaign to save the park knew that another round of public awareness was necessary to keep the pressure on public officials.

Nothing had occurred to restrain persons who killed wildlife for skins or tossed cans and other debris into the geyser holes. Although the improvement company would succeed in obtaining a lease, its officials were not satisfied with conditions in the park. They wanted more money devoted to building roads, increased law enforcement, and greater authority to develop commercial interests.

The war continued.

5

The Race to Open a Hotel

PARTIES TO THE BATTLE OVER DEVELOPMENT OF
Yellowstone National Park barely paused in pursuit of their interests after approval
of federal legislation. Senator Vest began work immediately on a bill to reshape park
boundaries. Secretary Teller, restrained only slightly by congressional action, proceeded
to put a lease in place for commercial growth. Nervous about the approaching tourist
season at Mammoth Hot Springs Hotel, the improvement company resumed its pressure
for improved roads and tighter security.

The increased intensity of Vest's legislative mission was expressed in a June 13
letter to Teller, voicing displeasure with the department and warning the secretary of
congressional action to come. Vest wrote, "I desire to urge the immediate attention of
your Department to the fact stated in the paper which I handed you a few days [earlier]
on the floor of the Senate. Since that time, I am in receipt of information corroborating
those statements, and I have no doubt that men are now at work in the Yellowstone Park,
cutting down timber, and living on game killed *under contract*. This should be stopped
at once. The bill reported from the Committee on Territories of the Senate, will pass as
soon as I can get it up, and its terms and provisions should require some attention by
Mr. [Rufus] Hatch and his associates, even *now*. As a quasi declaration of the views of
Congress, coming from a Senate Committee, it should not be entirely ignored."[1]

Vest's thinly veiled threat probably had its motivation on March 9 when Teller
and improvement company executives—Hobart, Douglas, and Hatch—announced
the signing of a lease for developments in the park. Carefully threading his way under
authority of the 1872 law and restrictions approved on March 3, Teller granted a
lease for ten acres of land. Rather than choosing one location for development, Teller
divided the acreage into seven parcels of a little more than one acre, each located
at or near one of the seven points of greatest interest in the park.[2] While Congress
denied the improvement company a monopoly, Teller found a way to give investors
a partial victory. In his announcement of the lease, Teller said it was done in the best

interests of the government, the park, and the public to hold business interests "to an absolute minimum."

Specifically, restrictions of law dealt with the size of ground that could be developed and access by the public to the park's geysers and Yellowstone Falls. Teller's careful waltz with the new law is contained in details of the lease. Article 1 of the lease declared seven sites for development and the size of ground for each. Most of the descriptions are familiar to visitors of the park today and are essentially the locations for facilities in the twenty-first century. The locations, with specific legal descriptions and specifications omitted in this account, were:

1. "Beginning at the centre of a building known as McCartney's Store," two acres of land, "more or less." This was the site at Mammoth Hot Springs.
2. "Beginning at a point due east from the center of 'Old Faithful,'" one and a half acres.
3. "Beginning upon the south bank of Madison River at a point one mile east from the corner," containing one and a half acres.
4. "Beginning at a point due east from the easterly side of Soda Springs and distant therefrom twenty-five feet," containing one acre.
5. "Beginning at a point due east from 'Tower Falls,' and distant therefrom twenty-five feet," one and a half acres.
6. "Beginning at a point due east from the head of 'Canon or Great Falls,'" one and a half acres.
7. "Beginning upon the bank of Yellowstone Lake, at the outlet," and along the bank, one acre.

The agreement covered access to the park's wonders by placing the parcels of land at least one quarter of a mile from the geysers and Yellowstone Falls and gave use of the land to the company for ten years, a period stipulated in the law.

Article 2 dealt with an agreement to build one large hotel, presumably at Mammoth Hot Springs, and an authorization to build hotels on locations 2 through 7. The "one hotel" was to contain not less than 250 rooms at a cost, including furnishings, of not less than $150,000, along with "outhouses, bath and ice houses and electric-light machinery." All plans for hotels and other buildings were to be approved by the secretary of the Interior. This article made it clear the secretary could approve leases with different parties at other park locations for similar facilities.

Article 3 specified a rental charge of $2 per acre per year, a figure widely criticized in Congress and by protectors of the park as being a gift. Article 4 described the default process by which the lease could be terminated and the improvements turned over to the government. This covered failure to pay the rent or keep the covenants of the agreement. The company agreed in Article 5 to submit an itemized schedule and tariff of charges to be paid for accommodations and services for approval by the secretary. Language made it clear that the company could not charge more than the approved amount.

Article 6 involved the conduct of company employees and the requirements for employment in the park. The company agreed to "require and enforce obedience . . . on the part of all persons employed by them or under their control within the said Park." No person declared "to be subversive of the good order and management" of the park could be employed by the company. Article 7 also addressed the legal procedures for control of the land by the government and the processes of default.

The delicate subjects of mining, cutting timber, and killing game were covered by Article 8. Protectors of the park raised these concerns frequently, and they would continue to be points of contention between the company and the department. The article said the company could not mine or remove from the land any gold, silver, copper, or other precious mineral, adding, "nor to mine any coal, nor cut or remove from said land any timber, excepting as may be authorized by the Secretary of the Interior . . ." The company agreed not to permit any employees "to injure or destroy any of the game, or any mineral deposit, natural curiosity, or wonder within the Park."

In one of the briefest but most important statements in terms of park usage, Article 9 prohibited the exclusion of the public from "the free and convenient approach" to geysers "or other objects of curiosity or interest" in the park. The final three articles dealt with correcting errors in land descriptions, prohibiting the transfer of the agreement without approval of the secretary, and stating that no member of or delegate to Congress could participate in or derive benefit from the lease. This excluded the likes of senators Roscoe Conkling and William Windom, both involved in creation of the Yellowstone National Park Improvement Company, from participation as investors or business partners while in office.

The lease arrangement received predictable commentary. On one side, including Assistant Secretary Joslyn, those who favored giving the improvement company a lease based on the original contract—4,500 acres and a monopoly of development—expressed concern for the loss of rental income under the restricted land lease. Joslyn noted that the original plan would have collected $9,000 at $2 an acre and, under the lease, would result in government income of only $20. *Forest and Stream* editor Grinnell responded in an editorial, "This is very true, but whether the loss of the $8,980 to the United States Treasury is as serious a matter as those sad-voiced scribes would have us believe is open to a little doubt. If the Interior Department had, as it seemed at one time likely to do, bartered away all the rights of the people for ten years to this lovely spot for $9,000 would it not have been thought that these dollars had cost the nation dear? We think so."

Grinnell preferred to consider the landgrab subject old news, saying, "The improvement company may yet try to seize on portions of the reservation, but it is for the officers of the Government to look out for this matter. The law is on the side of the people." He voiced pleasure that Teller had expressed some interest in calling on Secretary of War Lincoln for a detail of troops to guard the park and the game. Grinnell moved to the subject of expansion of the park, an unresolved issue originally championed by Sheridan. He wrote, "With the opening of the next session of Congress we hope to see a bill introduced embodying the essential features of Senator Vest's bill of last session, and providing for the enlargement of the Park on the east and south, as suggested by us recently."[3]

Any doubts about interest in commercial development within and near the park were dispelled by a review of requests for leases and permissions from a variety of people across the nation to Teller. In the wake of change in development law and the signing of a lease with the improvement company, letters flowed to the secretary's office proposing all manner of small- to medium-sized business ventures. There is little evidence that the department looked favorably on many of them.

A request from St. Louis expressed interest in building a facility in the park to display mining specimens and for a grocery and produce business. A man from Cincinnati asked for an acre or two for a hotel, without providing any plans. Another, from Minnesota, asked for ten acres for an unspecified purpose. A Montana man wanted a license to trade in the park, and a Bozeman writer sought permission to keep dairy cows in the park and promised them that would not interfere with tourist travel. Another Bozeman request sought land for four small buildings to sell fruits, confectionary, newspapers, and periodicals. A man from Virginia City, Montana, asked to use land near the Lower Geyser Basin to erect a tent and provide items for sale, promising he could beat the prices of any other providers. All of these surfaced within days of the signing of a lease.[4]

During this time, work continued on the Mammoth Hot Springs Hotel although approvals and paperwork lagged. According to the lease, Teller had the responsibility of approving final plans for the facility. On May 7, Hobart submitted drawings and details prepared by Leroy S. Buffington, a St. Paul architect for a number of mansions and referred to as the Father of the Skyscraper.[5] The plans called for a structure 414 feet long, 54 feet deep, and four stories high. In the summer when tourists began arriving, the hotel had 141 "commodious" rooms, according to Hatch, who also declared the facility "substantially built." That, of course, was open to a variety of opinion.

The department, activated by Teller, wasted little time in review and approval. Thomas Hassard, a department civil engineer, wrote Teller on May 9 that he had examined the plans and "in my judgment the cost of the building when completed according to the plans, and furnished, will exceed $150,000."[6] That was the minimum cost established by the lease. Teller issued an approval letter the same day as Hassard's report.

Signing a lease and approval of the architectural plan inspired Hobart to write park officials and Teller with requests—actually, more like demands—for action and improvements in park security and interior roads. With the Mammoth hotel scheduled for use by tourists in the summer, these issues obviously caused concern for project officials and investors. On both subjects, Hobart's letters appeared to generate government action, some of which may have been under way previously.

Hobart's letter of May 15 dealt primarily with the security matters.[7] He noted that the superintendent and assistants who were to be hired had no authority to make arrests or punish people for violation of U.S. laws or those of Wyoming Territory, in which the park rested. Citing an increase in tourists and completion of the Northern Pacific rail line near the park, Hobart requested Teller's assistance in encouraging Wyoming to assume responsibility for park law enforcement. "There should be more additional and more practicable means of prevention of violation of law and order and for the protection of life and property within the Park," Hobart stated.

Hobart's concerns did generate a response from Teller—beginning with a letter to William Hale, governor of Wyoming Territory, asking for comments.[8] County, local community, and territory officials addressed the issue, unanimously concluding nothing could be done. The Uinta County attorney's reply from Evanston, in the far southwestern corner of the territory, summed up the difficulty in getting cooperation from Wyoming. C. D. Clark, the county official, wrote that he was unable to find any law that would authorize an officer to enforce territory laws in the park. The officer, at best, "would have but a shadow of authority under which to act, and which, in my opinion, could be successfully attacked. I believe the matter can only be fully reached before the next general election by some action of the legislature . . ."[9] The security issue was resolved much later by providing a military presence in the park.

The roads concern, addressed by Hobart in a letter to Teller on May 28, received more positive attention. He had received a notice from Interior through Secretary Lincoln that an engineer would be appointed to work on improving roads.[10] Hobart said roads "at present time are unsafe for any sort of transportation" and urged the engineer not to wait until the fiscal year started on July 1 to survey the situation and start planning for improvements. The methodical bureaucracy was about to frustrate Hobart.

Teller forwarded Hobart's request to Secretary of War Lincoln, who answered on June 19, referring the matter to the Office of the Chief of Engineers of the army.[11] A reply dated June 15 from John G. Parke, acting chief, stated that the park was in the jurisdiction of the Military Division of the Missouri and that command should assign an engineer for park duty.[12]

Government officials appointed an engineer for Yellowstone duty in July, well past Hobart's requested time. Lt. Dan C. Kingman of the Corps of Engineers received the assignment to design and construct a road system in the park that everyone hoped would make the place more inviting to visit. Teller instructed Conger that all matters regarding engineering subjects would be Kingman's responsibility and the superintendent would have no direct authority over the engineer's work.[13] Given the huge task facing Kingman, no one really expected a miracle on the short term.

Hobart continued his barrage of letters to Teller complaining of problems in the park, calling attention "to what appears to be a great injustice, if not a violation of our privileges," granted under the lease regarding transportation to and from the hotel.[14] Hobart said the company intended to provide conveyances for tourists throughout the park at the rate of $25. He complained about "a man named Chadbourn[e]" who planned to provide similar services in competition with the improvement company. A. W. Chadbourne informed Hobart that Superintendent Conger said the same rights and privileges existed for him as for the company. Obviously irate, Hobart contacted Conger, who confirmed the conversation and statement about equal rights. The lease stated the secretary could grant development on land not specifically provided to the company.

Hobart used all the reasons he could find in an appeal to Teller. "Our case, for ourselves, and as against all other parties claiming such privileges, is this: We have invested and are investing large sums of money under your contract or subject to your approval and supervision. We are aiming to construct buildings and furnish a service for the public which will be creditable to the Park . . ." Noting that visitors and tourists would complain about the company if unhappy about service, he pointed a finger at those who had objected earlier when the improvement company arrived. "Already several parties who have been systematically robbed by the old gang who have run matters here for years have gone away highly indignant because the National Park Improvement Company treated them so unjustly," Hobart said. No documents survive that reflect Teller's response, although subsequent department actions tended to sympathize with Hobart.

The improvement company, in this case headed by Hatch, in July complied with another portion of the lease: submission of tariffs and charges for services and accommodations. Building as strong a case for the prices as possible, Hatch spoke to the issues of fairness, competition, and research. He compared charges with services provided at the time by guides in the park, concluding, "the rates charged are in every instance lower."[15] He added, "The list as now handed to you is the result of our best judgment on the subject, and I assure you that the rates are fair, reasonable and just." Hatch acknowledged rates were experimental to some extent and might be subject to later revision. Hatch obviously prepared the prices, then sent his private secretary to Yellowstone to get Hobart's approval.

The pressure of opening for business in the summer of 1883 resulted in a contract arrangement with Wakefield & Hoffman of Helena, Montana, to provide stage transportation. Hatch referred to the firm as "old and experienced Montana state managers, and amply responsible in a pecuniary sense." The improvement company intended to provide its own stage services in 1884.

At each of the places authorized for use under the lease, arrangements were made for overnight accommodations using tents. Hatch wrote, "We shall have fixed or permanent hotel camps of from ten to twenty five tents in each place, with large dining tent, cooking tent." Each tent for tourists would have carpeted flooring and bedstead "to be as comfortable as a room in hotel." The company planned to keep a small herd of cows at each station to provide fresh milk, "a luxury at present unattainable in any part of the Park." Unable to predict when the Northern Pacific line would be completed to Cinnabar, Hatch included a footnote to charge a prorated portion of the round-trip rate of $25 to Mammoth Hot Springs. The stated rate from Cinnabar was $1.

For a one-night stay at the Mammoth Hot Springs Hotel or in a tent at a fixed camp, a tourist would pay $5 for lodging in a single room, 75¢ for a private bath in the room, and 50¢ for each meal served in the room. For a trip from the hot springs to the Upper Geyser Basin, the fee was $9. The charge was $10 for a trip from the geyser basin to the canyon falls. A tourist could hit all the scenic spots and return to the hot springs for $25. The rate proposal was approved quickly.

As July ended, tourists arrived, and a visit to the park by President Chester A. Arthur was looming. The Yellowstone National Park Improvement Company was in business and partially ready.

Chester A. Arthur, President 1881-1885
Library of Congress

Lt. Gen. Philip H. Sheridan, U. S. Army
Library of Congress/Mathew Brady photo

6

A "Perfectly Safe" Presidential Expedition

INITIAL CONVERSATIONS ABOUT A JOURNEY BY President Chester A. Arthur to Yellowstone National Park likely occurred during the winter of 1882 to 1883. From that point, plans for the excursion evolved under guidance of General Sheridan and Senator Vest, partners in the park's protection. The first recorded communication is a letter from Sheridan to Vest dated January 31, 1883, referring to previous comments from the senator on January 22.[1]

Vest may have raised the subject with Arthur before contacting the general. Sheridan wrote, "If you and the President would like to go to the National Park the coming summer, I will place myself at your service and will only be too glad to do so. I have all the means on hand to take you in a comfortable manner without making any fuss about it." Sheridan's detached phrasing sounds as if he was not involved in the first talks, but that does not necessarily mean he was uninformed. Both men could see the value of a presidential expedition to Yellowstone as a means of elevating the park's image to the general public.

Demonstrating his enthusiasm for the journey, Sheridan presented ideas for the president's participation. These changed somewhat over the months until August, but the general's original basic concept remained the same. He grabbed the idea and ran with it, even to the point of mentioning the gear for which the government would not be responsible: ". . . [T]he fishing tackle and guns which every man must provide for himself."

Sheridan suggested a limited number of invited guests, including the president, primarily to minimize a strain on the care and feeding of important people. "The President can ask to go with him three persons, I one, myself making the sixth," he wrote. To reach the desired number of eight, Sheridan included two personal military aides, Lieutenant Colonel Gregory and Lieutenant Colonel Sheridan, the general's brother. Presumably, Vest would be among the president's guests, although that was not stated.

Sheridan also mentioned having a doctor along, the same surgeon who accompanied him on the 1881 and 1882 trips. He suggested leaving for Yellowstone on August 1, about the time of year he made the trip in both previous years.

For months, reports circulated in the press that Arthur had been diagnosed with Bright's disease, a fatal affliction of the kidney. The president's aides and friends denied the claims and pronounced the president's problems simply as fatigue resulting from the burdens of office. Biographers George Frederick Howe and Thomas C. Reeves documented the progression of Arthur's failing condition in 1882 and 1883, which coincides with his decision for a park excursion to get away from Washington and the pressures of the presidency.[2]

Howe described an incident in April when Arthur was stricken and unable to perform ceremonial activities. In order to play down the seriousness, aides called the reports exaggerated. This ongoing concern over Arthur's health may have raised a question about the president's physical ability to make the trip. In a letter to Vest early in April, Sheridan mentioned the president's participation but wrote as if the trip would take place with or without Arthur, saying at one point, "Should the President not be able to go, I will take you and General [Illinois Senator John A.] Logan, And four others you may select . . ."[3]

In the months after Sheridan's first letter to Vest, the two had opportunities to meet and discuss plans on occasions when Sheridan traveled to Washington from his office in Chicago. They also corresponded on the subject, as in a letter from the senator to Sheridan early in April. Sheridan responded on April 9 with more specific ideas for the journey and assurances of good times and little strain. He wrote, "It will be, my dear Senator, a fine trip, perfectly safe and comfortable, and cannot be taken in this world except under the same auspices . . . . On our return, my dear Senator, I am sure you will feel as if your longevity had been increased 20 years."[4] That was surely a message for Vest to transmit to the president.

Sheridan had expanded the list of specific names to include Sen. John Alexander Logan of Illinois, a general during the Civil War and hero of volunteer soldiers. Earlier, Logan and Vest had been placed on a select Senate committee to study the condition of Indian tribes in the Montana and Dakota territories during the late summer of 1883. Under the leadership of Senator Dawes, members planned to meet with tribal leaders in the Montana and Dakota territories and to report their findings to Congress.[5] Aware of this potential conflict with the Arthur trip, Sheridan said in the letter that Logan had committed to the Yellowstone trip and would write Dawes to be relieved of the assignment. The general asked Vest to do the same. "I wish you would do so also, or better perhaps divide the duties of the commission and you and General Logan take the Shoshone [tribe] for your part."[6] This conflict was not resolved until nearer the expedition date.

Sheridan spelled out plans for the trip in detail, saying he would meet the Washington contingent in Chicago on August 1. The entire party would leave Chicago by railroad for Rawlins, Wyoming Territory, where military wagons would be ready for the 120-mile, a day and a half, overland journey to Fort Washakie and the Shoshone and Arapaho Indian reservations along the eastern edge of the Wind River mountain range.[7]

Noting the wilderness aspect of the trip, Sheridan wrote, "On leaving Washakie we will bid adieu to civilization, and in fifteen or sixteen days will reach the Upper Geyser Basin." The route would include the Lower Geyser Basin, Grand Canyon of the Yellowstone, Mammoth Hot Springs, and outside the park to Fort Ellis and a Northern Pacific train connection south of Livingston.[8] Hoping not to alarm Vest or others about potential discomforts, the general said, "This distance will be made in easy marches and we will encamp on a trout stream every day, and those who want to hunt, after two or three days out will find plenty of game. This will probably be the most interesting part of the trip." He must have known of Vest's enthusiasm for fly-fishing. Sheridan promised all provisions and accommodations would be provided, "except the clothing you may want to wear, which should be some of your old clothes suitable to horseback riding."

The commitment by Arthur to the Yellowstone journey apparently occurred late in the spring of 1883, although there are no published accounts. It is obvious the decision was made by June 14 when Sheridan sent a lengthy letter to the president's private secretary, F. J. Phillips. He said, "I learn from Senator Vest and Gov. Crosby, that the President continues of the opinion . . . that he would be able to take a trip to the Yellowstone National Park during the month of August."[9] The general sketched the expedition from Rawlins to Livingston much as he had done in the April letter to Vest.

Sheridan provided the following list of "articles of personal outfit" for the president:

- four sets of winter underclothing
- four sets of summer underclothing
- four outer woolen shirts with pockets
- two suits of rough clothes, one heavy and one ordinarily light
- one heavy winter overcoat, ulster-style preferable
- one rubber coat
- one pair riding boots or shoes with leggings
- one dry pair of socks

The clothing needs may appear skimpy for an overland journey away from the normal comforts afforded a president. Sheridan planned for orderlies, or army enlisted men, to accompany the party and care for the dignitaries, keeping them in relatively clean and dry clothing.

Sheridan left it open that Arthur might prefer some other personal items. He said everything should be contained in two steamer trunks about thirty inches long, sixteen inches wide, and fourteen inches deep. Sheridan suggested a hand satchel for toilet articles, adding, "fishing tackle for trout fishing, and guns, can be taken in an extra package."[10] Arthur was known to favor trout fishing as a sport and had earlier ordered new equipment, presumably anticipating the journey. As he had done in letters to Vest,

Sheridan promised that, en route to the geyser basin, the party would camp every night on a trout steam; and if hunting was of interest, there were plentiful supplies of elk, bear, deer, and antelope.

Further evidence of the specific members of the party, numbering ten, was contained in the letter. He named Arthur and a "personal secretary," senators Vest and Logan, Montana Territory Governor John S. Crosby, two officers, and the general—making eight.[11] Arthur chose not to take a personal secretary. Sheridan offered the president and Vest an opportunity to name one additional person. Sheridan enclosed a map with the route from Fort Washakie to Livingston marked with a blue line. Departure day from Chicago was only six weeks away, and many decisions remained to be made and orders to be issued.

One of the matters concerned the involvement of Vest and Logan as members of the Senate subcommittee investigating the condition of Indian tribes. Logan resolved his participation by withdrawing from the president's expedition and committing fully to the Senate task.[12] Interestingly, the subcommittee planned to leave Chicago for its trip on almost the exact day as Arthur's group. Vest decided to combine the two responsibilities. He felt an obligation to the Senate responsibility, but Vest also had much at stake in the presidential journey and its consequences for the campaign to pass further legislation in Congress. Dawes, concerned about the future of Yellowstone, would have been sympathetic to Vest meeting both obligations. Vest traveled with the president until they reached Montana Territory, and then joined Martin Maginnis, territorial delegate to Congress, for meetings with Montana tribal officials. Sheridan replaced Logan with Anson Stager of Chicago, a brigadier general in the Civil War and a corporate officer of Western Union.[13]

Sheridan acknowledged another late addition to the list in a letter of July 7 to Daniel Rollins, a surrogate of New York City and a close friend of Arthur's. The general repeated most of the requirements sent to the president, adding that a rifle for hunting elk, deer, and antelope, and a shotgun for mountain grouse were appropriate. Another of Arthur's friends, George Vest, Jr., son of the senator, joined the group. At some point, Secretary of War, Robert T. Lincoln, who had missed the 1882 journey, signed up. As Sheridan's civilian boss, he could have been the choice of either Arthur or Sheridan, or both.

The final list of participants included:

1. President Arthur
2. Secretary of War Lincoln
3. Senator Vest
4. Lieutenant General Sheridan
5. Montana Governor Crosby
6. Daniel Rollins
7. General Stager
8. George Vest, Jr.
9. Lieutenant Colonel Gregory

10. Lieutenant Colonel Sheridan
11. Major Forwood, surgeon
12. Captain Clark, Second Cavalry

Also accompanying the party was photographer F. Jay Haynes, who provided the only pictures of the expedition and is believed to be the only participant who kept a diary.

With the party members determined and all informed of their responsibilities by Sheridan, military authorities turned their attention to communication, security, supplies and rations, and other items critical for a successful journey into mostly unsettled territory. Hiram M. Chittenden, captain in the Corps of Engineers who wrote *The Yellowstone Park*, described the total effort:

> The most elaborate expedition that ever passed through this region took place in August, 1883 . . . The interesting part of the journey lay between Fort Washakie, Wyoming, and the Northern Pacific Railroad at Cinnabar, Montana. The party traveled entirely on horseback, accompanied by one of the most complete pack trains ever organized in this or any other country, and escorted by a full troop of cavalry. Couriers were stationed every twenty miles with fresh relays, and by this means, communication was daily had with the outside world . . . . The elaborate equipment of this expedition, the eminent character of its personnel, and the evident responsibility resting upon those who conducted it, attracted a great deal of attention at the time, and gave it a prominent place in the annals of Western Wyoming.[14]

Perhaps the most important military assignment, other than Sheridan's, belonged to Capt. Edward M. Hayes, commander of Troop G, U.S. Fifth Cavalry. Hayes's seventy-five-man troop escorted the dignitaries throughout the trip, providing a variety of services that included security.[15] Those attached to Hayes's troop included fourteen enlisted soldiers brought by Captain Clark from Fort McKinney, Wyoming Territory, to serve as orderlies. In a communiqué listing responsibilities for Hayes, Lieutenant Colonel Sheridan stated the importance of doing a flawless job:

> "I am directed to impress on you confidentially that the President and Secretary of War will go with this expedition, and you are expected to have everything in the most complete and compact shape."[16]

In most cases, Sheridan and his aides reached out to military officers and civilians who had reputations for efficiency and success under difficult circumstances. One such person was Thomas Moore, the packmaster for General Crook. Moore had proved himself innovative and dependable in providing mobile mule packtrains in Crook's successful campaigns against the Apache Indians in Arizona and also in providing packtrains for Sheridan's 1882 excursion to Yellowstone. Moore assembled 175 mules and horses from Cheyenne Depot, Wyoming, and Fort Custer, Montana Territory.[17] Huge amounts of rations and grain were ordered and deposited at the supply camp not far from Fort Washakie.

Leaving no subject to chance, Lieutenant Colonel Sheridan asked a trader at Fort Washakie for the names of a "good guide" and an "active willing man who is a successful hunter" to provide fresh game for invited guests. For the right person, the military would pay $5 per day with rations. However, the guide and hunter had to provide their own horses.[18]

As Lieutenant Colonel Sheridan issued orders in the general's name to various military people, he also communicated on July 6 to Maj. J. H. Lord, quartermaster at Cheyenne, regarding the movement of Arthur's party from Rawlins to Fort Washakie.[19] Sheridan said that three mule-drawn spring wagons would be available and that the trip to Fort Washakie would take two days, moving about ten miles an hour to cover the 140 miles. He noted there would be "considerable baggage" to transport on the wagons. This was the route scouted in 1882 by Lieutenant Colonel Gregory who called it the best available from the rail line. Sheridan identified the Sweetwater River crossing as the best place to stop overnight. Nevertheless, Sheridan quoted Gregory as saying accommodations at the crossing were "very poor."

Throughout preparations, General Sheridan had stated the overland portion of the journey would begin at Rawlins after debarking the Union Pacific train. At some point after July 6, the decision was made to depart from Green River Station rather than Rawlins, which added about one hundred miles to the rail trip. No explanation has been found. Despite the change, arrangements for transporting Arthur and party were the same, and the overnight location was still scheduled for the Sweetwater crossing.

One of the most critical arrangements was for communications with the outside world by telegraph. Sheridan, with the urging of Arthur and Lincoln, had made the decision not to allow any newspaper reporters to accompany the expedition. In a telegram to Lincoln a few days before the trip began, Sheridan said, "I am of your opinion that if we have a newspaper man along our pleasure will be destroyed. Since telegraphing you I have made arrangements . . . to have Colonel Sheridan send news daily for the Associated Press and I think this will settle the matter."[20]

That did not settle the matter. Newspaper editors and reporters across the country complained bitterly about being left behind and attempted to gather information from unofficial sources. That led to articles containing serious errors and misstatements. Nonetheless, dispatches for the Associated Press were prepared daily by Lieutenant Colonels Sheridan and Gregory, who were approved by the president, and were sent by courier to a telegraph location. Details of the journey not included in the AP dispatches were lost to history, except for newspaper accounts that were soundly condemned by military officers.

Daily articles to the Associated Press were transported by courier to Fort Washakie during the first few days of the journey. After that, couriers took telegraph material to Fort Ellis in Montana Territory. Similar arrangements were made for receiving and sending mail. As an example, for the last half of the expedition, Capt. J. T. Wheelan at

Fort Custer was instructed to set up a daily courier system for mail and telegrams between Shoshone Lake in the southern part of the park, and Fort Ellis, in Montana, for use by August 1.[21] Wheelan was to establish relay stations from the Upper and Lower Geyser basins to Mammoth Hot Springs, twenty miles apart, each staffed with a minimum of three men. The captain got the clear message as to the importance of the courier system when Lieutenant Colonel Sheridan wrote, "The Lieut. General relies on your knowledge of the country and good judgment, to carry out all the details in accordance with what you know of his desires."

About a week before the expedition started, a reporter for the Associated Press interviewed the general in Chicago.[22] Sheridan laid out the schedule and route to Yellowstone Park, sharing planned activities and dates at certain locations. He inferred the president had made a decision to go on the journey just days before the interview that was published in newspapers on July 24. Sheridan explained, "The arrangements made for this expedition are exactly the same as heretofore [1881 and 1882], and the expedition would have occurred whether the president had gone or not." Perhaps Arthur had recently agreed to join the trip as Sheridan suggested, but the plans for his participation had been in the mix since spring.

In essence, Sheridan said this excursion was no different from many he had taken over the years into different parts of the West. The value of his expeditions, he said, was demonstrated by the increase in settlement to remote areas after he visited them and wrote a widely published report. "Ever since 1870, I have almost without exception annually made one of these exploring expeditions in any division, from Texas and New Mexico to the dominion [Canadian] line, in order to gain information from actual observations and make reliable reports on the sections visited, with a view to encouraging their settlement." Sheridan used two examples to make his point. "After my exploration of the Big Horn mountains the entire eastern base of that range was settled, and now thousands of cattle and fine farms are seen in that region. The valley of Gros Ventre and Teton basin have already been invaded by pioneers, following my exploration of last year . . ."

In one comment, Sheridan alluded to his interest in expanding the park and the connection of that idea with the journey. "I particularly wish the president and secretary and Senator Vest to learn something from observation about the National park. It should be enlarged as recommended by me last year. The extension I propose is principally on the south line, a country over which we shall pass and I am in hopes that the information these gentlemen may acquire will have a tendency to induce congress to adopt my views."

Sheridan went out of his way in the interview to show that the cost of the expedition, with or without Arthur along, would not be an additional expense to taxpayers. This is how the Associated Press paraphrased Sheridan's explanation: "There would be no expense attached to it, and had been none to any of the expeditions the general had made in former years. Pack trains and cavalry were on hand, having to be kept always in readiness in anticipation of Indian troubles. Men receive their actions and horses their forage when at posts, and as the guides are usually taken from those in government employ, the matter of expense is not greater than would occur should the president not go at all." Historian Richard A. Bartlett rephrased that explanation in today's terms, saying, "This was the nineteenth century counterpart of the politician using an Air Force plane which 'had to make the journey anyway.' Substitute horses for airplanes and the situation remains the same."[23]

Sheridan said all guests on the journey would pay for their own meals (referred to in military talk as "mess") and any incidental expense. As to the cost of train travel to Green River and from Montana, Sheridan explained, "The railroad companies knowing their value have always kindly furnished complimentary transportation for parties who have accompanied me. They do it in this case." The general said he mentioned the cost subject "because some criticisms have heretofore been made in this respect."

While Sheridan emphasized the pleasure aspect of the trip and the opportunity for Arthur to see a new part of the country, the underlying reasons beyond Sheridan's support for expansion of the park were apparent to others. There was more at stake as recited in an editorial by George Bird Grinnell on July 26 in *Forest and Stream*.

Grinnell noted crowds of tourists were visiting Yellowstone National Park during the summer, thanks largely to promotional trips on the Northern Pacific Railroad. He voiced no objection to sightseers in the park but stated that the most important visitors were in the President Arthur party who were about to begin the excursion under the command of Sheridan, including some of the nation's most important public officials.[24]

"No doubt they will have a good time, will catch a lot of fish, and, without the boundaries of the Park, kill some game," he wrote. "But the important point of the excursion will be that members of the government, whose influence should be strongest in shaping legislation on this important subject, will be able to see for themselves a part of the needs of the Nation in respect to the Yellowstone Park," he said. There is not time on such a trip to understand all that is necessary to preserve the park, "but intelligent men cannot fail to acquire much useful knowledge especially when they are accompanied by one who is so familiar with a considerable portion of the reservation as is Gen. Sheridan."

Much of the remaining editorial was devoted to support for Sheridan's idea of expanding boundaries of the park. Grinnell surmised that Arthur might be so impressed as to recommend enlargement of the park in his next message to Congress.[25] Calling for expansion on the south and east sides of the park, Grinnell added, "On both sides there are wonders which should be preserved to the people at large." Cattlemen in the region targeted by Grinnell could be bought out for a few thousand dollars, "an expense which should not be considered when the importance to the country at large is realized." Grinnell specifically pinpointed Jackson Hole and the Teton Mountains as likely prospects. The Arthur party would pass through Jackson Hole with a full frontage view of the magnificent Tetons.

Concluding on a hopeful note, Grinnell declared, "We are confident that this pleasure trip will next winter, in Washington, bear abundant fruit."

7

The Presidential Journey

Washington, DC, to Green River Station, Wyoming
July 30 to August 6, 1883

PRESIDENT ARTHUR WAS ALREADY A DAY LATE FOR the Yellowstone Park expedition when he departed Washington for Louisville, Kentucky, on the morning of July 30.[1] The ripple effect meant that planned social events as far away as Chicago were drastically altered.

There was, of course, political sniping as Arthur and cabinet officials began a trip of more than a month away from the nation's capital. As the journey began, one news account of Arthur's departure carried this comment: "A few Democratic editors have begun to carp at what they call the President's junket, but there certainly is no citizen of Washington who does not wish him health and pleasure on his vacation."[2] That rather soft landing by the writer probably reflected knowledge in Washington of the president's delicate health and his unlikely candidacy for president in 1884.

Arthur's itinerary before reaching Chicago (Sheridan had hoped for an August 1 departure) included a stopover to help launch the Southern Exposition in Louisville, the first of five annual celebrations in the city. This was no small-time event. The exposition, mostly an industrial and mercantile show, was held for one hundred days each year on forty-five acres south of Louisville's Central Park.[3] At the time, only the 1876 centennial celebration in Philadelphia was a larger show. With high expectations for a presidential visit, Kentuckians hoped Arthur would be on hand for several days. When the schedule changed, a fishing outing had to be cancelled in addition to numerous parties.[4]

The president arrived on July 31 as a battery of artillery on the riverfront fired a salute. Arthur brought a trainload of dignitaries from Washington, including War Secretary Lincoln; Treasury Sec. Charles J. Folder; Postmaster Gen. Walter Q. Gresham; Daniel Rollins of New York; Delaware Sen. Thomas F. Bayard; and U.S. Reps. Perry Belmont, E. H. Green, and C. C. Baldwin. Joining the celebrities in Louisville, after a train ride from Chicago, were General Sheridan, his brother Lieutenant Colonel Sheridan, and their wives. All, including Kentucky State and Louisville City officials, attended the grand opening at the exposition building, a banquet and reception.

Even with curtailment of Louisville events, Arthur's schedule in Chicago faced serious alteration. In a telegram to Chicago officials on August 1, Lincoln said, "At the last moment the president is compelled to change his plans. We will not reach Chicago until to-morrow evening. This will require the postponement of all Chicago arrangements until his return from the west. We will have no time on Friday, except to prepare to leave on the special train."[5]

Reporters from Chicago newspapers covered Louisville festivities as if they were backyard events, primarily because of the president's expected stop later in the Illinois city.[6] Hoping for glimpses of the president or even a quick interview, reporters grabbed at any anecdote to record their presence. A *Chicago Tribune* reporter started coverage of the trip from Louisville to Chicago by observing, "President Arthur quit Louisville yesterday morning in a bad mood."[7] This was attributed to the president having stayed up until 2 a.m. attending various parties and arising at 7 a.m. to prepare for leaving the city.

The same reporter noted details of the special train: "[A]n ordinary coach, a dining car, the President's coach, and the private car of Col. Bennett Young, president of the Louisville, New Albany & Chicago Railroad." George M. Pullman provided his private "palace on wheels" for the president's trip to Chicago. Nevertheless, another reporter observed, "The head of one of the greatest nations on earth travels with less luggage than a commercial drummer . . . and has but a single servant, who seems to have abundant leisure."[8] Flags decorated Engine 55, pulling the special train, with the headlight covered by a picture of the president. Beneath that was a wreath of evergreens with an elaborate centerpiece of flowers.

Much of the trip to Chicago passed through Indiana countryside and towns, and the train halted at several locations for the president and others onboard to offer greetings. At New Albany, a cannon roared, and hundreds of citizens crowded around the train. The president stepped out of his car, bowed, and said nothing. At Salem, the president bowed again and said, "I am very glad to see you all." About one thousand people gathered at Lafayette to hear Arthur give his longest talk of the day. He thanked the people and predicted that Indiana would soon be one of the greatest states in the Union.[9] The train reached Chicago's Polk Street station at 7 p.m., covering the mileage in ten hours and ten minutes from Louisville. The president left the special train, wearing a blue flannel suit and a silk Scotch cap.

Chicago Mayor Carter H. Harrison led the official greeting party for Arthur and associates, with about four hundred people gathered to watch, according to newspaper accounts.[10] Pullman headed a group of businessmen. City workers had decorated the depot in bunting, although no special event had been announced. Carriages whisked the presidential party to the hotel where all gathered in a special suite for a private reception. With the visit shortened, Arthur would spend less than twenty-four hours before boarding another train.

The small group adjourned to an adjacent parlor for a quiet dinner, with conversation carefully confined to personal and nonpolitical chatter. Meanwhile, a crowd of reporters gathered outside the door waiting for an opportunity to question the dignitaries. One reporter writing in a Chicago paper described the scene:

> The corridors in the vicinity of the President's dining-room swarmed with press representatives. There were German reporters, and English reporters and Scandinavian reporters, and Milwaukee reporters. There were tall and gaunt reporters, and brief and podgy reporters. There were blonde reporters, and fiery-hued reporters and raven-black reporters. There were muscular reporters, and effeminate reporters. But there were very few modest reporters. After long and tedious waiting the President got to toothpicks and then to cigars. Then the pressmen gathered around the unfortunate doorkeeper and the fun began. A number of gentlemen who were waiting the President's leisure sent in their cards and were admitted. A few of the muscular reporters forced their way in past the doorkeeper at the same time.[11]

As dinner guests such as Senators Dawes and Logan started to leave, a *Tribune* reporter squeezed into the room and approached the president. In an article the following morning, the reporter made this observation about the president's personal appearance: "There is far less of the flabby—some might say beefy—appearance which then [Arthur last appeared in Chicago during 1880] somewhat forcibly struck the average beholder . . . . Should the Presidential dignity go on unlimbering itself until the party reaches the Yellowstone there is no telling how many fish will be impaled on the President's hook."[12]

As expected, Logan and Dawes were headed to Montana and Dakota territories to meet with Indian tribal leaders. As Logan left the dinner, the reporter caught this quick exchange between the senator and president:

Arthur: Why, how are you, old fellow? See here, I thought you were going along with us. Can't you? Come, now I don't want any one to go back on my Administration in that way.

Logan: I can't go this time, Mr. President. I'm on an Indian committee and have got to look into the Indian question up in the Northwest.[13]

With the way cleared to Arthur, the reporter began with mild questions about the presidential reception in Louisville.[14] Arthur answered, "We had a charming time. It would have been impossible for the people of Louisville to have treated us any more kindly."

The reporter asked, "How about that other glory of Kentucky?" He meant bourbon.

The president, a teetotaler, responded, "Oh, we didn't seek much of that." The reporter followed with similar questions about Chicago, and the president said,

"Chicago is a great city." Arthur obviously was being cautious with his answers. Next, the newspaperman moved to a Yellowstone question, which received Arthur's stock answer: "I have left all the details to General Sheridan."

Having waltzed through polite chatter, the reporter started to ask a political question, specifically related to the 1884 presidential race. The president regained his balance quickly, saying, "Ah, you really must excuse me. I make it a habit not to talk politics with you gentlemen of the press. When I have anything to say to the country, I shall probably say it in black and white. By the way, I hope you are not interviewing me—I believe that is the word—or intending to quote what I have been saying. Do you know, I dislike very much to open a newspaper in the morning and find a column or so of a conversation in which I have taken part the day before. In Washington and New York, you know, the president is never interviewed." When the reporter persisted in asking a question about the upcoming journey, Arthur curtly referred him to Sheridan.

The *Tribune* did not stop with queries of the president. A reporter found Lincoln before dinner and peppered him with questions. Before serving in the presidential cabinets of Garfield and Arthur, Lincoln had practiced law in Chicago and was quite familiar to reporters and to citizens of the city. The reporter asked questions about Louisville and tried to engage the secretary in speculation about being on the presidential ticket in 1884. That received a terse reply that boiled down to "no comment." The reporter pushed his luck at that point.

The reporter said, "Recurring to the subject of politics—"

Lincoln interrupted with, "But don't recur. I don't talk politics."

The reporter responded, "This doesn't seem to be much of an interviewing Cabinet, does it?"

That set off Lincoln. "Well, not as far as I am concerned. See here, do you know Chicago is getting up a reputation as the headquarters of the 'interviewing nuisance' as they call it. Why, people who have passed through here on their way to Washington have told me that the thing was becoming perfectly awful. I can't understand it. Why, I am never interviewed in Washington; and when I go to New York, the reporters never think of coming near me. No, the thing seems to center in Chicago. I suppose it's enterprise, but I don't like it."[15] Lincoln walked away.

These encounters with Arthur and Lincoln might not have appeared in print or seemed so testy, except Sheridan, the president, and the secretary had agreed earlier not to allow any reporters on the trip to Yellowstone. While this rankled reporters who normally cover the president in Washington, it especially irritated Chicago newspaper people. Chicago was the western big city jumping-off place for the expedition, and reporters there considered it a right to be included. The officials did not. Further confrontations seemed likely.

Sheridan, keeper of a tight schedule throughout the journey, planned a noon departure of the Yellowstone contingent. With no official events in the morning, everyone took a long breakfast. Lincoln and other members of the cabinet ate about

8:30 a.m., but the president did not make an appearance until 10. As might be expected, officials and associates made their way to the hotel and began an impromptu reception with Arthur and other popular figures.[16] Finally, at about 11:20, Sheridan announced the approaching departure by carriages for the Wells Street depot of the Chicago and Northwestern Railway (C&NW).

Arthur left the hotel with about one hundred spectators hoping to catch a glance of the chief executive. When the party arrived, three coaches, specifically for Arthur and his guests, were waiting at the depot. The president entered the rear car, provided by Union Pacific President Sidney Dillon. None of the cars was decorated on the exterior, but workers at the roundhouse had given the brass and steel parts of engine No. 26 extra polish.[17]

The other cars for the full train included a baggage car No. 41, fixed with sleeping berths to accommodate servants; two cars for officials of the Chicago and Northwestern; and Pullman car, "U.P." Each car was furnished with its own kitchen, cook, and servants.[18]

While dutifully covering details of the train and guests, newspaper reporters were consumed with being left out. The *Chicago Daily News* included this comment in its coverage of the departure: "Newspaper men were emphatically denied admission to even the baggage car by Mike Sheridan who ordered even the platform cleared of their objectionable presence." The sting remained from the announcement earlier that Lieutenant Colonel Sheridan would be the expedition's "reporter." Actually, Sheridan shared the responsibility with Lieutenant Colonel Gregory, but reporters rarely blamed Gregory or gave him credit. The *Tribune* said of Sheridan's responsibility, "It must not be supposed, however, that the party were able to get off without a representative of the press going along with them, with instructions to stick to the President till he returns to this city next month. At the last moment the services of a competent person were secured and the public will be kept fully advised of all the movements of the President, and of his exploits as a fisherman and hunter. Col. Mike Sheridan was commissioned as a representative of the Western Associated Press, and given directions, which he's too good a soldier to disobey, to use the wires freely and to send everything that happened, so that the Nation might know every morning what its Chief Magistrate has done the previous day. Col. Sheridan has exceptional advantages for getting at the news, and his full and graphic dispatches will be read with interest."[19]

Before departure, reporters tried a variety of schemes to get aboard, in spite of the ban. One *Tribune* reporter wrote the following day of his failed attempt under the headline: THE GREAT MISTAKE.[20]

The reporter had noticed an open door to the commissary and baggage car and figured he might successfully stow away. He entered and hid behind a trunk and valise alone until another person entered. The reporter wrote, "A brusque gentleman with a straw hat and a white handkerchief in a blue coat-pocket whirred in. He was short in stature, but as he whistled the 'Pirate's Serenade' his stature seemed to increase . . . . He glanced about as he was leaving and saw the unfortunate man behind the trunk. The vision of a reporter flashed upon his mind, and in one more second he had grown until his head bumped against the ceiling of the car . . . . He glared at him [the reporter] and said, 'Git.'"

The man, obviously Lieutenant Colonel Sheridan, said, "I know you. You can't play that this time," and slammed the door, turned the key and disappeared.

Undaunted, the reporter sought another way of hiding aboard the train. Brushing himself off, he approached the train's engineer, claiming to be a member of the engineer's union. He hoped that would gain him entry. The reporter explained, "The story seemed to work until the engineer began to make mysterious signs and grips. Then the engineer said, sorrowfully, for he was not a colonel: 'You will have to get off the engine or I will be bounced.'" The writer concluded, "Progress was impossible. Every gate was shut except the one that led into the street and that was packed with people, who were falling back. The train moved out and the vision of reportorial horror vanished from the party." What the reporter did not say was that the *Tribune* maintained pursuit.

Joining Arthur onboard the special train were Lincoln, General Sheridan, Rollins, General Stager, Surgeon Forwood, Lieutenant Colonel Sheridan, and Senator Vest and his son—all who would make the excursion to Yellowstone Park. Train conductor, John L. Kellogg, who often ran trains from Chicago to Omaha, Nebraska, was in charge; and Sam Wheeler was the engineer. Special Chicago and Northwestern officials on board were Gen. Supt. J. D. Layng, and Division Supt. Charles Murray.

Although the train was the responsibility of Chicago and Northwestern from the starting point, the journey was a joint effort with Union Pacific. The Chicago and Northwestern line stopped at the Missouri River, where it linked with UP for the remainder of the trip across Nebraska and into southern Wyoming. Through Iowa, only one stop was made by the C&NW other than for water, fuel, and changing of engineers. At Clinton, Iowa, J. H. Shattock, superintendent of the Union Pacific's dining cars, joined the party with the expectation for gourmet meals.[21]

There was little advance notice of the presidential train at locations along the line, and on those rare occasions when a crowd gathered, the train did not slow down and the president did not acknowledge the assembled. Newspaper correspondents along the line reported faithfully, sometimes with detail, when the train passed. After the train whisked through Sterling, Illinois, a *Tribune* correspondent observed, "The anxiety to get a look at the President and Secretary Lincoln was so great that the people all turned out, and the operatives left the factories. As the train came thundering into the city the excitement among the people was very great, but when the train went through with nobody in sight on the train, the crowd was simply unutterable."[22] Most reports just stated the time of day and that the train did not stop. The train was expected to run at thirty-five miles an hour, making the journey in about seventeen hours, or about five less than normal.

Editorial pages of the Chicago's newspapers summarized the whirlwind visit by Arthur in August 4 editions. Generally speaking, they spoke kindly. The papers acknowledged it had been three years since Arthur had been in the city, and that was during the Republican national convention at which James Garfield was nominated for president, with Arthur as his running mate. The *Tribune*'s commentary was representative of all papers in noting the president "has paid the city a handsome compliment by refusing to proceed upon his western trip except by way of this city."[23] Sheridan did have other alternatives, especially the Northern Pacific Railway, but he had an agenda too, and the overland route to Yellowstone would receive more press notice than a train ride to the northern outskirts of the park.

The *Tribune* graciously acknowledged the expedition leadership position of Chicago resident Sheridan. "The President proceeds upon his trip to the Yellowstone under the guidance of Chicago's most popular and illustrious citizen, Gen. Sheridan. His escort is a guarantee that he will be well cared for and properly entertained," the paper said. All papers seemed to believe that Arthur deserved a vacation from duties in Washington. The *Tribune* stated, "He is entitled to rest. He has set out upon a journey which will reveal to him the vastness and grandeur of the country over whose political destinies he is presiding . . ." They all wished him well and stood ready to welcome the president back to Chicago in September. Not a word was written on editorial pages about the rebuff of reporters.

While the kind and courteous comments could be taken at face value and probably reflected the fact that Arthur was a lame duck, the fact remained that newspapers were furious about being left out. The *Tribune* and *Times* refused to take "no" for an answer as revealed when the train stopped at Green River Station.

The news columns, which in the 1880s often were hard to separate from editorial comments, took the liberty of sounding negative notes, minor though they were. The *Chicago Times* passed along what it termed "local comment and criticism" of the presidential journey.[24] First, the paper noted that Lincoln was the only cabinet member in the party and that some of a similar rank in the administration felt there was too heavy a hand by the military. The paper stated, "It was said that Gen. Sheridan determined to keep the president from creating public sentiment and had set down on everything looking like a popular ovation to the chief magistrate along the route."

Senator Vest also received a jab with the paper suggesting he had "abandoned at the last moment his duties as a member of the Indian committee, now on a junketing tour among the Indians, and joined the semi-civilian and military escort accompanying the president."[25] The paper failed to mention that Vest planned to join the committee studying the condition of Indian tribes but did allude to his responsibility for legislation curtailing monopoly commercial development in the park.

The *Times*'s brief mention of issues was among the few published during the short presidential visit. The paper did provide an extended review of the sights Arthur would visit in the park in a page-one display on the day of departure from Chicago, but the material omitted any political subjects. Noticeably, leaders of the expedition avoided comments about the park, other than to mention its beauty. Sheridan, Lincoln, and Arthur may have felt it better to emphasize the natural splendors than anything that would reveal political wrangling.

While the Arthur train moved across Iowa, some members of the party had been at Fort Washakie since July 27. This small group met at Rawlins, including photographer F. Jay Haynes, invited on the journey by Sheridan, and Lieutenant Colonel Gregory. With Gregory and Haynes were a military ambulance and driver; five government six-mule wagons; and six cooks, wagon masters, and soldiers.[26] They began the trek to the fort on July 21—traveling to Bell Springs, Lost Soldier Creek, Crooked Creek, and, on July 24, to Sweetwater Bridge where the main Arthur party would cross later. The small group made additional stops at Twin Creek, Big Popo Agie River, and finally Fort Washakie. They covered about 140 miles.

By arriving more than a week ahead of the Arthur party, Haynes had an opportunity to get acquainted with some of the helpers on the expedition. Also arriving early had been Captain Clark, Captain Hayes, Tom Moore, and Lt. H. De H. Waite. Moore, the chief packer, helped Haynes work out a system for fastening his large and heavy camera equipment on mules. The photographer spent time in the nearby mountains, caught fish, and realized how luxurious things might be on the expedition. Haynes wrote in his diary, "I have two assistants. My orderly makes my bed, brings water and keeps the tent in order. The other is my packer, and attends to my riding horse and the pack mules. It takes two mules to carry my outfit and bedding."[27]

The stretch of Union Pacific road from the Missouri River to Green River Station, Wyoming, is part of one of the grand transportation epics of American history: the transcontinental railroad. Leaving the river at Omaha, Union Pacific cut across Nebraska, Wyoming, and part of Utah to meet the Central Pacific line approaching from California to complete the road at Promontory Point, Utah, in 1869. Construction across Nebraska and Wyoming exposed workers to hostile Indian tribes, nasty winter storms, and industrial accidents that claimed countless lives and slowed progress. In his book about the six-year project across the northern plains, author Stephen E. Ambrose wrote, "Next to winning the Civil War and abolishing slavery, building the first transcontinental railroad, from Omaha, Nebraska, to Sacramento, California, was the greatest achievement of the American people in the nineteenth century."[28]

From the Missouri River, the Union Pacific roadbed cut northward where it joined the bend of the Platte River and remained near the north bank as it spread across the southern portion of Nebraska. In those days, most of the settlement of the state was in the eastern and southern portions. At North Platte, where the southern and northern branches of the river come together, the UP continued to Julesburg, Colorado. The line progressed across the southernmost portion of the Nebraska panhandle until reaching Cheyenne in the southeastern corner of Wyoming Territory. After heading west to Laramie, the line drove north to avoid the southern mountains, and then struck a westward drift to Rawlins and Green River Station. Even fourteen years after completion of the transcontinental road, this stretch of Wyoming was lightly settled by whites.

In western history, Wyoming country holds a unique place, not just for its Union Pacific rail line, but for being the historic heart of the American fur trade, the battleground between Indians and whites until the early 1880s, the dirt highway famously called the

Platte River Road, the Oregon and California trails, and the routes to the California goldfields.[29] Those episodes were in addition to the discovery by white explorers of the wonders of Yellowstone and Jackson Hole country. Military travelers such as the Sheridan brothers, Kellogg, and the many officers who provided support for the Arthur expedition knew Wyoming from their expeditions in the 1870s and early 1880s. They understood the dangers and respected the delights of the wilderness as well as the thrill of being among the earliest travelers to map and track roads that once were little more than Indian trails.

While General Sheridan headed a crew of veterans that knew what it took to survive and enjoy an overland trek, others on the expedition were tenderfeet, unfamiliar with anything west of Chicago, and were not sure of themselves in the wild. City dwellers could speculate about the heavy hand of Sheridan and his military subordinates, but the burden of protecting the president of the United States in a less-than-friendly environment weighed heavily on those responsible for safety and pleasure on the trails. Sheridan kept tight control, but the alternative was unacceptable for the president, the secretary of war, a U.S. senator, and others.

In his role as keeper of the timetable, Sheridan sent a telegram to the well-meaning officials of Cheyenne while traveling across Nebraska, saying he appreciated plans they made for a reception, but the stop would be brief. In spite of Sheridan's dash of cold water, a crowd of citizens waited at the station when the special train pulled in about 9:15 a.m., Saturday.[30] Community officials and officers from nearby Fort Russell entered the presidential car, first making apologies for the absence of Territorial Governor Hale who was ill. With the crowd outside cheering and a band from the fort playing, Arthur stepped to the back of the train. Characteristically, he spoke briefly, saying, "I am glad to see you, and thank you for your warm welcome. I am sorry I cannot stop longer with you. Let me introduce to you Secretary Lincoln."

Thus began a handoff that brought three additional speakers to the platform. Lincoln echoed the president's remarks, noting that he had appeared in Cheyenne sixteen years before. The crowd cheered loudly, which had been the case for the secretary whenever he spoke along the route. Next to address the crowd was Sheridan, making a rare public appearance. He thanked the crowd for its lusty greeting, mentioned that he too had been to Cheyenne before, and introduced Senator Vest.

If the crowd expected more platitudes, they got a surprise. Vest broke the pattern by delivering more than mere thanks and introduced—for the first time on the journey, in public at least—a measure of seriousness and humor. As one person in the audience shouted, "Don't take the park away from Wyoming," Vest responded quickly, "I am going to the park just for the purpose of informing myself as to what ought to be done. I hope to have the matter settled in the next congress."[31]

With tongue partially in his cheek, Vest added, "Gentlemen, I have the distinguished honor of being the only Democrat in this party. [Loud cheers and laughter] I am very lonesome, politically, and feel far from home. They have brought me along to give the affair a non-partisan appearance, I suppose. But I am being well treated, and if this country is to be afflicted with four years more of Republican rule, I hope it will be under the administration of Chester A. Arthur." The crowd burst into shouts and applause.

Sheridan allowed a number of men and women on the platform to meet Arthur and Lincoln. When a reporter for the *Cheyenne Daily Leader* stepped forward to shake the president's hand, Arthur started quizzing him about the community. The president admitted knowing little about Cheyenne, thinking it was just a settlement on the far frontier. The reporter proceeded to extol the virtues of the community, to the apparent amazement of Arthur. Clearly, he intended his surprise to register positively with local people. The greetings continued for several minutes as more people came to the platform, and some went inside the presidential car. Eventually, Sheridan asked citizens to leave, and the train moved on toward Green River Station. The party had spent about twenty-five minutes in Cheyenne.

En route to Laramie, forty-five miles from Cheyenne, the UP train climbed to the highest point on the presidential train trip. The train stopped in Green River Station at about 10:30 a.m., Sunday, the last stop in upholstered comfort for about three weeks. A welcoming group greeted the presidential party and spent time discussing Wyoming and the impending journey. Among them was Edgar Wilson "Bill" Nye, who was owner of the *Boomerang* newspaper in Laramie and was considered a frontier humorist. An attorney, he also served as a judge. Over his career, Nye wrote several books, including a collection of his humorous columns. Upon introduction to Arthur, the president said to Nye, "Nye? Bill Nye? Oh, one of my postmasters, I believe." Arthur may have remembered Nye's letter of acceptance when offered the postmaster position. Nye had written the following to Gen. Frank Hatton:

My dear Gen:

I have received by telegraph the news of my nomination by the president and my confirmation by the Senate as postmaster at Laramie, and wish to extend my thanks for the same. I have ordered an entirely new set of boxes and post office outfit, including new corrugated cuspidors for the lady clerks. I look upon the appointment as a great triumph of eternal truth over error and wrong . . . I do not know when I have noticed any stride in the affairs of state which so thoroughly impressed me with its wisdom . . . [32]

The first of official press communiqués written by army officers in the Arthur party appeared from Green River Station. It offered a brief account of the arrival, noted the party would remain in town overnight, and gave a brief summary of the expected departure on Monday morning, August 6.[33] A more complete report of the Green River Station time appeared in the *Cheyenne Daily Leader*, including comments from people who observed events of the day.[34] Joining the president at the train were Maj. Gen. Alexander McCook from Camp Douglas, Utah, and, the last member of the expedition, Montana Territorial Governor Crosby, who arrived by train. After conversations aboard the train, the president and others strolled about the community, which encouraged Arthur to say it was the best day's rest for him in more than a year.

In the course of afternoon pleasantries, Sheridan and Arthur learned that two men representing themselves as reporters for the *Chicago Tribune* and *Chicago Times* had booked seats on the next day's stage to Fort Washakie, the expedition's destination. Sheridan confronted the two and said that if they insisted on arriving at Fort Washakie, they would be arrested as soon as they entered the Indian reservation. The *Daily Leader* reported that the reporters said they would take the risk, only to learn the federal government had "chartered" the stage. Bill Nye had the final word on the episode in the *Boomerang*. He wrote, "If these men had been competent reporters they would have bought horses and ridden to Washakie."[35]

Green River Station, Wyoming, to Yellowstone National Park August 6 to 23, 1883

Beginning with the morning of August 6, Arthur's party discovered the military way. The Sheridan regime on the trail was firm. Unless the president interceded, the party arose at 6 a.m.—the president was often up earlier—and hit the trail after breakfast. The day's journey usually ended about noon; and the afternoon was devoted to hunting for food, fishing for pleasure, and resting. This was especially true after they left Fort Washakie on horseback. An extra day now and then allowed more rest and enjoyment of the scenery.

As they were about to learn upon leaving Green River Station, this was no garden-variety semiluxurious excursion to see token Indians and geysers. Statistics tell some of the story: The overland journey from Green River Station to the train for the ride back to civilization covered almost five hundred miles of roughest Wyoming and a small portion of Montana. Arthur and friends were gone from familiar surroundings more than a month, spent twenty-two consecutive days in the saddle, traversed the main chain of the Rockies, and crossed the Continental Divide three times.[36]

As instructed by Lieutenant Colonel Sheridan in July, Captain Lord—depot quartermaster at Cheyenne—took charge of arrangements from Green River Station to Fort Washakie. He had procured three spring wagons, also called military ambulances, for the party and one wagon for baggage. Each wagon was drawn by four mules. Arthur, Lincoln, and Sheridan rode in wagon number 1; Vest, Rollins, and Stager in number 2; and Crosby, Vest, Jr., Forwood, and Lieutenant Colonel Sheridan in number 3. Captain Lord and soldiers on horseback provided security and handled chores. The first day's objective was a camp on the Sweetwater River, about 101 miles from Green River. At the rate of ten miles an hour, the party arrived in the afternoon.[37]

The Associated Press dispatch called the Sweetwater "a beautiful mountain stream," overlooking the historic aspects of the region where the party crossed the river. Twenty or thirty years before, the river was part of the great emigrant highway from the Missouri River to Oregon and California. Thousands of men, women, and children seeking new lives on the West Coast, followed the Platte River across Nebraska into western Wyoming and the Sweetwater.[38] The Oregon Trail then angled toward the southwest corner of Wyoming. By 1883, only the ghosts of those wagon trains and an occasional wagon wheel rut could be detected.

Many who kept diaries and journals on the trip west described the Sweetwater as a swift, clear, and full stream, easier to follow and enjoy than the more rambunctious North Platte left behind to the east. The stream also was a welcome relief from the sagebrush and alkali that pestered the traveler in that portion of Wyoming. The river derived its name from an accident that occurred to a trading expedition many years earlier.[39] Apparently, a pack containing all the sugar for the expedition was dropped in the water and lost.

In the relative comfort of their ambulances, Arthur and party watched the passing scenes, including the native game of antelope, jackrabbits, and sage hens. The AP report waxed fully about the president, saying he "enjoyed the ride greatly," and described how he rode outside the wagon with the driver for the last forty-five miles to camp. Although some might have seen just monotonous and dreary desert, the writer saw "smiling valleys, rolling prairies and rugged bluffs, and the gravelly loam of the soil," which made "a splendid natural road, use only being necessary to perfect it." The reporter may have been a military man, but his superiors gave him the latitude to report more than the facts and figures of the march.

Along this stretch of the first day's travels, an incident occurred that has been passed down through the decades although it never made any official or even unofficial reports. There were a number of such occasions on the trip, but there was no way to determine the accuracy of the reports. A few were cited in newspapers; and others, simply the word-of-mouth record. A representative few are repeated here and later in the journey's narrative as curiosities: maybe true, maybe exaggerated, maybe false. Lieutenant Colonel Sheridan and other officials on the expedition firmly denied anything happened that did not make the official reports for the Associated Press.[40] A few of the rumored incidents sound perfectly plausible.

A. G. Clayton, a Washakie National Forest ranger in the Sheridan District, which included much of the region covered by the expedition in its first days, wrote an article entitled "A Brief History of the Washakie National Forest and the Duties and Some Experiences of a Ranger." It appeared in the *Annals of Wyoming* issue of October 1926.[41] He described an encounter with the Arthur party en route to the Sweetwater, which had ominous beginnings and, apparently, a happy ending.

Clayton said word had been sent by telegraph north of Rawlins to an unnamed location that the Arthur expedition had left Green River with a military escort. The ranger wrote, "Two cowpunchers . . . being desirous of seeing the president had ridden out to meet it [the party]. At a point near South Pass they met, the cowboys having since been joined by a few others."

The president and others in the wagons thought they were being approached by bandits, according to Clayton. "Upon being told the visitors' mission, Sheridan, who

Presidential ambulance train used from Green River Station
to Ft. Washakie, Wyoming
Abraham Lincoln Presidential Library & Museum
F. Jay Haynes photo

Shoshone tribal chiefs at Ft. Washakie; Chief Washakie on horse at right
Abraham Lincoln Presidential Library & Museum
F. Jay Haynes photo

was in civilian clothes at once dismounted from the coach and introduced all hands to the president." Clayton said they were not far from the campsite when this happened, so Sheridan asked the cowpunchers to join the party for dinner. Continuing, Clayton said, "A shooting match was held; hats were thrown up and shot at and likewise cards. Sheridan proved himself expert with the revolver and since the president had never seen a real bucking horse one of the men gave a splendid exhibition in riding." Clayton provided few details that might help determine accuracy of the report. No hint of such an occurrence made the daily news report, except a vague reference to having eaten "a most elaborate dinner."

The location of the encounter had a historic past. Explorer Robert Stuart and a party were the first white men to discover South Pass in 1812, not far from where Arthur and company met the Sweetwater. The pass provided relatively easy low elevation passage east and west across the Rocky Mountain terrain and became the principal wagon highway of the Oregon Trail.[42]

Although Lieutenant Colonel Gregory had warned other officers that accommodations at the Sweetwater left something to be desired, the news report applauded the work of Captain Lord, in whose hands the party had been placed by General Sheridan. The dispatch stated upon reaching the Sweetwater "Captain Lord, Depot Quartermaster at Cheyenne, had, by direction of Gen. Sheridan, pitched tents for our use, and accumulated all the conveniences necessary for our comfort . . ." In honor of the captain's work, Sheridan named the location Camp Lord and began a ritual naming most camps along the route to Yellowstone.

After a "bountiful" breakfast on August 7, the party loaded the wagons and headed for Fort Washakie, fifty-five miles beyond the Sweetwater, with the president again riding with the driver.[43] En route they discovered a few people clinging to existence at old settlements. The first was South Pass City, described by the reporter as two or three occupied buildings, "the rest were fast falling into decay." Four miles farther, Arthur and company came to Atlantic City, "also nearly deserted, a stage station, post-office and saloon sole relics of the activity and prosperity which a few years since thrived and pulsated with all the vigor which bad whisky and rich anticipation could give the reckless inhabitants of a new mining camp."

Beyond Atlantic City, the travelers saw an occasional placer—and quartz-mining activity although it appeared to the visitors that efforts were nearly futile. They stopped at a group of huts and frame buildings called Miner's Delight, "but the name seemed the acme of irony and sarcasm." A few miners came to the president's wagon with a pan of dirt that they washed in hopes of finding gold, but only "a few glittering grains resulted."

Moving on to the Little Popo Agie River, the party stopped for lunch. A bit farther, they came to the Popo Agie River at the town of Lander. The party's correspondent again painted a picture of despair among those holding on in hopes of finding riches. He wrote, "Here women were to be seen and little children were running about. The valley seemed smiling and happy, while in the mining camps only men herded together and now only the ashes of their fierce dissipation and blasted expectation remain."

A few miles beyond the town, they were greeted by a welcoming party of Shoshone and Arapaho Indians, who "turned out in large numbers to welcome the Great Father, and dashed around the President's party most gaudily and fantastically arrayed, displaying their skill in horsemanship and gratifying their curiosity." Arthur and friends planned to spend the remainder of that day and another full day among the tribes while preparing for horseback travel over the rugged Wind River Mountains.

The Arthur party devoted much of the full day to special ceremonies involving the Shoshone and Arapaho tribes in costume and demonstrating horse-riding skills. Arthur, Sheridan, and Vest also took advantage of the time to talk with tribal leaders: Washakie, chief of the Shoshones, and Black Coal, chief of the Arapahos, whose tribes shared the reservation.[44]

Washakie, in his eighties at the time of Arthur's visit, had a long history of cooperation with U.S. military and elected officials that had minimized armed conflict on the Wyoming plains. During his life, he experienced the best and the worst of whites. As a tribal leader, he first knew Americans as fur traders in the West, later as explorers, as exploiters, and as honest, unfaithful, and friendly. The years included tensions too. For example, Washakie fought hard to establish a Shoshone reservation and did not easily accept the government's assignment of Arapahos to the Shoshone lands in 1878.[45]

The chief led Shoshone warriors against neighboring tribes in order to keep the tribal land near the Wind River Mountains. On infrequent occasions, when some Shoshone warriors battled U.S. soldiers, he kept most of the tribe out of the fight. To remain on relatively good terms with the government and its officials was not easy and often led to disappointments and frustrations. His expectations may have been too high for the whites.

In writing about Washakie, Peter M. Wright said, "Washakie was not a white man's Indian. He had fought with the Anglo-Americans against the Sioux because the latter posed a traditional and immediate threat to the Shoshones and their homeland . . . . His loyalty was first to his family, then to his band, and finally to his tribe. A realist, Washakie was willing to utilize any alliance that would serve his people's purpose." Washakie died on the reservation in 1900.

This meeting at Fort Washakie was the rarest of opportunities for Washakie and Black Coal to visit with a president, a secretary of war, and a high-ranking general in the army. Privately, there may well have been thanks expressed on both sides for assistance given by the Shoshone tribes in U.S. battles with Sioux tribes.

Tribal leaders had asked Arthur for a meeting and ceremony of welcome during the afternoon. With the president and party standing in the open, about five hundred mounted warriors dashed one thousand yards at full speed toward the president before pulling up abruptly. Washakie, Black Coal, and lesser tribal leaders dismounted and approached Arthur. The official report said, "The President thanked his visitors for calling upon him; congratulated them upon their fine appearance; assured them of his interest in their welfare and of the satisfaction with which he had heard of their exemplary conduct and growing attention to the practice of industrial pursuits." Tribes throughout the West were being pressured to take up the tools of farming and raising livestock.

An English-speaking member of the Shoshone tribe, educated at the respected Carlisle Indian Industrial School in Pennsylvania, interpreted the president's remarks for his elders. The interpreter translated the chiefs' comments into English for Arthur, aided by Captain Clark of General Sheridan's staff who had studied Native sign languages. The report said the interpretations "were full of expressive metaphors, and were at times positively eloquent."

Following the exchanges, Black Coal stepped forward with a pony, placed the bridle in Arthur's hands, and said the gift was for the president's daughter. Members of the party also received gifts of moccasins and leggings. The day's ceremonies ended with a war dance performed by twenty young Indians, eight of whom beat drums and chanted "a weird song for exciting the efforts of their fellows." The report explained, "Some of the dancers were nearly naked, their skin being painted in various colors; others were gaily dressed in flashy-colored costumes, no two of which were alike." The president and associates appeared fully entertained.

Not all events that day were ceremonial. Vest carried a message from the U.S. Senate to the chiefs regarding a proposal taking shape in Congress to disassemble reservations and to offer Indians individual landownership for farming and raising livestock. Called severalty, the plan also included reimbursement by the government for reservation lands in the form of annual payments. Congress approved the scheme and President Grover Cleveland signed an act in 1887, after many years of negotiations with tribes in the West.[46] Vest wanted a reaction to the idea of severalty from the chiefs to take back to Senate colleagues. If he thought the peaceful Shoshone and Arapaho tribes would jump at the chance of individual landownership and life without a reservation, he got a surprise. The AP dispatch reported, "All the Chiefs expressed themselves against tenure in severalty."

August 9, 1883: Official First Day of the Expedition

The nature of the expedition changed dramatically when leaving Fort Washakie. The main party was on horseback and would travel in that manner until leaving the park. The military escort, Troop G of the Fifth U.S. Cavalry, commanded by Captain Hayes kept close at hand, ready to deal with any eventualities on the trail. Strung out behind these elements were the supply trains of wagons pulled by pack mules, with feed for the animals and food for humans. The trail from south of Lander, past Fort Washakie and on toward the next campsite, followed the route of today's U.S. Route 287, skirting the eastern side of the Wind River Range. On this first official day of the expedition (Fort Washakie was Camp No. 1), the party went twenty-one miles before stopping at Camp No. 2 on the north bank of the Bull Lake fork of the Wind River, about five miles southwest of where the rivers met.[47]

Before reaching the campsite, they crossed a divide just nine miles out of Fort Washakie and paused to take in the view of Crow Heart Butte and the Owl Creek, Wind River, and Shoshone Mountains—all to the north of the divide. Those landmarks remain, for today's travelers, as U.S. 287, which merges with U.S. 26 and heads northwest. The riders had their first experience with rocky country, "climbing and descending alternately high and stony hills" until reaching camp. The poor footing for horses provided the dispatch writer an opportunity to compliment those who showed solid horsemanship on the trail. "Surrogate Rollins distinguished himself in horsemanship on this march of twenty-one miles, and in compliment to him Gen. Sheridan named our first camp 'Rollins,' which honor was thoroughly approved of by the whole party."

The first day's travel ended with ample time for Arthur and others to try their hands at fishing. The reporter wrote, "Immediately after our arrival at this place, which is near a beautiful trout stream, the President took his rod and soon landed the first trout, keeping up his old reputation of being a fine fisherman."[48] Another portion of the daily report addressed the president's camp habits and wearing apparel. The dispatch read, "He [Arthur] enjoys camp life very much, is up and out of his tent among the first at 5 o'clock each morning, and with flannel shirt and large hat, roughs it with the rest."[49]

F. Jay Haynes was allowed to photograph the president's first catch but not the president in action. Of the many pictures taken by Haynes, there were none of the president setting a hook in a trout. Arthur feared a negative reaction to a photograph of him adding to the fish kill. The following day's news dispatch, which left camp by courier before the fishing had concluded, noted, "Both the President and Senator Vest brought into camp fine creels full of trout as the result of their afternoon's sport." Fishing became a staple of the daily news report, probably because many tried and succeeded.

August 10, 1883

The camp reporter called this day "very uneventful."[50] The party traveled mostly over sagebrush and bunch grass mesas where horses found unsteady footing. Easing some of the strain were sights of Wind River and Owl Creek Mountains. The reporter said they made camp on Spring Creek, due west of Crow Heart Butte, with plentiful wood, water, and grass. There is some dispute over the exact location of the camp. Photographer Haynes, writing in his journal, said it was an unnamed tributary of the Wind River. Led by Arthur and Vest, fishermen quickly found their way to the stream, whatever its name. Sheridan named the camp for Vest, partly out of respect for his fishing abilities and acknowledging his help in protecting Yellowstone Park.

The daily report ended with this curious statement: "There are no special or professional correspondents with the party, and all dispatches purporting to be from such persons are spurious."

The disclaimer probably resulted from newspaper stories similar to one appearing in the August 10 issue of the *Chicago Tribune* under the page one headline THE PRESIDENT. RUMORS OF A PROPOSED ATTEMPT TO SEIZE AND HOLD HIM FOR RANSOM.[51] Information about a kidnap threat actually appeared near the end of the article, with most of the space devoted to a running disagreement with Arthur party personnel over access of reporters to the expedition. The story carried a dateline CAMP BUFFALO LAKE, WYO., AUG. 9, the day the party left Fort Washakie. The introduction, referring to President Arthur rising from sleep at 5 a.m. to witness preparations for departure, read as if the reporter was close at hand. The *Tribune* part of the story began with this introduction:

> The Presidential party had breakfast . . . when an incident occurred which caused general consternation. Although the time at Washakie was rapidly approaching 6 a.m., it was past 7 in Chicago. A courier came up with a dispatch in haste addressed to Gen. Sheridan from his constant adviser in your city [Chicago]. The missive was handed to the President, who swore, actually swore. It stated that the *Chicago Tribune* "had published a report in full of the proceedings the day before, with an account of the proposed issuance of Government bonds to Indians."

The mention of a proposal to provide severalty for Indians referred to the discussion between Shoshone and Arapaho chiefs with Senator Vest in which Indians would sell reservation lands to the government. That information in brief appeared in the official report.

Continuing, the newspaper report said Sheridan gave orders to conduct a search of the camp and arrest any correspondent found on the reservation but added, "Up to the present writing the intruder has not been found." The remainder of the article presented an account of the trail ride by the party and the president's first fishing outing, most of which could have been gleaned from the day's official report. The final paragraph addressed the kidnap rumor. "There are those who predict that an effort will be made by Indians or bands of robbers which are thick around here now to seize Mr. Arthur, carry him into the mountain and hold him for ransom. The oldest stage-driver the *Tribune* correspondent has met is certain an attempt will be made and thinks if conducted rightly the attempt will succeed."[52]

The account carried one clearly erroneous statement, claiming that Secretary Lincoln planned to remain at Fort Washakie for several days. He did not leave the party at any time during the expedition. Another article on page one carried the headline THE OFFICIAL REPORT and was a statement about the full day at Fort Washakie.

August 11, 1883

At 6:30 a.m., the party began a three-day change of direction in the trail, angling slightly north and west from Camp Vest, under cloudy skies that had produced showers overnight.[53] The reporter, easing into a travelogue mode, praised the dampness as offering "a delightful freshness and coolness to the air . . . . The rest from the burdens of official and social life, the exhilarating effects of the climate, the wearing away of the little soreness that some of the party had felt from the riding—all the good effects, in fact, of this outdoor life were seen in the buoyant manner in which the members of the party mounted and rode away."

They rode about fourteen miles for the day over gentle, rolling countryside, making camp at Dinwiddie Creek, which was "a noisy mountain stream rushing down in a boisterous way to join its waters with Wind River." While en route, some members of the party broke away and headed into the adjacent foothills in search of game. They reported seeing just one deer and one antelope, and the reporter stated, "The game had nearly vanished, it is well nigh exterminated." Sheridan named this camp for Montana Territorial Governor Crosby.

The reporter wrote at length about the nearby land formations, including a natural bridge in a canyon formed by waters of the creek:

> The Indians call the stream the creek with God's Bridge, and some ten miles above its mouth is a natural bridge about 300 yards wide [that] spans the chasm through which the waters rush. This bridge is scarred and marked by trails made by Indians and game, which are distinctly visible from the heights a mile above it. The canon is grand—so grand and beautiful in fact that one of the party who has wandered much in foreign lands said of it: "Nothing there can in any way compare with it." This gorge in the mountains carved by the Master's hand is hard to describe, but one cannot look at it without some awe of the Great Architect.

As the afternoon progressed and the tents were pitched, fisherman in the party grabbed their gear and prepared for another outing. At that moment, from the northwest, "a great black cloud came sweeping over the bluffs, and a hail and rainstorm really made the party feel that they were enduring hardships, but they are just mild enough to be agreeable." The camp scribe was quick to advise his readers, "The entire party is enjoying the best of health."

Although fishermen stayed off the stream, hunters had a measure of luck in the hills, bringing in two antelope. General Sheridan approved hunting outside the park only to put food on the tables.[54]

August 12, 1883

The party rode just twelve miles this day, heading straight west to the southeast bank of Torrey Creek, about four miles southwest of the Wind River and due south of today's town of Dubois on U.S. highways 26 and 287. The destination offered a better opportunity for grazing horses and mules. The creek was named for Capt. Robert A. Torrey, who served with the Thirteenth U.S. Infantry Regiment during the 1870 wars with Indians in Wyoming and Montana.[55]After leaving the military, Torrey purchased nearby rangeland where he ran large herds of cattle. Camp was made on the creek, and Sheridan named it for Stager.

Although the shortest ride of any day so far, the journey introduced the riders to rugged mountain landscape that required fording the river twice and avoiding a number of small streams that flowed into the river. On one of the river fords, the reporter described how it felt to make the crossing, "The first crossing was made by fording in a diagonal direction up stream where the water was so rapid in its flow that one's neighbor seemed to be moving up the river with the speed of a running horse." At one point, the party dismounted and led the horses while descending one of a number of treacherous banks.

The party saw the last of Crow Heart Butte, thirty miles east. The remaining scenery caught the fancy of the reporter, this time looking west toward the Shoshone Mountains. He reported on a history lesson about the mountains from one of the Arapaho guides who said the butte got its name from a battle between the Shoshone and Crow tribes. The guide said the Shoshones celebrated the victory by burning the hearts of the dead Crows on the summit of the butte. Meanwhile, fishing and hunting continued by members of the party, usually reported by the camp reporter in glowing terms. Sometime later, one of the party set the record straight about fishing during the first days of the trip.

Writing in *Forest and Stream* magazine after the journey, Senator Vest told of a fishing lesson the president and he learned, with great humility, near Torrey Lake. In a long article about fishing on the expedition, Vest, a veteran of the waters who brought all the proper equipment for the outing, told of his early disappointment.[56] "My flies, reel, and split bamboo rods were, it seemed to me, faultless, and the President's array of tackle was enough to bewilder an entire fishing club. You can imagine our surprise, not to say consternation, when at the first three camps we came in with only a dozen trout each, the largest not weighing over a pound, while the soldiers and teamsters with their snake poles or sticks, and a piece of twine tied on the end, brought into camp large strings of fish, many of them weighing over two pounds."

Vest, still confident of his experience and gear, decided to see if the "lesser" fishermen had a secret for catching more and larger fish. He wrote, "At the next camping place, near Torrey's Lake, in Wyoming, I quietly reconnoitered the banks of a mountain stream where a number of teamsters were fishing with tackle improvised for the occasion, their only bait being grasshoppers." When he saw the men crawling around the rocks and bushes, dropping their bait quietly into the eddies of the current "and then yanking the wary trout out of the water without a second's delay, the mystery was fully explained." With the lesson learned, Vest and presumably the president, approached every stream "with the watchful treat of an Indian, taking advantage of every means of concealment . . ."

Vest's account ended with a measure of redemption. "I am glad to say that the struggle between fancy tackle, as it is derisively called, and the hoop-pole, twine string system, went each day in our favor to the end. I mention this to emphasize the statement that caution, skill and work are as necessary to successful trout fishing in the Rocky Mountains as elsewhere."

August 13 and 14, 1883

The party continued its steady approach to the summit of the Wind River Range with a nineteen-mile push from Camp Stager on August 13.[57] The reporter again wrote admiringly of the vistas and scenery along the Upper Wind River "where gorgeously colored and fantastically shaped mountains alternate with those which are covered with grassy slopes and timbered ravines." The weather had improved as had the hunting. The game tally for the day included three antelope, a bear, several grouse, and a rabbit—inspiring the reporter to add with a touch of humor, "So there is at present no immediate danger of starvation for anybody."

General Sheridan named the location for H. R. Bishop of New York who made the 1882 journey to Wyoming and the park. This was the last camp before ascent to the Continental Divide and marked the point where they turned west, away from Wind River. Photographer Haynes provided the camp locations in a journal, and his son, Jack Ellis Haynes, used that information for this description of Camp Bishop: "West of the Wind river near the confluence of the unnamed creek rising in Lincoln Pass and the Wind River. Lincoln Pass is about fifteen and one half miles directly south of Togwotee Pass, and both are on the Continental Divide. The unnamed creek referred to joins the Wind River about five miles upstream from the confluence of Warm Spring Creek. This camp was on the north bank of the unnamed creek and southwest of its confluence with the Wind River."[58]

The party remained at the site all the following day, August 14, for rest, relaxation, and preparation of packs for traveling farther into the wilderness. Supplies sufficient for the remainder of the trip had been stored there by army personnel. Most members of the party took advantage of the respite to fish and hunt. Arthur and General Sheridan took a three-mile horseback trip up the main fork of the Wind River, where the president had caught fish the first day. Arthur returned to camp with "the heaviest catch of the party." Surgeon Forwood bagged a large elk; and other hunters returned with two antelope, mountain grouse, and ducks.

A report in the *Chicago Times* dated August 14 offered details not mentioned in the official report, without identifying a source of the information.[59] The account said the party, traveling from Camp Stager over tough and broken country, reached a meadow about two miles from the forks of the Wind River. "It is the property of a settler, who came into camp last evening [August 13], bringing his wife and seven children, ranging in age from a babe at the breast to the stalwart son as large as his father. The settler was greatly delighted at the honor which, he said, had been done the country by the visit of the chief magistrate, and created much good natured amusement by the familiar manner in which he 'presented' the members of his family."

One other adventure reported in the *Times* concerned several members of the party and an antelope that came close to the campsite. The article stated that the antelope, after startling Senator Vest who had stopped by the riverbank, gave a merry chase to the president, Rollins, Stager, and Arapaho guide Bill. After almost eluding the armed persons giving chase, the animal was felled from a shot by Stager.[60]

The paper said one reason for the additional day in camp related to weariness of the travelers. The report claimed, "Several members who were not used to horseback riding found that a week in the saddle had told on them rather more severely than they had anticipated after the lameness resulting from the first two days had worn off. Surgeon Forwood's medicine chest was opened and the sufferers were given a generous supply."

August 15, 1883

For purposes of reporting the party's activities, this day ranks among the most ceremonial, close to the exclamations over the Teton Mountains and the wonders of the park.[61] This was not because the scenery rivaled those monuments, but rather that it was the crossing of the Continental Divide, and the camp and pass were named for Secretary of War Robert Todd Lincoln. Sheridan named the pass for Lincoln on the 1882 journey in the absence of the secretary who was detained in Washington.

Current maps show this location as Sheridan Pass. Those who have written about the journey and the pass suggest that while General Sheridan and Arthur wanted the pass named for Lincoln, it probably never was officially announced. Researchers for the state of Wyoming Board of Geographic Names and the U.S. Geological Survey say that on U.S. topographic maps published before 1965, there was no name for the pass.[62] Afterward, it was shown as Sheridan Pass. In his comments on the naming, Jack Ellis Haynes quoted an article by Daniel W. Greenburg from 1926 that stated, "The party followed the Wind River nearly to its source . . . . It was thought then to be the shortest route between the valleys of the Wind and the Snake. They camped at what is now locally known as Sheridan Pass; however, the camp was named 'Camp Robert Lincoln,' and the pass was named by President Arthur as 'Robert Lincoln Pass,' and the name should have been retained, but probably was never officially announced."[63]

The official report described the party's arrival, "The camp is named Robert Lincoln, and is situated on the crest of the backbone of the Rocky Mountains, at an altitude of nine thousand feet above the level of the sea. Within a hundred yards of the camp are streams which flow respectively into the Atlantic and Pacific Oceans."

The report went on at length about the beauty of Lincoln Pass:

> Picturesque Camp Lincoln, with its banks of snow lying placidly and slowly melting near the trail, and near the snow flowers, which had all the freshness of early spring, tender forget-me-nots, wild asters, buttercups, columbines, the latter with a delicate and scarcely perceptible shade of blue in its rich white, and for which many deem it the most beautiful of the wild flowers found in the Rocky Mountains, a carpeting of scarlet and blue and gold, added to this the White Mountain flox, nestling close to mother earth, and in such profusion as to suggest the idea that the hand of Nature had grasped some of her myriad stars and scattered them in wanton profusion on the grassy slopes of this romantic region.[64]

Another description of the Continental Divide south of Lincoln Pass to Union Pass, to the state's tallest mountains and glaciers, and back east close to where the Arthur party traveled to Torrey Lake appeared in the article by A. G. Clayton, Washakie National Forest ranger, previously quoted.[65] He traveled the Wind River country in the summer of 1925 and wrote about it in an article published a year later. While his journey did not follow the Arthur trail precisely, his account provides a sample of the territory and the mysteries of traveling alone, something not experienced by the Arthur expedition.

Clayton began the trip about ten miles south of Sheridan or Lincoln Pass along the divide. He described the feeling of loneliness in a vast world of trees, boulders, glaciers, and other obstacles. "Perhaps because, due to the bigness of the country, I had a feeling of being the only one in it. True there are not many travelers in that part of the world, nevertheless it has been pretty well explored at different times for many years back." Clayton traveled with three horses to carry his packs and for riding. They encountered canyons two thousand feet deep, slippery snowbanks, and, worst of all, nearby lightning strikes as a storm passed.

"To one who has not camped alone amid the high peaks, it is quite impossible to describe the feeling that comes over one in such a dreary waste of land as this," he wrote. "Everywhere rocks, cold and grey interspersed with snowbanks and glaciers. No sign of life anywhere evident and one feels as though he had been removed to a dead world . . . . A feeling of utter loneliness and such loneliness as I have never felt before—as though every living soul had left and gone to a brighter world."

On his way down from the peaks, Clayton encountered soft ground in which all the horses lost their shoes. Suddenly, he came upon a boulder field. "Soon the soft ground was passed entirely and in its place was a jumble of large boulders broken only by interspersing snowbanks. All of the boulders in the world, apparently." At camp that night, the tender-footed horses stood in a snowbank in preference to the "cruel jagged rocks [that] were everywhere."

After travel above timberline and on flats covered by boulders, Clayton worked his way close to the Torrey Creek drainage, not far from the route taken by Arthur and party. He seemed relieved. "How good those trees looked and the abundant short grass surrounding them. For a while I felt as though I was again in the heart of the forest in spite of the fact that this was on the extreme upper edge of timber line. And I could not help but think of what a horrible place this world would be if trees were taken away from us."

August 16, 1883

After the usual early wakeup and breakfast, the party left Camp Lincoln and Lincoln Pass and began a difficult descent to the headwaters of the Gros Ventre River. The reporter could not resist one more look at 360 degrees of scenery from the divide, saying, "Camp Lincoln was a beautiful spot, presenting to the eye, towards the east and north, all the grandeur of the Shoshone Range of snow-clad mountains, and to the west and south the snow-capped peaks of the Gros Ventre Range. Pines and tamaracks cover the base and lower lines of the ranges opening at intervals into beautiful grassy parks."[66]

Gen. Anson Stager at Trout Point
Library of Congress
F. Jay Haynes photo

Presidential escort, Troop G, Fifth Cavalry, crossing the Gros Ventre River
Library of Congress
F. Jay Haynes photo

The expedition's view of Grand Teton mountain
Library of Congress
F. Jay Haynes photo

The going was slow down the mountainside but was accomplished without accident. The group dismounted at a location described by the writer as "steep and difficult." Approaching the chosen campsite about eighteen miles west of Lincoln Pass on the south side of the river, a depression in the mountain range enabled the party to get a glimpse of the Teton Range to the west, the first of many that would elicit a variety of descriptions in the days to come.

The usual fishing and hunting activities began after arrival at the camp named for Edward S. Isham, a Chicago attorney and good friend of Lincoln and General Sheridan. The reporter noted the absence of Lincoln and Captain Clark in pursuit of elk but did not mention the results. A day later, the official report mentioned Clark's return after two days' hunting without luck but did not say whether Lincoln accompanied the captain.

The final line of the daily report appeared to summarize a nearly perfect setting: "The weather is cool, the air delicious and invigorating, and the scenery grand."

On this date in Chicago, the *Times* newspaper published a brief item without a dateline regarding events involving the Arthur expedition. Given when it was printed, the notice, if true, probably related to events that occurred when the party ascended to headwaters of the Wind River. No sources of information were provided, and consequently, the information must be given little credibility. However, it is another example of a newspaper's attempt to keep up with the journey, perhaps at the risk of fabricating. The statement read:

> The presidential party is meeting with even larger game than white house poker. In the wilderness through which the tireless Sheridan is now leading it, Colonel Mike [Sheridan] came across a monster bear, the other day, and proved that in his hands the gun is scarcely less mighty than the pen by killing it at the first shot. The next day General Stager discovered a wild cat crouched on the limb of a tree just ahead of his horse, ready for a spring. Happily, a well-aimed shot from the general's rifle brought the dangerous animal to the ground. The president, who was just behind, was in at the death and became thoroughly excited by the incident . . . . The president devotes himself mostly to the safe and quiet amusement of trout-fishing, but where game is so abundant he is quite likely to win something of a reputation as a hunter by killing a bear, wild cat, jackrabbit, or some other large and ferocious animal of the Rockies, before he returns.[67]

August 17, 1883

Having entered the Gros Ventre River Valley (*Gros Ventre* is French for "big belly"), the party traveled mostly due west with a slight drift northwest to the Snake River at the foot of the Teton Mountains.[68] The river valley changes colors rapidly, with a segment of red hills especially dramatic. It also changes character: at times narrow with dangerous footing and sloping canyon walls, at other times spread out with gradual approaches to the water. Travelers today can get an idea of what confronted the expedition on the portion of the road that is not paved and continues on the north side of the river to the headwaters.

The river in the twenty-first century is not exactly as it was in 1883. The major change in the river and valley occurred on June 23, 1925, after a period of heavy rainfall when a huge landslide dammed the river.[69] The mud came from the north face of Sheep Mountain, containing fifty million cubic yards of sandstone, limestone, shale, and rock. The dam was about one mile long and two thousand feet wide. The dam rose 225 feet high for a half mile across the river, creating Lower Slide Lake. It held until May 18, 1927, when a portion of the dam gave way, producing a wall of water six feet deep that flowed down the canyon, destroying ranchland and flooding the small town of Kelly. Six people died in that community.

This was the first full day of travel in the Gros Ventre Valley, and it provided a challenge to everyone. For ten miles, the party worked its way through canyons and across mountains, away from the river. The official report captured the sensations coming down to the river: "At one point we wound round the precipitous side of a mountain, at the base of this nearly perpendicular bank, about 1,000 feet below, the green waters of the river rolled and tumbled and lashed themselves into a white fury. A stumble, and horse and rider would have gone headlong to almost certain destruction." No one took a tumble, but the group moved cautiously. After another four miles, the travelers got their first introduction to the changing personality of the valley. The reporter wrote, "About fourteen miles out we rose to the crest of a high bluff, from which a most beautiful crescent-shaped little valley met our gaze."

Again, Lieutenant Colonel Sheridan unleashed a word description of the changing colors designed to make readers salivate. "The beautiful blue sky above, the dark green mountains to the left, the rich red hills to the right, the russet brown grass of the valley, relieved here and there by the bright green willow bushes and small cottonwoods, the stream of pure cold water made a grand picture of an ideal camp . . ." The party "voted" unanimously to make this spot a campsite. The first thought obviously was to try fishing the Gros Ventre, and reportedly, all went to the water with equipment in hand. The fishing derby scorecard at the end of the contest read: First, Stager (mostly white fish); second, Senator Vest; and third, Arthur. But the total catch turned out so bountiful that everyone—including soldiers, packers, and Indian guides—sat down to a fish feast.

Sheridan named the location Camp Arthur.

August 18 and 19, 1883

Following the routine of early rise and early breakfast, the party was traveling the north side of the river by 6:30 a.m. Apparently, the satisfaction with yesterday's campsite remained as they headed west, "not without longing, lingering looks behind." Compared to earlier travels over fallen timber, down rocky sidehills, and up steep ascents, the trip today seemed almost dull.[70] The main exception was described in the official report:

> We had climbed to the summit of a long hill about five miles from Camp Arthur, when there suddenly burst upon our view a scene as grand and majestic as was ever witnessed. Below us, covered with grass and flowers, was a lovely valley many miles in extent, through which was threading its way the river in whose banks we had just encamped. Along the whole westerly edge of this valley, with no intervening foothills to obstruct the view, towered the magnificent Teton Mountains, their snowy summits piercing the air 13,000 feet above the sea level and 8,000 feet above the spot on which we stood in reverent admiration.

The sight repaid everyone for the effort to reach this point of the journey. The party camped about eight miles from the Gros Ventre confluence with the Snake River, approximately fifteen miles south of the south shore of Jackson Lake. General Sheridan made an exception in naming the site, choosing to call it Camp Teton rather than naming it for an individual. The reporter referred to the location as "our least attractive camp," adding that while there were magnificent views, weather conditions left much to be desired. He wrote, "The river at this point has an excellent reputation as a trout stream, but the wind has been blowing at too many miles an hour to permit much success in angling." Wind gusts were powerful enough to break the ridgepole of the mess tent. That night temperatures dropped below freezing, and the travelers awoke to ice a half-inch thick on water buckets outside the tents.

Requiring rest and preparation for the route into Yellowstone National Park, the party remained at Camp Teton another full day. The camp reporter did not file an account for August 19. The official report on the twentieth mentioned a continuation of unpleasant weather on the day of rest. It recorded "hot weather in the middle of the day, and severe gales of wind throughout day and night, accompanied with blinding clouds of dust."[71]

A curious report appeared in August 19 edition's of the *Chicago Times* about a journey on dates that did not jibe with the actual record. The report, with dateline CAMP NEAR JACKSON LAKE, AUG. 17, told of a march along the valley of the Snake River.[72] Actually, on that date, the travelers spent their first full day on the Gros Ventre, a number of miles from Jackson Lake and the Snake. The article related how members of the party had to dismount to ascend a hill and said that Lincoln became so exhausted that he dropped down on the narrow trail to catch his breath. The account also mentioned numerous fords on the Snake River and "many mishaps," including when a mule fell on a packer, bruising the man.

That same edition of the *Times* carried pointed criticism of Lieutenant Colonel Sheridan, the primary reporter, claiming he did not "rise to the demands of the situation. As the historian of the present campaign, he is a partial failure." The article said Sheridan failed to report an incident between the reporter and a bear, and "the climax of inefficiency was reached with the failure to forward the Stager wildcat [story] . . ." The war with the newspapers was continuing.

August 20, 1883

Members of the party rode in the saddle about eighteen miles, finally coming to the banks of the Snake River and facing the Teton Mountain Range in all its glory. They had reached the "Sheridan Trail," which led into the park and today is followed by U.S. highways 26, 89, and 191. After the blustery weather two days before, the reporter recorded the day as "clear and bracing."[73]

General Sheridan named the camp for U.S. Sen. Wade Hampton, a Democrat from South Carolina. The reporter said he was expected to make the journey although his name did not appear in correspondence prior to the expedition. Jack Ellis Haynes located the campsite as "about one and one-half miles south of the confluence of the Buffalo Fork and the Snake River, on the east bank of Snake River, seven and one-half miles due east of the southeast corner of Jackson Lake."[74] Anticipating another cold night and frosty morning, many in camp slept under three blankets.

August 21 and 22, 1883

The assemblage pushed hard northward toward Yellowstone National Park, traveling over a dusty, timber-strewn trail for thirty miles, the longest day trip since leaving Fort Washakie. They took a route into the hills rather than risk the treacherous marshy bottoms of the Snake River. The official report termed it "rough and rugged country, covered for nearly a quarter of the distance traveled by dense tracks of burned and fallen timber."[75]

Along the way, about noon, the party reached a "sparsely timbered knoll that commanded a view of Jackson's Lake, with snow-covered Tetons rising from its shores in the background." They pushed beyond that scenic spot to a campsite about two miles from the south boundary of the park and a mile west of the Snake River, near a small stream. General Sheridan named this location Camp Strong for retired Gen. William E. Strong, who accompanied Sheridan on his 1881 and 1882 journeys.

With tents placed in a grove of pines on the banks of the stream, those so inclined took to the waters for fishing. Apparently, Arthur wanted more time at leisure and fishing as he decided they would spend another full day at the location. He, and others, may have needed a day of rest after the strenuous march from Camp Hampton.

According to the official report, the president went to the Snake River and scored one of his greatest fishing triumphs. "The President and Senator Vest, our two most expert fishermen, made the best of our stay, and scored the greatest victory yet achieved over the finny tribe." At one cast, Arthur landed three trout, weighing a total of four and a quarter pounds, the report said. On each of six other casts, he caught two trout.

Vest, writing about the demonstration later, said, "It is hardly necessary to say that with a six-ounce rod it required both skill and patience to accomplish the feat."[76] The total weight of the day's catch by Arthur and Vest reached 105 pounds. The report also credited Vest with the single largest trout of the full journey at three and a half pounds.

Lieutenant Colonel Sheridan's report of August 21 included another critical remark about newspaper reporters, no doubt adding to the tensions. He referred to the *Chicago Tribune* article that placed Lincoln at Fort Washakie for several days while the travelers moved ahead. Sheridan wrote, "The omniscient reporter who claims to be with us, and who has been purely a mythical personage since we left the railroad at Green River, carefully and considerately located the Secretary of War at Fort Washakie for an indefinite period after we had started on our present trip across the mountains, and as the Secretary has never been absent, it is a matter of much curiosity as to how the inventive genius of this fictitious correspondent would be able to restore him to us." Sheridan added that Lincoln "is constantly and pleasantly reminding us of his presence."

By continuing the warfare with newspapers, Lieutenant Colonel Sheridan assured his leaders of further clandestine and fictitious accounts.

Presidential party at the Upper Geyser Basin: seated from left, Montana
Gov. Schuyler Crosby, Lt. Gen. Philip Sheridan, President Chester A.
Arthur, War Secretary Robert T. Lincoln, Sen. George Vest; standing from
left, Lt. Col. Michael Sheridan, Gen. Anson Stager, Capt. Philo Clark,
Surrogate of New York Daniel Rollins, Lt. Col. James F. Gregory.
Library of Congress
F. Jay Haynes photo

8

Inside the Park, At Last

THE ARTHUR EXPEDITION SPENT THE BETTER PART of seventeen days in Wyoming Territory—traveling first by train, then by army ambulance, and finally on horseback. Participants experienced the full range of Wyoming landscape: sagebrush, sand, desert, roaring rivers, and majestic mountains. They fished, hunted, struggled in the saddle, and drank in the scenic wonders.

But they still had not set foot in Yellowstone National Park.

Finally, on August 23, fifteen days after leaving Fort Washakie, the party entered the park. There were no brass bands, official greeters, or anxious reporters. Their elation was tempered by the challenge of the trail. But the objective was met—if only they had enough energy left to fully appreciate the wonders still to come.

Yellowstone National Park to Chicago, Illinois
August 23 to September 5

August 23, 1883

Rested and presumably content after bagging a quantity of fish, Arthur and party awakened to thick frost on camp surroundings. The night had been the coldest of the trip, with the temperature at twenty degrees as the party gathered at 6 a.m. The official report stated, "And in the mess tent the water which had been served a few moments before the party sat down for breakfast formed a beautiful network of ice on the inner surface of the glasses."[1]

The trail continued to be a challenge for the horsemen, but that did not detract from the historic moment that occurred not long after they started north from camp. They passed into Yellowstone National Park, making Arthur the first president of the United States to set foot there.[2] Reporting that enough game had been killed to satisfy the needs of the party before entering the park, the general's aide, Lieutenant Colonel Sheridan, said, "But to-day we entered the sacred precincts of the park, and the buffalo and elk can look at us with perfect safety, for Gen. Sheridan has given strict orders that nothing shall be killed." Whether just outside or inside the park, the trail remained a challenge, angling west of the Lewis River to Lewis Lake. The reporter described it this way:

> The trail was very crooked to-day, and led over a low range of mountains covered with pine forests. At intervals we found open, grassy parks, but the most of them were only a few acres in extent. About twelve miles out we came upon the lower falls of Lewis or Lake Fork, a dark gray gorge cut through solid walls of volcanic rock, its sides nearly perpendicular. About 600 feet below us the stream rushed and tumbled over its dark bed, broken white by its fretting. The upper falls, some six miles from the lower, we saw at a distance through an opening in the evergreen trees; it seemed to drop from out the dark foliage behind it like a flood of lace.

Five miles farther, they discovered an open area at the head of the lake, "the only spot on the shore line which is not densely timbered." They made this the campsite, described by Jack Ellis Haynes as "on the northeast shore of Lewis Lake, fifteen miles southeast of Upper Geyser Basin."[3] General Sheridan named the camp for U.S. Sen. John Alexander Logan of Illinois, who had been invited to make the journey but declined and chose to devote his attention to the Senate committee investigating the condition of Indians. The official report offered this description of the pleasures of camp: "The sound of the swirl of the waves on the beach mingles pleasantly with its twin sister sound, the [sighing] of the winds in the trees near by."

In his report, Lieutenant Colonel Sheridan reviewed the two weeks spent by the party in the saddle from Fort Washakie. He wrote, in part, "Looking back over our course from Fort Washakie, where we first mounted our horses, abandoned wheeled vehicles, and took the Indian trail which has led us through some fertile valleys, across some bad lands, and over rugged mountains, many memories linger pleasantly in the mind of every member of the party." He mentioned specific highlights along the trail including a hailstorm, the picturesque setting of Camp Lincoln, trails of fallen timber, the indescribable beauty of Camp Arthur on the Gros Ventre, Jackson Lake, and Mount Moran in the Tetons. He concluded, "Yes, the scenery along our route will furnish many pleasant memories in the years to come."

August 24 and 25, 1883

The trail from Lewis Lake to the Upper Geyser Basin offered little relief. For twenty-six miles, the party rode over a rough and dusty trail to the first of many spectacles in the park. From Lewis Lake, the trail led along the east shore of Shoshone Lake, through Norris Pass to Spring Creek, and to the Firehole River and Upper Geyser Basin. No sooner had they arrived and dismounted for camp near Old Faithful, they were greeted by one of the geyser's hourly eruptions. Since the travelers expected to be around awhile, there seemed no need for many to watch the first show. Instead, the tired and hungry ate lunch and began taking advantage of such pleasures as resting and bathing.[4]

They camped about a fourth of a mile west of Old Faithful, near the center of the present hotel. The official report declared, "After our ride on horseback of 230 miles every member of the expedition is in the best of health, and not an accident of the slightest character has occurred on the whole journey to mar our pleasure." That final phrase might have been aimed directly at various newspaper reports of mishaps.

The party remained at the basin another full day, taking in the awesome sights of the geysers, bubbling waters, peculiar sounds, and vapor. Lieutenant Colonel Sheridan declined to provide details of the sights, the whole park having been adequately and often described in various published reports. They had intended to stay a second full day but discovered the camp area did not provide sufficient forage for the animals. As a result, the party headed eastward to Yellowstone Lake after being joined by Collins Jack Baronett, who provided guide service for the president through the park.

Unknown to anyone traveling in the Arthur expedition, the *Wood River Times* newspaper of Hailey, Idaho, published an article on August 24, claiming that a number of cowboys had started for Yellowstone Park with intent to kidnap President Arthur.[5] Various reports of kidnap plots had been published by newspapers since the journey began, without any visible evidence of an attempt. This account, offered by the resident sheriff, stated the group left Hailey secretly on the stage road to the park.

The article, based on testimony of a man who had been asked to join the cowboys but had refused and escaped, said, "The object of the expedition is to corral and capture President Arthur and party, and to spirit them away into the mountains and caves, where they will be fed, but kept prisoners, while members of the party act as pickets to prevent being surprised and captured." The escapee said there were sixty-five men in the outfit, armed with rifles and scalping knives, who hoped to gain a million-dollar ransom. The leader was reported to be a Texas desperado. As far as ever known, the outlaws never proved a threat to the expedition or the president. However, the army took the threat seriously and provided an additional troop of soldiers to protect the president.

August 26, 1883

The party followed its usual early morning routine at the geyser basin, loaded up, and headed back along the trail they had followed to the park two days earlier. The destination was the West Thumb bay of Yellowstone Lake. The trail contained no surprises and few new vistas, prompting the reporter to offer this mild complaint, "Our journey to-day has been somewhat tiresome. Its difficulties can perhaps be most effectively summarized in the statement that we have twice crossed the Continental Divide in the space of twenty miles."[6]

Presidential party crossing Lewis Fork of the Snake River
Library of Congress
F. Jay Haynes photo

Old Faithful in action
Library of Congress
F. Jay Haynes photo

Lower Falls of the Yellowstone River
Library of Congress
F. Jay Haynes photo

Always looking for the bright side, however, Lieutenant Colonel Sheridan added, "Our camp is one of the most attractive spots which has greeted our eyes since we began our tour through the wilderness." He spoke of the view across the lake. General Sheridan named the camp for Gen. Delos B. Sackett, inspector general of the army and a participant on both the 1881 and 1882 journeys with the general.

Lieutenant Colonel Sheridan's official report for the day included mention of paint pots, mud geysers, hot springs, and flowers in the vicinity of camp. About the hot spring waters, he said, "Their waters are clear as crystal and close to their edges grow flowers as rich in color and as dainty in structure as those which carpeted Camp Lincoln."

No mention was made in the official report of angling on the lake, perhaps reflecting a weariness of the fishing marathon over previous weeks. Lieutenant Colonel Sheridan closed with a report on the sunset and a "refreshing rain" overnight that promised to dampen the dusty trails.

August 27, 1883

President Arthur's group, with the full-support complement, traveled twenty-two miles around a portion of Yellowstone Lake, through timber from the southwest corner to the northwest about where the Lake Hotel later was established. Lieutenant Colonel Sheridan remarked about agreeable shade and the absence of dust that made the journey pleasant. The camp location was about one and a half miles from the outlet and was named Camp Campbell.[7]

While many of the party chose to spend the afternoon resting and enjoying the scenery, Arthur and Captain Clark fished the lake. The president caught thirty-five fish weighing forty-five pounds, but no fish count was given for the captain. Major Forwood, camp surgeon and naturalist, spent his afternoon productively, finding what he identified as the head of an extinct species of rhinoceros and two vertebrae of a large fossil saurian on the bank of the lake near camp. Forwood declared them prime examples and promised to send them to a professor in Philadelphia.

The campsite provided a comprehensive view of the lake and the Absaroka Mountains bordering the water, causing Lieutenant Colonel Sheridan to observe, "Many of the peaks are snow-capped, and by the light of the setting sun are made visible for many miles."

August 28 and 29, 1883

Judging from the official report of August 28, the glories of the Grand Canyon of the Yellowstone and the Upper and Lower falls captivated the party. The trip followed a trail west of the river for eighteen miles to the falls. The writer called the route "a splendid trail. The road was equal to any turnpike in the states."[8] This comment clashed with reports from commercial interests in the park that constantly complained about the poor condition of roads, along with requests for financial fixes by congressional appropriations.

En route to the falls, the party stopped briefly to view mud geysers to which they gave names. One was known as Editor's Hole, and another as Devil's Caldron. The official reporter could not avoid a caustic comment about Editor's Hole: "As we looked into the first and listened to the rush and roar of the seething water and mud that eternally boils, but finds no outlet, it was generally remarked that the place was properly named."

The party picked a campsite between the Upper and Lower falls within view of the canyon and named it Camp Allison. While the official report offered no explanation, the naming most likely was for U.S. Sen. William B. Allison, Republican of Iowa and a supporter of the park. Jack Ellis Haynes gave the location as south of Cascade Creek near the canyon's rim.[9] The official report mentioned visitors to the park for the first time although they must have seen people at Old Faithful and the Upper Geyser Basin or even at Yellowstone Lake. The report said, "Mingled with these scenes of nature, we find here also the inevitable tourists, male and female, each of whom is anxious to see not only the canyon but the President, and it is wickedly suggested by some that the eyes of these lovers of nature are directed more frequently to the latter than to the former."

Arthur and General Sheridan decided to remain at the site one more day to allow explorations of viewpoints. The reporter called the day "very interesting, but uneventful." While that terse description covered happenings at camp, Lieutenant Colonel Sheridan, with approval of his leaders, addressed at length what had become the least pleasant aspect of his duties.[10] His preface to the commentary read, "As our trip is drawing to its end, this is probably as good an opportunity as will be presented to refer to the inventions of newspapers which have continuously published pretended special telegrams purporting to be from correspondents with our party. No special correspondents have been with us." He called the alleged reports "falsehoods," citing conflicts between dates of dispatches and actual dates spent at locations, and added:

> Their silly stories of personal incidents are not of sufficient consequence to be denied, but stories of danger to the President and of his being in bad health go beyond the bounds of permissible hoaxes as misleading the public in a matter of general interest, and for this reason it should be known that there has not been at any time the slightest ground for any such stories. The President is and has continuously been perfectly well, and has traveled the whole journey on horseback, being excelled by none in his enjoyment of our marches and camp life.

Lieutenant Colonel Sheridan addressed occasional newspaper stories that inferred the president, the secretary of war, and General Sheridan had conferred to develop a new policy for dealing with Indian tribes. He said, "If such matters were to be dealt with, the Secretary of the Interior would have been present, and it is sufficient to say that many newspapers have been fighting a man of straw. A simple illustration of the deceptions of these specials [articles] is found in their having made our party arrive at the Upper Geyser Basin on a day when we were four days march distant from it."

Reports contrary to official reports about the president's good health appeared in newspapers during and after the journey. According to one, Arthur gave up riding horseback in the park for an army ambulance. In a later candid moment, Lieutenant Colonel Sheridan admitted the president appeared weary in the saddle during the long daily rides.[11] It is understandable that Arthur would not approve an official report that indicated he was anything but in top condition and fine health. The same goes for other activities that occurred on the journey, which the official report omitted. One example was Governor Crosby's record of winnings at the nightly poker games.

August 30, 1883

Arthur's party spent a final day along the Yellowstone River en route to camp at Tower Falls. The route north took them through Dunraven Pass, along an Indian trail to the crossing of Tower Creek, and down to the valley of Tower Junction, a trip of twenty-one miles. They took one of two trails, eliciting this comment in the official report, "One follows the canyon, along its brink, for five or six miles, then leaves it and passes to the eastward of Mount Washburn. It is a very difficult route, the last twelve miles of which are a constant descent. The other and better one we followed, and passed over the westward slip of the same mountain."[12] The route took them to the summit of Mount Washburn and a "comprehensive view of the park scenery."

While at the summit, the party discovered a cairn of stones, which contained cards and notes written by visitors who provided detailed accounts of depredations—including cold winds, snow, and sleet. The official report did not say whether members added their accounts to the record. General Sheridan first encountered this cairn on his 1881 trip into the park. Lieutenant Colonel Sheridan reported on the view from the summit, "The Grand Canyon, from this point of vantage, looks like a narrow gorge fringed with dark pines. In the distance can be seen some of the great geysers sending forth puffs of steam and giving their locations the appearance of an aggregation of busy factories."

The campsite was near Baronett's Bridge, named for guide Baronett, a celebrated character and habitué of the park, who was known as Yellowstone Jack. He first saw the park as part of the Yellowstone Expedition of 1866. A peak located in the far northeast corner of the park bears his name. Baronett built the first bridge across the Yellowstone River at the confluence with the Lamar River and charged a toll for its use. At the time of the Arthur expedition, Baronett's Bridge was in place and run by Yellowstone Jack. Sheridan used Baronett to guide his military excursion of 1881 from the bridge to Yellowstone Lake.

General Sheridan named the camp for former Sen. Simon Cameron, a Republican from Pennsylvania and good friend of the president. The president and Vest went to the waters again and had modest success bagging trout. The score: Arthur, 8; Vest, 6.

August 31, 1883

The party followed a wagon trail rarely used by tourists in 1883 to Mammoth Hot Springs and the last campsite of the long journey. They traveled over an area called Pleasant Valley, crossed Blacktail Deer Creek, and passed along the base of Mount Everts to park headquarters. This route follows today's northern portion of the park's loop road. Fortunately, as the AP correspondent noted, rain fell overnight and dampened an otherwise dusty road. The day's official report noted "the march of 350 miles is finished."[13] That referred to the miles from Fort Washakie to Mammoth Hot Springs.

Upon reaching the campsite, near the park superintendent's residence, most of the group first sought a hot bath. Others visited the new hotel that just opened to tourists, about three hundred yards away. Senator Vest and Governor Crosby preferred to fish first and, after catching seventy-five trout, joined the larger group in the afternoon. The evening activity included an impromptu reception at the hotel—organized by Rufus Hatch, an official of the Yellowstone National Park Improvement Company, with wines and cigars provided. It became festive after the lighting of a huge campfire of logs and fallen timber. A party of tourists from the hotel joined the group, mainly to pay respects to the president, but they also serenaded the prominent visitors with songs.

Because there were many people who saw President Arthur at the hotel and other locations near Mammoth Hot Springs, it is not surprising that written accounts of the festivities surfaced. William Hardman, editor of London's *Morning Post*, provided one story of the evening in his book *A Trip to America*. George Thomas, a hotel employee who attended the reception, provided his version in writing.

Thomas's eyewitness account told of an incident that must have been embarrassing for the president and General Sheridan.[14] Thomas said Lieutenant Colonel Sheridan, the expedition reporter, was the only member of the traveling party not at the reception when it began; but he appeared later, apparently drunk. Thomas said Sheridan was discourteous to the president, causing Arthur to leave the reception, and brought an end to the event. Thomas said Sheridan's behavior was prompted by not receiving a promotion from the president.

Hardman encountered the Arthur party after touring the park with foreign visitors.[15] He wrote of the evening:

> After dinner that evening we went in a body to serenade the President, who received us by his camp fire. It was a sight never to be forgotten, so wild and strange was it. Later in the evening President Arthur returned our visit, bringing with him General Sheridan, Secretary Lincoln, and the other members of his party. We were all especially interested in making the acquaintance of General Sheridan, who is not only a remarkable man, but a remarkable looking man, being short and stout, in fact, almost as broad as he is long . . . . I was favored by being placed on the President's right hand when we adjourned for a cigar to a private room. I found him a most courteous and agreeable man, ready to speak of public matters with less reserve than I should have anticipated . . . . I found from him that his grandfather had fought at Waterloo, and that he still preserved as a valued heirloom a decoration which had been bestowed upon his ancestor by the Duke of Kent.

Hardman described the condition of Arthur's clothing and a physical condition resulting from the president's long overland journey and extreme exposure to the sun. "We had both been out of the vicinity of Washerwoman [a bath] for some weeks; but I flattered myself he looked the shabbier and dirtier of the two as we sat side by side; besides, the skin hung in strips on his nose, which did not improve his appearance."

The editor obviously considered it an honor to be in the president's company during the evening. He concluded his observations, "I enjoyed a very pleasant chat with him, for three-quarters of an hour, and I doubt if any other Englishman ever before had an interview under similar circumstances with any of the Chiefs of the Great Republic across the Atlantic."

September 1, 1883

After breakfast and the striking of tents, the party moved quickly to the main line of the Northern Pacific at Livingston and on to Chicago. All were aboard except Crosby, who returned to his office in Helena, and Senator Vest, who joined the Senate committee investigating the condition of Indian tribes. As the train passed Billings, Lieutenant Colonel Sheridan sent his final dispatch: "All are well. This is the last telegram you will receive from the representative of the Associated Press accompanying the Presidential party."[16]

President Arthur and General Sheridan made good on their promises to spend time in Chicago at the end of the expedition. The party's train arrived about 2 p.m. on September 4 and was greeted by an entourage of city officials and business people. Some two hundred members of the Chicago Union Veterans Club led the parade to the hotel.[17] With no formal statements by the arriving dignitaries to offer readers, newspaper reporters talked about how individuals looked after a month away from the centers of industry and politics. One paper referred to them as "distinguished picnickers." Some examples:

Arthur:	"The president is quite well. He is looking better even than when he passed through the city en route to the west. His face is tanned and he says he feels invigorated."[18]
General Sheridan:	"The general was burned to the hue of a boiled lobster, and his eyes looked smaller under a high white hat than they did when he left the city a month ago. He was stouter, however, and appeared to enjoy excellent health."[19]
Lincoln:	"Secretary Lincoln, too, was sunburned . . . wore a corduroy suit and looked not unlike a Highland deer-stalker."[20]

Reporters followed the carriages to the hotel and, after some coaxing, left the visitors to relax and prepare for scheduled events. The coming and going of some members of the expedition gave reporters an opportunity to ask questions. Lincoln reportedly left the suite and went to the hotel's front desk to claim the president's mail. Reporters gathered around. "Glad to get back?"

"Yes, sir, very glad to get back; never felt better in my life; never had such a good time; president well, very much tanned; he had a good time."

The *Times* captured a few comments from General Stager, including one that warmed the hearts of the newspaper's staff and added a new element to the matter of reporters following the expedition. Stager said, "We had a splendid time and I think we were all improved by the trip. We crowded more hard work and real pleasure into that compass of time than most anyone could imagine."

A reporter asked Stager, "Any accidents?"

The general said, "None whatever except to the *Times* correspondent, who was on our trail. It was not serious, however, for he only overslept himself one morning and on awaking found that we had packed our tents and silently stolen away. But he overtook us during the day, so it was not much of a mishap." About the *Times* reports from the trail, he added, "They were exhaustive and those of the *Times* were especially commended for their fidelity . . ."[21] A rare contradiction to the official reports had surfaced.

An editorial in the *Daily News* portrayed Arthur's experience as more than a simple stroll. "He has been roughing it in the true sense of the term, and has taken a trip that even old travelers think twice before embarking on. No president, while in office, has ever before made so extended a journey, and we dare say there have been times when Gen. Sheridan thought himself a simpleton for undertaking it. For it is no child's play. To one unaccustomed to camping out, to climbing mountains and descending into ravines on a mountain pony or in a mountain wagon, the trip that the president has made is one of real hardship . . ."[22]

A *Daily News* reporter managed to corral the object of disdain by many newspeople: Lieutenant Colonel Sheridan. He announced, "I have dropped journalism. I utterly refuse to be interviewed. As I said before, I've had enough of it! I will now get back to my legitimate sphere." He did make an additional comment—after declaring it was not in an interview. "I find nothing but happy recollections of our trip. It was, indeed, pleasant. There, I must attend to my mail."[23]

The only other comment recorded by newspapers regarding the controversy over news reports from the trail was made by Lincoln. The *Daily News* quoted the secretary as saying, "The so-called special correspondents of certain Chicago papers, from the presidential party in the Yellowstone Country, was invention, pure and simple. The stories were lies from beginning to end—not one word of truth in them."[24]

Official festivities on September 5 began at noon when Arthur and General Sheridan joined members of the Chicago Board of Trade before lunch. After brief remarks by Arthur, members gave a cheer for Lincoln, who addressed the group, "As a citizen of Chicago, I thank you cordially for your reception today of the President of the United

States. For the last two years, as one of his constitutional advisers, I have been trying to make Mr. Arthur, who lives in New York, believe that Chicago is the center of the world. You have done more today to convince him of this fact than I could in two years."[25]

Arthur, Lincoln, and General Sheridan joined Illinois commanders of the Military Order of the Loyal Legion for lunch when "the old soldiers drank bumpers to the president and Lieut. Gen. Sheridan and sang campaign songs." Arthur toasted the general, calling him "that distinguished soldier, gallant gentleman, and true friend," whom he loved as a brother and who had piloted the president safely through his Yellowstone journey.

That night, Arthur and other members of the expedition greeted thousands of Chicago citizens for two hours at the long-awaited public reception. At the end, Arthur offered a short comment and urged Lincoln to respond after someone offered three cheers for the next president. Lincoln said, "I hope I shall always be able when shooting to hit the mark better than the man who called for these cheers. I am grateful for the reception given the President by this great throng."[26] At 11:30 p.m., Arthur and Lincoln left for Washington by train.

A few final details remained to close the door on the Yellowstone National Park expedition. As announced in advance, members of the party received bills for food and incidentals. Lincoln's tab totaled $246.30, for example.[27] Letters went to those who General Sheridan praised for their work in behalf of the expedition. Receiving such notice amounted to high praise for soldiers in the ranks. In one, Lieutenant Colonel Sheridan—writing for the general to Brig. Gen. O. O. Howard, commander of the Department of the Platte—expressed thanks to Capt. E. M. Hayes, Lt. H. De H. Waite, and Troop G of the Fifth U.S. Cavalry "for the very efficient manner in which they performed their duties while escorting the President of the United States from August 9th to September 1st."[28] The general also thanked Troop A of the Fifth Cavalry for forming the courier line from Fort Washakie to Shoshone Lake.

Looking back on the excursion, all objectives seemed to have been achieved. Arthur had a lengthy, and healthy, respite from the chores of the presidency. Sheridan and his associates, in the effort to protect and expand the park, received extensive publicity on the wonders of Jackson Hole and Yellowstone National Park through the daily accounts written by Lieutenant Colonel Sheridan, which were published throughout the nation. People across the country who had hardly given the park a moment's thought had access to the daily reports. There seemed to be few, if any, serious leftover controversies from the journey. Whether the trip advanced Sheridan's idea for expansion of the park awaited further consideration by Congress.

9

An Abundance of Chaos

MAMMOTH HOT SPRINGS HOTEL, THE CENTER OF controversy for more than a year and still in unfinished condition, opened to tourist trade in August 1883. While the president and his party toured the region and brought attention to the park, the geysers erupted and sprayed, the Yellowstone River flowed inexorably, and the canyon displayed its awe-inspiring colors. But the park had its problems. Behind the scenes, backbiting and sniping continued among officials of the Department of the Interior and the Yellowstone National Park Improvement Company. The future of the park seemed as threatened as before in spite of higher public awareness.

John M. Hartman of Philadelphia and his family visited the park in August.[1] After returning home, he wrote Teller with this lament:

1st. The visitors are rapidly destroying the craters, edges of pools, &c., for relics.

2d. The roads are barely passable and are daily growing worse. Last Sunday a lady was thrown out of the carriage and badly hurt at Fire Hole River. Between the two fords on Gibbon River my wagon was turned over sideways and my wife thrown out. The driver did all he could to escape the chuckhole, and no blame can be attached to him. We rolled stone down the mountain, mended the road, and prevented any further trouble for others. The roads are terribly worn down on one side, which makes it difficult to keep in a wagon.

3d. From the high rates charged by the Yellowstone National Park Improvement Company, is it not desirable to maintain the Marshall Hotel at Fire Hole River as a check on the Improvement Company, as there are far better accommodations at a much less rate at Marshall's than at the Mammoth Hotel.

A few weeks later, E. S. Reddington, a dealer in baled hay and livestock at Whitewater, Wisconsin, wrote President Arthur about the condition of game in the park.[2] On January 15, 1883, Teller had admonished park officials to protect the game. Reddington expressed concern for keeping buffalo, moose, elk, deer, and antelope safe in the park. "They are fast passing away," he said, "and a very few years will see the last one of them all destroyed." He proposed building a fence around the park. While his suggestion for saving the game might have been extreme, Reddington clearly wanted Arthur to do something. He wrote, "You will now, after seeing for yourself, be able to judge whether the Park will sustain such animals through the year, and also if the natural formation will hold them when in."

Although these were the concerns and opinions of just two citizens, they reflected the still unmet need for law enforcement and conservation in the nation's first park. The record, as reflected in documents and correspondence during the remaining months of 1883, did not provide much encouragement for addressing the concerns of Hartman and Reddington.

With the influx of tourists in August, Rufus Hatch, president of the improvement company, left his New York office and came to the park. Hatch had done his part in reassuring Teller and others in Washington that everything would be just fine with the hotel in operation. At the same time, he supported the continuous pleading of Hobart, serving as project manager at Mammoth Hot Springs, for protection from outlaws and poachers and the need for improved roads.

Anxious to make the hotel a financial success, Rufus Hatch donned the hat of master promoter by bringing a trainload of foreign and domestic press representatives and wealthy visitors from Europe and scattered U.S. cities to the park during the month. Reporters represented newspapers in England, France, and Germany; and Hatch mixed them with newspaper people from New York State. With Hatch as spokesperson for the venture, the train's movements from eastern cities to Niagara Falls and Chicago captured adoring newspaper headlines and gave the impresario an opportunity to praise his company's venture in the park. The *Chicago Times*, among others, published names of all sixty-two persons on the train and quoted "Uncle Rufe" extensively, referring to him as "the prime mover" of the improvement company.[3] These were high times for a financial venture already on shaky legs.

While Hatch came across in correspondence with officials and in meetings with members of the press as a reasonable man who had the interests of investors and tourists in mind, his reputation included a tough side. An incident in the park during August revealed how forceful Hatch could press his case when necessary.

While the Arthur expedition worked its way across Wyoming into the park, a group of U.S. senators met in Montana Territory with representatives of the Crow Indian tribe. This was part of efforts by a Senate select committee to gather information on the condition of tribes in Montana and Dakota territories. Hearing testimony from the Crow chiefs were Senators Henry Dawes of Massachusetts, chairman of the committee; John A. Logan of Illinois; and Angus Cameron of Wisconsin—all Republicans. After several days with the Crows, the three took a side trip to Yellowstone National Park where they camped. No record of this made its way into the official report of the committee or other proceedings of Congress.

National Hotel and Cottage Hotel as seen from top of the terraces
at Mammoth Hot Springs, c1895
Courtesy National Park Service, Yellowstone National Park, YELL 9278

Wylie Camping Company permanent tent camp,
guests in foreground, c1885
Courtesy National Park Service, Yellowstone National Park, YELL 713

F. Jay Haynes, at right, expedition photographer,
leaning on platform loaded with equipment, pre-1889
Courtesy National Park Service, Yellowstone National Park, YELL 147915

An account of their visit to the park and the reaction of Hatch was prepared by a reporter for the *Chicago Tribune*, who was nearby waiting to catch a glimpse of President Arthur as that party moved toward the north boundary. In an article carrying the dateline HATCH'S HOTEL, YELLOWSTONE PARK, AUG. 20 VIA LIVINGSTON, MONT., AUG. 20, the reporter said the senators had left the park a day earlier having "camped out and roughed it all through the park."[4] Without attributing information to a specific source, the article continued, "The chief thing accomplished was to hold a meeting and agree to present the next Congress with a protest against allowing one company to control the park to the exclusion of competition."

The senators' complaint may have been prompted when they tried to hire transportation outside the park in Montana for a journey inside the national preserve. Park officials had declared that only transportation provided by the improvement company could be used in the park. While this eventually was exposed as a misinterpretation of a Department of the Interior statement, it appeared to senators that the government was protecting the interests of one company and stifling competition. The senators obtained a military ambulance at Fort Ellis, Montana, complete with soldier escort, for their adventure in the park.

A few days later, the reporter met with Hatch at the hotel and told him the senators' intent. Angered and defensive, according to the report, he replied that competition was impossible. "We hold a contract for ten years. If there is any big Indian who wants to take it off our hands he can be accommodated."[5] Preferring to take the comments personally, Hatch said he could paddle his "own canoe against the sneak thieves of both parties." He concluded by saying the select committee was composed of lawyers who knew that a contract was signed by the government, and he doubted the report that senators were intent on introducing more competition.

Quarrelsome statements from August through December 1883 exchanged by officials of the improvement company and the Department of the Interior often reached personal levels and spared no feelings. While interesting reading, they might be put aside by some as just another example of bureaucratic government infighting, with no real consequence other than personal bragging rights and political gain. There may have been some of that, but the ramifications of accusations and complaints came at a critical time in commercial development of the park and had serious impacts for years in laws and financial outcomes for persons and corporations. In some respect, these were continuations of contentiousness outlined in 1882 and earlier in 1883, but the intensity reached new heights.

Unresolved issues still on the table between the company and the government as fall approached included the condition of roads, status of law enforcement, illegal cutting of timber, poaching of game, further controls over development, and expansion of park boundaries. With conclusion of the Arthur expedition, pressure mounted from Sheridan, Vest, and conservationists led by Grinnell for greater protection of the park and for extension of the eastern and southern boundaries. Meanwhile, despite the rhetoric from Hatch, the company was hurting in a financial way.

During the summer, concerns within the department about management of the park, especially regarding the work and behavior of Superintendent Conger, led officials to take a drastic step. Teller and his assistant, Joslyn, decided they needed the viewpoint of someone inside the park who could gather information without arousing the suspicions of Conger and his assistant superintendents. On August 3, W. Scott Smith, a special agent for the government land office, received verbal directions to conduct official business in the park from his superior, the commissioner of the General Land Office. When Interior officials learned of the planned visit, they asked Smith to make inquiries regarding park management and to report to the secretary. Smith was told not to disclose his connections to the department.

After reaching the park, Smith spent several days observing the superintendent and assistants and determining whether instructions of the secretary in regard to preservation of the park were being properly carried out. In a report dated October 15, Smith stoked the fires of controversy with strong criticism of the superintendent. The communication from Smith to Teller reverberated in angry correspondence through the end of the year and put Conger's job in jeopardy.

Smith's observations may not have included much more information than was already available or reported earlier to Teller and Joslyn. However, Smith put the material together in such a way to conclude that Conger was insubordinate and incapable of carrying out the secretary's directives to protect game, timber, and the natural beauties of the park. Smith did not identify his sources of information other than to note that rumors among guides, hunters, teamsters, and members of the Geological and Geographical Survey parties provided stories that Smith believed. Without further identification, it is possible that some of those he talked with, including improvement company officials, had axes to grind with the authority figure in the park.[6]

The report contained six accusations or claims of inaction against Conger and the assistants. The superintendent had been admonished previously to post signs throughout the park prohibiting the unauthorized killing of game. Smith said he found no notices posted. He wrote, "As a result of careful inquiries, I became satisfied that the superintendent has made no attempt to obey these instructions, but has shut his eyes to the fact that hunting has been going on openly during the past summer within the Park." He added that hunters were employed by the Mammoth Hot Springs Hotel to kill elk and other game for the hotel's visitors.

Smith wrote that one of the "most important duties appertaining to the office of superintendent is to see that the wonderful curiosities about the springs and geysers are protected from destruction at the hands of vandals and curiosity seekers." Upon visiting the geyser basins, Smith said there were no assistant superintendents on duty to prevent vandalism. More damaging was Smith's report that some assistants had lifted artifacts from the geyser areas and sold them to tourists. Smith said, "The further I inquired the more I learned that some of the assistant superintendents have used their knowledge to obtain the choice specimens to sell to visitors for good prices . . . . It seems almost incredible that such a condition of affairs should long continue without coming to the knowledge of the superintendent."

This led Smith to the conclusion that assistant superintendents were not qualified for duties in the park. "The duties of the office require men possessing both judgment and nerve, men who have the physical courage to do their full duty in the face of the rough element that is to be found in the Park . . ." His recommendations called for the appointment of men "who have lived on the frontier and are accustomed to hardships." The first assistants named earlier in the year were mostly from midwestern and eastern U.S. locations.[7]

Smith cited one example of what he believed was overt favoritism for the improvement company and restraint of competition. Conger apparently had misinterpreted a directive from the department designed to prohibit people within the park from transporting visitors without a permit. Instead, Smith claimed Conger had prohibited transportation companies from bringing visitors into the park and taking them back out again. He apparently said once visitors were within the park, the improvement company should provide transportation. Smith recalled a report that three U.S. senators wanted to hire a team and drive into the park from Bozeman, Montana. They were notified they could not do so. Smith offered no names; but they must have been Senators Dawes, Logan, and Cameron.

The report included Smith's recommendations for changing performances by the superintendent and assistants. He called for posting notices conspicuously throughout the park and for one assistant to be stationed at the Mammoth Hot Springs Hotel to prevent any hired groups from leaving to hunt game for the hotel. This recommendation also suggested an order forbidding persons authorized to transport visitors in the park to carry rifles or carbines upon threat of losing their permit. He questioned whether this would be practicable.

Smith believed assistants should be replaced, and he did all but call for the immediate removal of Conger. He wrote in conclusion, "I think the interests of the Government demand a more active, energetic, and competent superintendent than the present one. Mr. Conger is well advanced in years, and while he might fill some positions satisfactorily, he does not, I am satisfied, combine the qualifications required to make an efficient superintendent." Smith called Conger's deficiencies "too serious to let go unnoticed."

Teller forwarded "extracts from a communication" to Conger on October 23, with a few comments on specific charges leveled by Smith.[8] His first reference was to the accusation that assistant superintendents had "engaged in the extraction of the curiosities for the purpose of selling the fragments to tourists." He ordered Conger to investigate. Secondly, Teller tackled the subject of killing game in the park and his directive to Conger of January 15, 1883. In essence, he expressed concern for Conger's behavior when the order was so specific. Teller said, "The Department cannot understand why the Superintendent has not exercised greater effort to enforce obedience to these regulations." Teller seemed stunned that the superintendent and assistants had not monitored hunting parties whose mission was to kill game for use at the hotel.

The secretary saved the bulk of his letter for the misinterpretation of the order limiting transportation within the park to businesses that had permission from the department.

Teller said the directive was designed to make sure the improvement company did not charge rates in excess of those approved by Teller. He restated the intent not to regulate transportation from outside the park to points in the park. Teller's tone left no doubt that he was puzzled by Conger's interpretation. In all, Teller's transmittal letter stopped short of threatened dismissal, but the criticism left little to the imagination.

In reply to Smith's report and Teller's comments, Conger unleashed three letters to the secretary in defense of his actions. The first dated November 4 expressed outrage at the accusations and denial of all charges. The second was a broadside aimed primarily at Hobart, who Conger believed instigated many of the items included in the Smith report. The final letter in the series was a plea for understanding from Teller that law enforcement in the park was virtually impossible under existing conditions.

Conger evidently was unprepared for Smith's report. Presumably, he did not know someone was in the park gathering information about his job performance. Since Conger did not mention Smith's name in his replies, Teller may have purposely omitted that information. However, unless Conger was naïve or simply out of touch, he knew Hobart and officials of the improvement company wanted him removed for someone more sympathetic to their cause. Hobart could hardly have forgotten that Conger disapproved of the company's original application for a contract and lease.

Conger recognized that Smith's report aimed directly at the superintendent's performance and declared it inadequate. Conger said, "I wish to enter my most emphatic, indignant, and positive denial."[9] He objected to being in the position of defending his honor instead of the accusers providing proof of the charges. Conger quickly turned to Hobart as the dealer of mischief behind the accusations. "This hostility comes, not for the reason of inattention to my duties as superintendent of the park, but from a knowledge of the fact that I guard too closely the interests of the Park and public to suit their designs," he stated.

The superintendent claimed to have spread the word in keeping with the secretary's January 15 order although he did not respond to the accusation that he had failed to post notices. Conger claimed he had warned people about rules and regulations regarding fires, destruction or injury of the geysers, and shooting or killing any animals or birds—"except bears and vicious animals with claws [all predators]."

Conger attached a copy of a communication from June 30 to William Chambers, an assistant superintendent, regarding reports that park employees had taken geyser specimens and sold them to tourists.[10] In the letter to Chambers, Conger ordered an investigation of the alleged incident and a report on items taken. Writing to Teller, he acknowledged one incident involving an assistant: "Upon investigation I found that one of the assistants had picked up a small but curious specimen away from the Geysers, and that a gentleman seeing the specimen and desiring to possess it offered the assistant one dollar for it, which he accepted. I cautioned them all and told them such traffic was highly improper, and commanded them not on any account to do the like again, and I do not believe that any of them have, except Mr. Henderson, who lives here at the springs, and whose daughter is postmistress. They keep exposed for sale a large selection of specimens in the post office. Where or how they obtained them I am unable to ascertain." A bit of larceny appeared to have occurred. He agreed to provide Teller with the name of the assistant who took one dollar for a specimen—if asked.

The superintendent's defense on the issue of hunters illegally shooting game in the park depended mostly on the often-stated concern about law enforcement authority. He admitted that unlawful hunting occurred and probably would continue to occur "in spite of all the vigilance that any officer can possibly exercise with the force at my command and under existing conditions." He related incidents where assistants responded to reports of illegal hunting and tracked people into the backcountry without success. He used that example to defend the assistants and asked for understanding of their situation, saying, "I must beg you to remember that they all are strangers to this section of the country, and that a number of them are quite young and inexperienced; and I think some allowance should be made on that account, not only on their own account but mine as well." In effect, Conger acknowledged one of the major criticisms made by Smith.

Conger returned to the subject of Hobart and the improvement company in a letter written two days later.[11] Obviously, the superintendent believed it served his purpose to attack, even though the letter would become part of the official record. Conger said concern for the public record had limited the information provided about activities of the improvement company. He also complained about not knowing exactly what conversations or correspondence had been exchanged between Hobart and Teller and what extraordinary privileges had been extended. When Conger got down to charges against the company, he revealed the depth of animosity that had influenced the relationship between his office and Hobart, Douglas, and Hatch.

"I only know that they help themselves indiscriminately to whatever they may want inside or outside of the Government inclosures without reference to any other interest than their own," he charged. "They have cut and manufactured nearly all of the timber available for building purposes anywhere near this place to build their great hotel and their numerous other buildings here." He mentioned the hotel's herds of horses and cattle had broken and destroyed fences he had erected to protect government stock.

On a personal level, Conger claimed that Hobart had been heard to say he would tear down the fences as often as the superintendent put them up, "that he would show me he had a right to do as he pleased here." Conger said this had driven up costs to the government of caring for stock outside the park because the company bought all the hay within twenty miles of his office at Mammoth Hot Springs. From that point, Conger expanded his quarrel with Hobart. "Mr. Hobart has obstructed me in every way in his power ever since he has been here . . . . Hobart has boasted in my hearing of his influence with you, and that he had frequent letters from you . . ." Conger feared the secretary, and Hobart had made private deals excluding the superintendent; and while the record does not disclose any "deals" or cozy sentiments as such, there was direct correspondence between Hobart and Teller throughout 1883.

After receiving Conger's references to what he believed was going on behind his back, Teller responded, blaming the superintendent for not mentioning his complaint in a personal meeting of the two government officials in Livingston.[12] Denying any dealing with Hobart, Teller said, "I have had no communication with Mr. Hobart or any one connected with his company, and it was your duty to promptly inform me of any and all improper acts on the part of the hotel company or their employes." He added, "I have not communicated with Mr. Hobart except in an official way." The final sentence, to which Hobart reacted later, stated, "You will notify Mr. Hobart that he must comply strictly with the conditions of his lease or steps will be taken to compel such compliance." Conger passed along that sentence in a note to Hobart dated November 25.

Conger's third letter in November dealt mostly with his frustration at not being able to obtain effective law enforcement in the park.[13] "I have not the legal right or power to arrest and detain any person charged with a violation of any of the rules governing the Park," he wrote. As if to figuratively throw up his hands in defeat, Conger said, "Now what am I do to? What can I do under this state of facts?" He suggested federal legislation to deal with the difficulty in securing legal proof of the violation of the law, especially as it related to the killing of game. "It would be next to impossible to take a man in the act, and none are so rash or foolish as to proclaim their purpose to do an unlawful deed nor to voluntarily confess their own guilt," he added. Everyone, it seemed, had some desire for improved law enforcement.

The superintendent ended his letter with an obscure reference to "very wise men" who find their way into the park. "They offer unsolicited their valuable advice and information upon all matters and things wherever they may go or happen to be," he said. "They print their learned views and whims in the papers and whisper them to the ear of powers. You doubtless have been tendered assistance by this class of persons in the discharge of the duties of your high office." He left the matter at that, inferring the secretary had been influenced by whispers and rumors included in the Smith report.

It was only a matter of time before Hobart heard of the Smith report and Conger's replies. If the Conger-Hobart war had been a private affair, no longer was that the case. The impact on working relations so critical to protection of the park and responsible growth of commercial interests was incalculable, especially in Washington where the Interior secretary and members of Congress watched. As the last to comment on the uproar of Smith's report, Hobart could be the voice of decency and reason.

In the November 30 letter to Teller, Hobart went through Conger's charges against the company and attempted to refute them by the number, all the while expressing innocent intent.[14] In summary, these were his statements:

1. The company has never violated any of its obligations under the contract or imposed by law. "If it be true that we 'have helped ourselves' to whatever we wanted, it has been only because we have 'wanted' nothing beyond that to which we were fairly and explicitly entitled."

2. The company cut only as much timber as needed for construction of buildings, and it was all taken from one gulch "in such a manner as not to be noticed in its effect upon the forest, and remote from any point of interest."

3. The company kept thirty horses and 110 cows for the transportation of tourists and for providing products for meals; no more than the necessities required. "That we should keep such stock as the nature of our business demanded was clearly contemplated by our contract."

4. "We absolutely and emphatically deny" tearing down fences around the government pasture.

5. If hay was eaten, it probably was because of the "dozen or more horses kept by Mr. Conger."

6. "I am not aware that I ever obstructed Mr. Conger in any way in the discharge of his duty; certainly I did not intentionally. I endeavored to treat him respectfully, and to facilitate his labors."

7. Hobart said he would like to acknowledge "intimate relations and friendly correspondence with the Secretary of the Interior," but that was never the case. He denied boasting of having Teller's ear.

After dispensing with the specific charges by Conger, Hobart aimed at the superintendent on a personal level. He referred to rumors passed along to Conger's "greedy ears and credulous mind" by the assistants as "too weak to be answered." At one point, Hobart referred to Conger's "groundless jealousy." Hobart attributed Conger's grievances to a feeling that he had not "received the social consideration to which the superintendent of the Park was entitled . . . . When the complaints against us are reduced to this, they have reached a point where they are no longer entitled to official consideration, because they do not affect public interests." Hobart did his best to characterize the superintendent as a man afraid of his own shadow and given to delusions.

The clash between Conger and Hobart simmered for the rest of 1883, rising to the surface on occasion but not matching the volume of this exchange. On December 21, Hobart wrote Teller in reference to the statement forwarded earlier to him by Conger that the improvement company must comply with provisions of the contract and lease. Hobart said he asked for a further explanation of the secretary's comment, and Conger referred him to Teller. Hobart stood his ground, saying, "As I have endeavored to observe the conditions of the lease in every particular, and am not aware of any default therein on the part of the Yellowstone National Park Improvement Company, I feel obliged to come to you for the information which I fail to get from Mr. Conger."[15] There is no reply from Teller among papers of record through the end of 1883.

As if the internal pressure on the embattled Conger were not enough, word of Smith's report received notice in publications reaching the public. One of those was Grinnell at *Forest and Stream* magazine. He was obviously not privy to the extended correspondence among principals, but he had access to the Smith report and found it damning regarding the behavior of assistant superintendents.[16] Grinnell wrote, "It is stated that they are, for the most part, Eastern men, wholly unacquainted with life in the mountains, and so, perfectly useless as protectors of the Park . . . . It is said also that they permitted hunting and allowed game to be killed in direct opposition to the Secretary's order. On the whole, if the report is at all to be trusted, the assistant superintendents have proved themselves wholly incompetent and generally worthless." In an editorial earlier in 1883, Grinnell had issued a warning to Conger about carefully watching out for the public interest at Yellowstone.

Harsh judgment aside, Grinnell's displeasure at reports about the assistants was mild compared to his conclusions about Conger. He said if the official was guilty of permitting the acts with which the assistants were charged, "it is clear that he is by no means the man for the place which he holds, and his prompt dismissal is certain." Later in the editorial, Grinnell said Conger "must go."

Rufus Hatch tried his best in an annual report filed December 1 with Teller to set an optimistic tone for the hotel, the company, and the future.[17] As a stock speculator, Hatch knew the language of hope that lured so many to invest in grand ideas, and he again demonstrated his promotional skills in the report. For example, he rolled out figures to support his statement: "There never has been a building of the magnitude of this one constructed in such a wilderness, so far from railroad facilities or a base of supplies, and where nearly all of the material, the workmen, and supplies had to be hauled by wagons, sometimes more than 100 miles, over the roughest of Rocky Mountain roads, amid alternating snow and mud or blinding dust." While perhaps given to exaggeration to impress the secretary, there undoubtedly was a measure of truth in his comments.

He never missed an opportunity to point out the poor condition of roads, a fact the company complained about constantly. In comments about the tents established at the Norris Geyser Basin, the Upper Geyser Basin, and the Great Falls, he wrote, "To establish these camps required the hauling of the equipments over the worst possible roads, distances varying from 27 to 85 miles, and all the edible supplies to carry on these camps had to be conveyed to them by the like means." Pointing out the hazards for tourists in the first season, Hatch urged the government to "make the roads not merely safe, but comfortable for travel." He promised better transportation services for the 1884 season, "and we respectfully urge that the roads be improved correspondingly."

Perhaps to reassure Teller that the company had the secretary's agenda well in mind, Hatch added, "The National Park Improvement Company are desirous to have the natural curiosities preserved and protected from the hands of vandalism, and the wild game within the Park preserved from destruction, and to this end will co-operate to the fullest extent with the officers of the Department in executing the laws, and the orders of the Secretary of the Interior."

In spite of Hatch's upbeat rhetoric, the picture looked gloomy for him and the improvement company as 1883 drew to a close. Perhaps his most embarrassing moment had occurred in September when the two lines of the Northern Pacific Railroad met in Montana and were connected with a final spike. Always working at raising funds from investors, Hatch had assembled a trainload of foreign money people for an excursion to the park at about the time of the joining of the two rail lines. Henry Villard, top official of the railroad, had a trainload of foreign capitalists of his own, following Hatch. The *New York Times* described the events:

It was while these two special trains were moving westward that news was received that there had been a raid on Northern Pacific stock, and it had gone tumbling down. Both Villard and Hatch were financially ruined in that crash, and the foreign capitalists whom they had taken out to interest in future investments laughed at them when they returned. From that failure of 1883, Mr. Hatch never recovered. He paid all but $25,000 of what he owed."[18]

In addition to his investment woes, Hatch spent approximately $35,000 of his own money to entertain foreign and domestic dignitaries and members of the press in August. The combination resulted in Hatch filing for bankruptcy and dropping out of official duties with the improvement company.

Another factor in the hard-luck search for investors in the company's future was the 1883 lease with the government that limited site development to ten acres as opposed to the earlier promise of 4,400 acres. Combined with a poor season's return because of a late start on construction of the hotel and start-up difficulties, the company ended 1883 in debt and unable to pay its employees or creditors.[19] There was no respite for the company in the months immediately ahead. George Carver, a Livingston businessman, filed suit against the company—attaching a company sawmill, a herd of horses, and 180 head of cattle to pay company debts. Hobart and Douglas continued to direct operations while the company was in receivership.

Meanwhile, on the legislative front, Senator Vest introduced a bill in December to revise the Yellowstone Park law enacted in 1872, which provided for extension of the laws of Montana Territory to the park. The proposal also made the park part of Gallatin County, Montana Territory. It called for giving the superintendent and assistants powers of U.S. marshals. This was the long-awaited bill left over from the early 1883 congressional session when the Senate refused to consider Vest's bill. The proposal also called for expanding the park to the east and south as recommended and promoted by the coalition that included Sheridan and Grinnell.

The year 1884 held some promise for correcting the problems of park management, slaughter of game, wanton cutting of timber, and the financial misfortunes of commercial development. The improvement company hoped that larger crowds of tourists in the 1884 season would provide profits that had remained elusive. In spite of optimism and renewed expectations, there always seemed to be an abundance of chaos.

10

The End of Noble Deeds

THOSE CONCERNED WITH PRESERVING
Yellowstone National Park waited anxiously as the 48th Congress opened for business
in 1884. Their hopes rested primarily with Senator Vest's omnibus bill to revise the act
of 1872, incorporating changes and reforms he and others thought necessary to expand
and save the park.

When Congress refused to consider Vest's legislation and resolution in the early
months of 1883—choosing instead to pass appropriations legislation directed at the
park—and Teller signed a ten-year lease with the improvement company, the senator
began drafting legislation to expand the park boundaries to provide law enforcement
that would prevent the destruction of natural wonders and game and to increase
and strengthen resources for park administration. Vest wanted to amend the original
legislation rather than continue a piecemeal approach to laws involving the park.

Since the partial victory of 1883, Vest had experienced the accomplishments of
the Arthur expedition in spreading the word of Yellowstone Park's wonders and had
enjoyed the strong support of friends of the park mobilized by Grinnell and the magazine
Forest and Stream. By forcing Teller to make public all documents related to granting
a commercial lease, Vest had brought light to secretive dealings between government
and the improvement company. Vest believed the moment had arrived early in 1884 to
correct twelve years of neglect, apathy, and poor judgment.

In an editorial on January 17, Grinnell lamented the sad state of affairs in the park
as reflected in the 1883 lease documents released by the secretary of the Interior.[1] The
papers included the Smith report and various exchanges of accusations and denials by
Teller, Conger, Hobart, and Hatch. "It is quite apparent that matters in the Yellowstone
Park are in a very unsatisfactory condition," Grinnell wrote.

After reciting concerns by Teller and others for law enforcement needs, Grinnell
pushed again for a military presence in the park, reiterating a stand he had taken a year

earlier. He wrote, "The need for this protection now is more urgent that ever before. An effort has been made to care for the Park, and this effort has proved wholly abortive. The Government is now the laughing stock of the Improvement Company and the skin-hunters and trespassers . . . . Until some legislation bearing on the civil government of the Park shall have been determined the proper legal means by which the violators of laws and rules shall be punished, there is no means of preventing these violations except by the use of troops."

In a final plea to Teller to take action on military assistance, which Congress provided in the 1883 sundry bill, Grinnell added, "The friends of the Park, and those are the people at large, would rejoice to see some vigorous measures taken by the Secretary of the Interior in behalf of their pleasure ground. Now that the Park has become so easily accessible, something must be done, and that soon."

That issue of the magazine also contained a letter to the editor, signed Ichthus, purporting to be written by an assistant superintendent in the park.[2] Mostly the letter was a plea for help in law enforcement. The writer said, "At present we have not the power to arrest violators of the laws, and only our presence has been the curb of restraint upon hunters, who question our authority, because there are no defined boundary lines to the Park." He claimed some success in corralling illegal activity "but not as much as a true sportsman would like to see."

The assistant also wrote in opposition to running a rail line into the park, an unresolved issue that had been before Congress since 1882. Rumors surfaced periodically that railroad officials had proposed lines for the Northern Pacific and Utah and Pacific into the park, but nothing had materialized. However, the fact that plans for railroads in the park had not been put to bed alarmed those who opposed. It was the kind of issue that could sneak through Congress almost unnoticed, so the best defense was to mention it periodically. "A railroad through the park means the destruction of its forests, which go further to make up the matchless beauty of the Park scenery than any other one thing," the assistant stated. Assistant superintendents often wrote letters to newspapers calling for military assistance and providing examples of depredations by vandals.

Another voice on the matter of trains in the park came from Arnold Hague, a geologist with the U.S. Geological Survey, in a letter to Vest toward the end of December.[3] He spoke to similar issues as Ichthus and called for a prohibition of trains. "Nothing would tend more to destroy the timber by fire than the passage of trains through the forest. Moreover, the locomotive whistle and the additional traffic caused by railway transportation would convert the place into a public highway and tend to destroy all aspects of a Park. It would most effectually drive out all large game."

The Committee on Territories reported Vest's bill to the full Senate on March 4 with an amendment to strike the enacting clause of the Act Establishing Yellowstone National Park (1872) and to replace it with nine new sections.[4] For much of two days, the Senate debated the bill whose essential pieces were:

Section 1: Primarily extended the southern boundary about ten miles and the eastern boundary thirty miles. Vest said the eastern extension would "take in a large extent of country which is the home of large game and covered with forest trees, the preservation of which is absolutely necessary to protect the sources of large rivers and without including that it is absolutely impossible to protect either the timber or the large game which there exist."

Vest added that General Sheridan and he had conversations with guides, hunters, and trappers who were familiar with the eastern country. "It takes in no country which is valuable for mineral purposes or for grazing purposes." One Senate exception in the extension involved the area adjacent to the northeast corner of the park. The extension boundary was moved ten miles south to accommodate an existing mining operation. "This is done to avoid any complication as to title, and in order to give those now engaged in that enterprise full scope and opportunity to proceed with their business."[5]

Although no government survey of the original park boundaries had been achieved in twelve years, officials estimated acreage at 3,300 square miles. During debate, Vest said the proposed boundary expansion would add another 2,000 square miles to the total, less than proposed by Sheridan.

Section 2: Reestablished the Interior secretary's authority and responsibility to administer the park under federal laws as a "pleasure-ground for the benefit and enjoyment of the people of the United States."

Section 3: The secretary's authority to make regulations and rules for protection of the natural wonders and game within the park was reconfirmed as stated in the original park act. Further, the secretary's choice to use U.S. military resources to maintain law and order was reiterated as it had been included in the 1883 sundry bill.

Section 4: Specific game to be protected were named. Violations declared as misdemeanors were subject to a fine up to $250 and jailed for three months for each act.

Section 5: Previous law regarding limits on the authority of the secretary to issue leases was spelled out as prescribed in the 1883 sundry bill. It precluded the secretary from granting any exclusive commercial privileges within the park, except on the specific ground leased. Any leases, contracts, or agreements reached previously that disagreed with the provisions were declared null and void.

Section 6: The laws of the territory of Montana were extended over the park; and for arrest, conviction, and punishment, the park would be considered a part of Gallatin County, Montana.

Under questioning by senators, Vest explained why Montana was chosen to protect life and property in the park instead of Wyoming Territory. He noted that the capital of

Wyoming was in Cheyenne, and persons arrested in the park would have to be transported to that city, requiring a trip of 175 miles on horseback. If suspects were taken to available train connections on the north or east of the park, the trip to Cheyenne would cover five hundred miles. The availability of train travel close to the north boundary of the park gave Montana the edge, he said, because most violations of the law are likely to occur near the hotel and geyser attractions. Suspects could be removed quickly to a judicial center in Montana by the northern route.[6]

During debate, Vest mentioned personal criticism of him by Wyoming sources. "I have been assailed in the newspapers of Cheyenne for attacking the Territorial sovereignty of that people. It is ridiculous. I have no personal interest in the matter, I could have no prejudice politically or personally against the territory of Wyoming. All that I sought to do was to save expense to the Government and to bring about a speedy administration of justice."[7] Faced with the proposed alternative of Montana laws applying, officials in Wyoming altered their previous position. Correspondence during 1883 with Teller indicated a reluctance of Wyoming law enforcement officials to take responsibility for the park.

> Section 7: The number of assistant superintendents was increased to fifteen from ten at the same rate of pay as before, $900 a year, and with the requirement of residence in the park. The superintendent's pay would remain at $2,000 a year. Assistants were given the authority to make arrests and "shall also have all the powers and duties conferred by law upon the sheriffs and constables for the Territory of Montana and their deputies." Expansion of the number of assistants was primarily to assist in coverage of additional park acreage.

Another provision of the section prohibited the cutting of timber for building purposes or for firewood, except with permission of the superintendent. This reflected previous law and Interior regulations, although concerns existed for enforcement.

> Section 8: Since July 1883, an officer of the Corps of Engineers had been assigned to plan and construct a road system in the park. However, all parties remained concerned about the commitment to improved road conditions, and the desire of this provision was to put the arrangement in law.
>
> Section 9: Approval of the president of the United States was required for actions taken by the secretary of the Interior.

During floor debate on March 4 and 5, Vest answered questions posed by a few senators about boundaries and Montana law enforcement. Much of the time involved exchanges between Vest and Sen. John J. Ingalls of Kansas, who mounted a serious protest about provisions of the bill and the continued existence of the park. Ingalls made it clear at the outset that he disapproved of a federal park, saying, "I doubt the propriety of the Government going into the show business, or engaging in the protection of an exhibition of geysers . . . ."[8] The degree to which Ingalls spoke for others in the Senate could not be determined by the limited debate. He seemed unable to rally sufficient support to stop Vest's initiatives.

Ingalls objected to language authorizing the secretary of war to provide troops at the request of the secretary of the Interior, and he proposed eliminating that part of Vest's bill. Ingalls complained about giving the secretary discretionary authority to call out the armed forces for what the senator described as a remote portion of the nation. "I cannot conceive that there is any such great danger of invasion, or insurrection, or violation of the primal rights of man, that the ordinary tribunals of the land will not be sufficient to punish those who may offend against the provisions of this proposed act," he said, referring to the provision as a declaration of "martial law."

Refusing to argue the past action of declaring a national park, Vest said the bill would resolve "whether the park shall be abandoned and left without law, without control, and given up to the vandals who go in for the purpose of destroying the game and the objects of curiosity and wonder in the park." He spoke to the inadequacy of a superintendent and ten assistants patrolling the park against parties of men "in numbers of five and ten and even twenty, armed to the teeth, for the purpose of destroying the game in order to ship it to market." Vest said giving the secretary authority to summon the army had been done in the 1883 sundry bill and is "no extraordinary power, because the National park is in such a condition that at times nothing but the Army amounts to anything, and it is absolutely necessary to have such a provision in order to protect it."[9]

Ingalls's response was to return parkland to the public domain "and allow the curiosities that exist there, the game that lives there, and the waters that flow there, to be taken care of as the other great objects of interest in this country are, by men who feel a special individual interest in them."

The Kansas senator also mounted an argument against the bill and the park, based on his concern for future costs. He predicted the eventual need for a department of government to control Yellowstone National Park. Citing the demand for expenditures to cover roads and bridges, to pay for additional assistant superintendents, and to potentially have army troops available, Ingalls said, "We are on the threshold of a very large and constantly increasing annual expenditure for the improvement of this property." His amendment to eliminate language for military assistance failed on a voice vote.

In response to Ingalls's attack on the idea of a national park, Dawes of Massachusetts—an early proponent of the park—said if he believed the idea was a mistake, then refusing to appropriate public money would be a way of killing it.[10] "I would suggest, as the Senator from Kansas very properly does, to take the vitality out of the bill, not permit the protection of the park . . . . I would not go through the pretense of it before the world, unless I was prepared to take care of it and preserve it. I would make haste to announce to everybody that the first who can light on it shall under some homestead or pre-emption right appropriate it to himself." Dawes obviously did not agree with Ingalls, but his statement drew a clear line for choosing sides on the bill.

Vest picked up on comments by Ingalls and Dawes for this final statement: "If we have the park let us treat it as a national park. If, on the other hand, we are to adopt the idea advanced by the Senator from Kansas, and throw it open as a part of the public domain, then as a matter of course not a dollar should be expended upon it for any purpose."[11] The Vest bill passed the Senate.

Supporters of Vest and the park quickly applauded the Senate bill. Grinnell wrote in *Forest and Stream* a few days after passage, "On the whole, the bill, as passed, is a vast improvement on the laws we have hitherto had in relation to the Park. While the area of the reservation is increased only two-fifths, instead of being more than doubled, as we had hoped would be the case, the enlargement is sufficient to greatly enhance its value to the people . . . ." He expected naturalists "of all nations" to welcome news that the park would be a preserve for wild animals and hoped for passage by the House.[12]

On March 11, the House referred the Senate bill to its Committee on the Territories. The deliberative nature of Congress was about to be demonstrated once again, complicated by delays for a presidential election in the fall. As a result, it was not until February 1885 that the House version surfaced for consideration with amendments.

The House made two substantial changes in the Senate bill. The committee preferred Wyoming Territory for law enforcement in the park instead of Montana Territory. No explanation was offered except to say, "Your committee believes it to properly belong" with Wyoming.[13]

The major change involved the existing northern boundary of the park. As part of its amendment to extend the eastern boundary, the committee preferred the park's northern boundary to follow the Yellowstone River and its eastern fork (known today as the Lamar River). This would cut off the northeastern corner of the original park and give further geographic definition to the northern boundary, supporters of the change claimed. The House version would extend the eastern boundary at that point, much along lines of the Senate proposal. In all other respects, the House concurred with Vest's bill.

During debate of the amended version, opponents to the northern boundary change expressed concern for tampering with the original boundary. Rep. J. Warren Keifer of Ohio, the past speaker of the House, observed, "If you recede the northern portion of the park to Montana you bring the boundary line almost to the very verge of this great natural curiosity [Mammoth Hot Springs]. We want to protect it." Keifer also objected to changing the original park boundary. "If we encroach upon the boundaries of this park as originally laid out, carefully and prudently, we are likely to encroach again whenever prospectors or others want to get in at one place or another."[14] The congressman noted that "some people" had discovered valuable minerals in the northeast corner vicinity, and that could be a reason for wanting to cut off that portion of the park.

Keifer found few supporters of his concerns as the House voted 69-17 to approve the boundary-change amendment and later approved the law enforcement amendment by voice vote. When the House version arrived in the Senate, Vest and colleagues refused to accept the changes and called for a conference committee consisting of members of both chambers.[15] The House agreed, and conferees met to resolve differences.

Unfortunately for Vest and other park protectionists, the conference failed to work out an agreement, and the proposal died. To many, it appeared the efforts at congressional action begun in late 1882 had failed miserably in spite of a few restrictions on commercial growth in the 1883 sundry law. Combined with other events occurring in 1884, the direction of public and private affairs regarding the park raised additional fears.

The single most serious defeat for park protectionists was Sheridan's proposal for expansion of the park, even as debated and altered. However, actions by Congress and Presidents Benjamin Harrison, Grover Cleveland, and Theodore Roosevelt accomplished Sheridan's purpose by designating vast areas adjacent to the park as national forest reserves by executive orders. Acting in 1891, 1896, and 1902, the presidents almost precisely set aside the areas proposed for expansion by Sheridan in 1882. Today, those areas are included in the Teton Wilderness on the south and the Washakie Wilderness, North Absaroka Wilderness, and Shoshone National Forest on the east.

While Congress struggled to find an elusive compromise bill, chaotic affairs continued in the park. The Yellowstone National Park Improvement Company began 1884 unable to pay its bills. Also hanging over the company was the lawsuit of Livingston businessman George Carver, asking recovery of money owed by the company. A Livingston banker was appointed receiver in the case, but Hobart and Douglas of the improvement company sought and obtained a change through the U.S. District Court in Wyoming Territory. The court appointed George Hulme, who remained in charge of the company through 1884 and 1885. Hobart and Douglas handled operations. Further complicating affairs for the company was a strike of hotel workers that put the 1884 tourist season in jeopardy. Through the efforts of Hulme, the parties reached a settlement in June, and the hotel opened to tourists in July.[16] Until the opening, the company provided tourists arriving by train at Cinnabar free lodging in sleeping cars and offered meals at 75¢.

Teller expanded development of commercial interests by granting additional leases. He approved a ten-year lease on four acres of ground at the site of Marshall's Hotel on the Firehole River, and plans were drawn for new buildings. This angered Superintendent Conger who wanted Marshall to vacate his house "for the reason of his outrageous treatment of tourists" and because Marshall refused to be governed by rules and orders. Conger added, "Marshall is a bad man and I do not believe a respectable man can be found in this section who is acquainted with him that would believe him under oath."[17] Disagreements among Marshall, Conger, and the improvement company continued through 1884 with no resolution about new hotel buildings.

In March, photographer F. Jay Haynes received a lease for eight acres at the Upper Geyser Basin with permission to erect buildings for preparing photographs and selling them to tourists. Later in the year, Teller permitted Haynes to split the eight acres with four at the Upper Basin and four at Mammoth Hot Springs. Other ventures, including plans for hotels, were pending as the year progressed.[18]

Tensions between Conger and the improvement company did not subside during 1884. One point of contention was Conger's opposition to any railroad access inside the park. Hobart and associates wanted rail service and applied continuing pressure on behalf of the Northern Pacific. Another disagreement between the parties concerned access to Mammoth Hot Springs for baths to accommodate hotel patrons. Conger banned the baths and ran off the company's men working on pipes to the baths and confiscated tents.[19]

Conger had other problems too. Criticism of assistant superintendents continued. Without appreciation for their work, several assistants returned to their homes in the East only to be replaced by other political appointees without knowledge or understanding of living and working in wild areas. Smith's recommendations for hiring assistants with a better understanding of the work and the environment failed to influence decision makers. With Congress refusing to provide law enforcement help and more assistants, the situation for Conger remained untenable. In a letter dated July 12, 1884, Teller cut the string.[20] He requested Conger's resignation "in view of the unsatisfactory condition of affairs in the Park and the improbability of improvement." Late in the park season, Teller appointed Robert C. Carpenter as the new superintendent.

Teller's action ended Conger's error-and controversy-filled tenure at a little more than two years. During that time, Conger managed to satisfy a few and to anger many people in the park, Washington, and other centers of influence. He would be remembered well by many for opposing a lease for the improvement company and refusing to bless rail service in the park.

Lack of support for Conger could be found in many places, including editorial columns of *Forest and Stream*. A few months before Conger's ouster, Grinnell wrote about the superintendent's mishandling of his assistants, especially hiring strangers to Yellowstone Country.[21] "We warned you last year against doing just this thing. There were plenty of good men to be had in Montana, Wyoming and Idaho . . . . Such men should have been appointed, and if they had been, their efficiency would have spared you a great deal of trouble and annoyance."

More change was coming. The end of Teller's term as secretary of the Interior followed Democrat Grover Cleveland's election as president in November. Succeeding the Coloradan as secretary was L. Q. C. Lamar. Complaints about Carpenter using the park as a source of profit for himself and his friends grew from the outset—ending his tenure in June 1885, after less than a year of service.[22] Vest, hoping for much improvement in park administration, nominated Col. D. W. Wear, a member of the Missouri State Senate. Lamar appointed him superintendent effective June 20, 1885.

Teller's tenure as overseer of the park left much to be desired. Essentially an honest and ethical man in his public service, he was not easily persuaded to favor one particular point of view about the park's future. He believed saving Yellowstone depended on a solid program of businesses serving an ever-increasing number of tourists. These services had to be provided by private concerns, Teller thought, because the government could not assume the costs and there was no specific department devoted only to preserving the park. Teller also had to balance other concerns and needs of the Department of the Interior along with demands from interest groups for Yellowstone Park. He never appeared as much of an advocate for preserving the park, but he also never expressed much emotion on the subject. Teller kept his feelings under control and, as a result, never earned the trust of protectionists or commercial interests.

Teller appeared to do the right thing—when pressed. He backed off cutting a deal with the improvement company for the whole park when challenged by Vest. Teller accepted the decision of Congress limiting his authority to sign leases; and again, once confronted by members of Congress, he made all documents related to leases for 1882 and 1883 available, which revealed that he had proceeded without fully informing the federal legislature about his ideas and plans. He offered neither excuses for his behavior nor refused to share requested information. Teller seemed thwarted in his efforts by conflicts within the park between the superintendent and officials of the improvement company. If anything, the secretary appeared baffled by the quarrels and unable to enforce his regulations and policies with employees. He must share responsibility for the lack of efficient park administration during his tenure.

When Teller took the position of secretary, he had little idea of the mess he inherited. Basically unfamiliar with the park (he visited it only a few times) and with the disparate interests contending for superiority within the boundaries, Teller kept his distance from partisanship. He also remained aloof and hesitant to build support for his initiatives, leaving mostly a mixed record of achievement as a legacy.

Jumping into the void created by a lack of law enforcement authority in the park, the territory of Wyoming passed the Wyoming Territorial Act on March 6, 1884, annexing the park into Uinta County, which today encompasses the state's southwestern corner.[23] The governor appointed two justices of the peace and two constables with Yellowstone jurisdiction, stating the territory's intent was to protect the park from vandals and poachers that were outside the reach of the superintendent and his assistants. As an incentive for law enforcement officers and for the territory treasury, the law decreed that half the fines assessed would be paid to the officer, prosecutor, or witness in a case and the other half to the territory. The door was opened to mischief in the name of law enforcement, and events soon proved that to be true.

Visitors and residents found territorial judgment to be overly harsh for minor offenses. The case that finally exposed weaknesses of the act occurred in 1885 when the justice of the peace sitting in the Lower Geyser Basin declared Lewis E. Payson, an Illinois congressman, guilty of leaving a fire burning at the campsite. The sitting judge fined the congressman $60 and $12.80 in court costs, causing Payson to post $1,000's bond and to appeal the verdict that he considered unjust.[24] A quick conference between the two resulted in a final judgment of court costs only as Payson refused to accept a fine under any compromise offer. The story appeared in the *Chicago Tribune* and became a measure of the ineffectiveness of the Wyoming law. The governor of Wyoming approved repeal of the law in March 1886, again leaving the park without any form of judicial or law enforcement administration.

Vest tried again to gain approval of Congress for a Yellowstone Park bill with a proposal submitted in December 1885. Due to internal politics of the Senate and his opposition to railroad interests that wanted access to the park, Vest could not summon enough support to get the bill considered on the Senate floor. Complicating the situation, from March 1884 to early 1886, Vest underwent a major change of attitude about the use of troops. Originally, a supporter of armed assistance, he concluded military intervention meant the failure of civilian authority.

Matters on many fronts had reached the point of stalemate, endangering civilian control and the park's future. Wrangling among senators and congressmen prevented an appropriation for the Interior secretary to pay civilian employees working in the park, which brought the use of soldiers in the park to a head.

On August 6, 1886, Secretary Wear contacted the secretary of war under authority granted in the 1883 sundry law. He requested "a Captain, two lieutenants and twenty selected mounted men from the Army be detailed for service in the park."[25] Because Interior had no money for military relief Wear deferred to the department of war to pay the bill. The secretary of war referred the request to General Sheridan who recommended sending Troop M of the First U.S. Cavalry from Fort Custer to Yellowstone Park. The troop commander, Capt. Moses Harris, relieved Superintendent Wear of his duties on August 20, 1886, bringing an official end to civilian authority in the park.[26]

The military presence remained until 1918 although the National Park Service was created in 1916. The collapse of civilian control and the advent of military administration saved the park from demise by administrative and bureaucratic bungling, although it also signaled the failure of many efforts to preserve the park from 1882 to 1886. Military protection might never have occurred without the concentrated efforts of Vest, Sheridan, Grinnell, and a host of others who believed, in spite of their occasional differences, that Yellowstone National Park should survive as a place for all the people of the United States to see, enjoy, and respect. Through the efforts of protectionists to elevate concern for the park's future—with the Chester A. Arthur expedition as a centerpiece—policy makers eventually realized the place known as Wonderland could be saved only by dramatic intervention.

Notes

Introduction: A National Park Emerges, 1807-1880

1. Gary E. Moulton, ed., *The Journals of the Lewis and Clark Expedition*, vol. 2, *August 30, 1803-August 24, 1804* (Lincoln: University of Nebraska Press, 1986), 515; and vol. 8, *June 10-September 26, 1806* (1993), 302. Consensus among historians is that Colter traveled through a portion of the park and talked about it to others. Clark wrote of Colter's departure from the expedition on August 15, 1806. Also, Burton Harris, *John Colter: His Years in the Rockies* (New York: Charles Scribner's Sons, 1952), 104-15; and Aubrey L. Haines, *Yellowstone National Park: Its Exploration and Establishment* (Washington: U.S. Department of the Interior, National Park Service, 1974), 4-5.

2. Gary E. Moulton, ed., *The Journals of the Lewis and Clark Expedition*, vol. 1, *Atlas of the Lewis and Clark Expedition* (Lincoln: University of Nebraska Press, 1983), 12-13. Moulton connects Colter's return to Missouri with information obtained by Clark for his 1810 map. According to Clark's map of 1810 (125), Eustis Lake on the map is considered by historians to be Yellowstone Lake.

3. Warren Angus Ferris, *Life in the Rocky Mountains: Diary of Wanderings on the Sources of the Rivers Missouri, Columbia, and Colorado 1830-1835*, ed. LeRoy Hafen (Denver: Old West Publishing Company, 1983), 23, 50, 328-29. Ferris visited Yellowstone area in 1834.

4. William F. Raynolds, *The Report of Brevet Brigadier General W. F. Raynolds on the Exploration of the Yellowstone and the Country Drained by That River*, 40th Cong., 1st sess., 1868, S. Doc. 77; and Raynolds, "Terra Incognita: The Raynolds Expedition of 1860," *http://www.cr.nps.gov/history/online_books/baldwin/chap2.htm*, 1-2.

5. Raynolds, *Report*, 86.

6. Charles W. Cook, David E. Folsom, and William Peterson, *The Valley of the Upper Yellowstone: An Exploration of the Headwaters of the Yellowstone River in the Year 1869*, ed. Aubrey L. Haines (Norman: University of Oklahoma Press, 1965), 6.

7. Ibid., 40.

8. Haines, *Yellowstone National Park*, 56.

9. Haines sets the stage for Langford's account of the Washburn expedition in his foreword to *The Discovery of Yellowstone Park* (vii-xii).

10. Nathaniel Pitt Langford, *The Discovery of Yellowstone Park: Journal of the Washburn Expedition to the Yellowstone and Firehole Rivers in the Year 1870* (Lincoln: University of Nebraska Press, 1972), xxxi.

11. Paul A. Hutton, "Phil Sheridan's Crusade for Yellowstone," *American History Illustrated*, no. 10 (February 1985): 11. Also, Paul A. Hutton, *Phil Sheridan and His Army* (Norman: University of Oklahoma Press, 1999), 164.

12. Haines, *Discovery*, ix; and Haines, *Yellowstone National Park*, 59.

13. Orrin H. Bonney and Lorraine Bonney, *Battle Drums and Geysers: The Life and Journals of Lt. Gustavus Cheyney Doane, Soldier and Explorer of the Yellowstone and Snake River Regions* (Chicago: Swallow Press, 1970), 201. Also, Langford, *Discovery of Yellowstone Park*, 4-5; and Kim Allen Scott, *Yellowstone Denied: The Life of Gustavus Cheyney Doane* (Norman: University of Oklahoma Press, 2007).

14. Bonney and Bonney, *Battle Drums and Geysers*, 203. Also, Haines, *Yellowstone National Park*, 66. Doane's report "is the best account written by a member."

15. "Wonders of the Yellowstone: II," *Scribner's Monthly*, June 1871, 113-128. Also, Chris J. Magoc, *Yellowstone: The Creation and Selling of an American Landscape, 1870-1903* (Albuquerque: University of New Mexico Press, 1999), 11.

16. Marlene Deahl Merrill, ed., *Yellowstone and the Great West: Journals, Letters, and Images from the 1871 Hayden Expedition* (Lincoln: University of Nebraska Press, 1999), 13. This story is repeated in almost every account of Hayden's Yellowstone survey in 1871. Also, Haines, *Yellowstone National Park*, 83-84; Mike Foster, *Strange Genius: The Life of Ferdinand Vandeveer Hayden* (Niwot, CO: Roberts Rinehart Publishers, 1994), 202-04. Foster takes issue with many conclusions expressed by historians about Hayden.

17. Richard A. Bartlett, *Great Surveys of the American West* (Norman: University of Oklahoma Press, 1962), 40; and Merrill, *Yellowstone and the Great West*, 14.

18. Hutton, "Phil Sheridan's Crusade," 164-65. The author says Sheridan met directly with Barlow and Heap to map out a six-week reconnaissance.

19. John W. Barlow to Ferdinand V. Hayden, telegram, 3 June 1871, quoted in Haines, *Yellowstone National Park*, 101. Also, Merrill, *Yellowstone and the Great West*, 18; and Bartlett, *Great Surveys*, 45.

20. Hiram M. Chittenden, *The Yellowstone National Park*, 4th ed. (Cincinnati: Robert Clarke Company, 1903), 82. Also, Bartlett, *Great Surveys*, 48.

21. Bartlett, *Great Surveys*, 51.

22. A. B. Nettleton to Ferdinand V. Hayden, 27 October 1871, in Hayden survey, general letters received, vol. 3, RG 57, National Archives, quoted in Haines, *Yellowstone National Park*, 109; and Bartlett, *Great Surveys*, 57.

23. Langford, *Discovery of Yellowstone Park*, 117-118. Also, Paul Schullery and Lee H. Whittlesey, *Myth and History in the Creation of Yellowstone National Park* (Lincoln: University of Nebraska Press, 2003), 87, 89.

24. Haines's *Yellowstone National Park* (112-124) provides a detailed account of the movement of bills through the Senate and House. Bartlett in *Great Surveys* recommends W. T. Jackson's "The Creation of Yellowstone National Park" found in June 1942's *Mississippi Valley Historical Review*, volume 29 (187-206), for a definitive story of the passage of the bill. Also, Bartlett, *Great Surveys*, 57-59.

25. Merrill, *Yellowstone and the Great West*, 13, 207-208.

26. *Congressional Globe*, 42nd Cong., 2nd sess., 1872, pt. 2:1244. The house vote was a roll call; however, Senate approval was by voice vote. *Congressional Globe*, 42nd Cong., 2nd sess., 1872, pt. 1:697.

27. As printed in *Congressional Globe* the day it was passed by the Senate (January 30, 1872).

28. H. Duane Hampton, *How the U.S. Cavalry Saved Our National Parks* (Bloomington: Indiana University Press, 1971), 47.

29. Haines, *Discovery*, xx; Also, Hampton, *U.S. Cavalry*, 34-39.

30. *Wikipedia*, s.v. "Northern Pacific Railway," http:en.wikipedia.org/wiki/Northern_Pacific_Railway. Also, Freeman Tilden in *Following the Frontier with F. Jay Haynes, Pioneer Photographer of the Old West* weaves information about Northern Pacific history related to the activities of the photographer during the railway's development to Montana.

31. Richard A. Bartlett, *Yellowstone: A Wilderness Besieged* (Tucson: University of Arizona Press, 1985), 30-31. Also, Kenneth H. Baldwin, *Enchanted Enclosure: The Army Engineers and Yellowstone National Park* (Washington: Office of the Chief of Engineers, United States Army, 1976), 1-3; and William A. Jones, "Two-Ocean Water and Togwotee Pass: The Jones Expedition of 1873," *http://www.cr.nps.gov/history/online_books/baldwin/chap4.htm*.

32. William A. Jones, descriptive journal, August 3, 1873.

33. Bartlett, *Yellowstone*, 30; and Baldwin, *Enchanted Enclosure*.

34. Richard A. Bartlett, introduction to *A Trip to the Yellowstone National Park in July, August and September, 1875*, by W. E. Strong (Norman: University of Oklahoma Press, 1968), x-xvii. Strong's condemnation of vandals and poachers is on pages 104-105 of the journal.

35. Francis P. Prucha, *American Indian Policy in Crisis: Christian Reformers and the Indians, 1865-1900* (Norman: University of Oklahoma Press, 1976), 72-102; also, Francis P. Prucha, ed., *Documents of United States Indian Policy* (Lincoln: University of Nebraska Press, 2000), 116-122. During much of the late 1860s and up to 1880, top officers of the army, including Sheridan, argued for Department of War control of Indian affairs—which, since 1849, has been the concern of the Interior department. Points against military control included concerns for separation of military and civilian responsibilities.

36. William Ludlow, *Report of a Reconnaissance from Carroll, Montana Territory, on the Upper Missouri, to the Yellowstone National Park, and Return, Made in the Summer of 1875* (Washington: Government Printing Office, 1876); Paul K. Walker, introduction to *Exploring Nature's Sanctuary: Captain William Ludlow's Report of a Reconnaissance from Carroll, Montana Territory, on the Upper Missouri to the Yellowstone National Park, and Return, Made in the Summer of 1875*, by William Ludlow (Washington: Historical Division, Office of Administrative Services, Office of the Chief of Engineers, 1985), v-xii. Also, Bartlett, *Yellowstone*, 31-32.

37. Hutton, "Phil Sheridan's Crusade," 339-40. Civilian administrative control of Yellowstone National Park ended in 1886. The military remained in the park until 1916 when the National Park Service was organized. Sheridan and Interior Secretary Carl Schurz tangled frequently over Indian policy and accusations of corruption in the department.

38. John F. Reiger, ed., *The Passing of the Great West: Selected Papers of George Bird Grinnell* (New York: Winchester Press, 1972), 1-5. Bonney and Bonney, *Drums and Geysers*, 441. Also, Hutton, "Phil Sheridan's Crusade," 165.

Phil Sheridan to the Rescue

1. Hutton, "Phil Sheridan's Crusade," 346-348. When Lt. Gen. Philip H. Sheridan made three consecutive excursions to Yellowstone National Park beginning in 1881, he was number 2 in command of the U.S. Army. He was outranked by Gen. William T. Sherman. Sheridan worked in Chicago offices where he commanded the Division of the Missouri. On November 1, 1883, Sherman retired; and Sheridan moved his office to Washington where he assumed command of the army.

2. Hutton says of Sheridan's interest in the West, "One benefit of the light duties attached to the commanding general's office was that Sheridan could continue to pay close attention to affairs in the West. He often traveled west on inspection tours, good excuses for fishing and hunting jaunts as well. His keen interest in Yellowstone country never slackened." Ibid., 354.

3. Philip H. Sheridan, *Report, Dated September 20, 1881, of His Expedition through the Big Horn Mountains, Yellowstone National Parks, Etc., Together with Reports of Lieut. Col. J. F. Gregory, Surg. W. H. Forwood, and Capt. S. C. Kellogg* (Washington: Government Printing Office, 1882), 3, 12.

4. Ibid., 3-4.

5. Ibid., 10. A map accompanying the report traced the route from Rock Creek Station (Office of the Chief of Engineers, USA).

6. Ibid., 5.

7. Ibid., 19.

8. Haines, *Yellowstone National Park*, 134-135. Haines provides an extended biographical note on Baronett.

9. Sheridan, *Report 1881*, 19-20.

10. Ibid., 21.

11. Ibid., 8.

12. Ibid., 21.

13. Ibid.

14. Ibid., 9.

15. Ibid., 25.

16. David J. Saylor, *Jackson Hole, Wyoming: In the Shadow of the Tetons* (Norman: University of Oklahoma Press, 1971), 113.

17. Philip H. Sheridan, *Report of an Exploration of Parts of Wyoming, Idaho, and Montana in August and September, 1882, with Itinerary of Col. James F. Gregory, and a Geological and Botanical Report by W. H. Forwood* (Washington: Government Printing Office, 1882), 1.
18. Ibid., 5.
19. Hutton, "Phil Sheridan's Crusade," 341-342.
20. Gregory, *Report 1882*, 22.
21. Ibid., 20.
22. Ibid., 8.
23. Ibid.
24. Ibid., 9.
25. Ibid., 35.
26. Ibid., 11.
27. Ibid., 17.
28. Ibid.
29. Ibid., 17-18.
30. Ibid., 18.
31. Ibid., 13-16, 31. Also, Bartlett, *Yellowstone*, 34-35.

A Picture of the Park in 1883

1. Osborne Russell, *Journal of a Trapper: A Hunter's Rambles Among the Wilds of the Rocky Mountains,* ed. Aubrey L. Haines (New York: MJF Books), 60, 55n, 56n.
2. Russell, *Journal*, 46.
3. "It was quite an event, 70 years ago, to course through the oldest and largest of the national parks." H. B. Wiley, "Yellowstone Park in 1883," *Montana the Magazine of Western History* 3, no. 3 (Summer 1953): 8-18. The editor's note says, "Although Howard B. Wiley is credited with authorship, this portion of the Wiley papers was obviously copied from the hand-written notes of his father, Abraham S. The narration, therefore, is the father's, with reference to 'How' pertaining to the son."
4. Wiley, "Yellowstone Park," 10.
5. Haines, *Yellowstone National Park*, 12-15. Haines describes the four trips to Yellowstone as part of the park's early history.
6. Bartlett, *Yellowstone*, 30, 32.
7. *Wikipedia*, s.v. "Northern Pacific Railway." Also, Freeman Tilden, *Following the Frontier with F. Jay Haynes, Pioneer Photographer of the Old West* (New York: Alfred A. Knopf, 1964), 66-77.
8. *Wikipedia*, s.v. "Northern Pacific Railway."
9. Ibid.
10. Bartlett, *Yellowstone*, 44.
11. Wiley, "Yellowstone Park," 8.
12. Ibid.
13. Ibid., 10, 13, 17, 18.

14. Ibid., 11.

15. Ibid., 13.

16. Wyoming Department of State Parks and Cultural Resources State Historic Preservation Office, "Queen's Laundry Bath House," *http://wyoshpo.state.wy.us/queen.htm* (accessed August 29, 2006). The structure, on the western end of Sentinel Meadows in the Lower Geyser Basin, is listed on the National Register of Historic Places.

17. Wiley, "Yellowstone Park," 18.

18. Ibid., 14.

19. Ibid., 14-15.

20. Ibid., 12.

21. Jerry Wallace, a former employee of the National Archives who now lives in Oxford, Kansas, provided the author with information from the *Winfield Courier* in 1883 and 1884 dealing with J. W. Weimer. Wallace discovered the material while working among archives of the Cowley County Historical Society. He provided the information in 2004 to Lee H. Whittlesey, Yellowstone historian, who placed it with other background on Weimer in the Yellowstone archives. Wallace's communications with the author were by e-mail in December 2006.

22. Lee H. Whittlesey to Jerry Wallace, e-mail, 15 December 2004. Weimer served as an assistant superintendent from 1883 to 1886. Also, Henry M. Teller to U.S. Rep. H. B. Strait, 20 December 1883, 1883 documents. This included a list of the people appointed assistant superintendent.

23. Before leaving Kansas for Yellowstone National Park, Weimer served a single term in the Kansas legislature. Editors at the *Courier* supported his candidacy and service.

24. Whittlesey to Wallace, e-mail, 15 December 2004. Whittlesey identified the companions, unnamed by Weimer in his article, as S. S. Erret and Edmund Fish, both also assistant superintendents.

25. J. W. Weimer, "The National Park: A Visit in the National Playground, or the Wonderland of America," *Winfield Courier*, 1 November 1883. Weimer dated his article 16 October 1883.

26. Weimer, "The National Park."

27. Ibid.

28. J. W. Weimer, "Wyoming Letter," *Winfield Courier*, 20 September 1883. Weimer dated the article 12 September 1883.

29. J. W. Weimer, "Yellowstone National Park Trip Continued," *Winfield Courier*, 7 February 1884. Weimer dated the article 12 January 1884.

30. Ibid.

31. Weimer, "Wyoming Letter."

32. Ibid.

33. Jerry Wallace to Lee H. Whittlesey, e-mail, 17 December 2004.

34. Lee H. Whittlesey, "Marshall's Hotel in the National Park," *Montana the Magazine of Western History* 30, no. 4 (October 1980): 44.

35. George W. Marshall, handwritten biographical statement, during 1885, original in R. H. Bancroft Collection, Bancroft Library, Berkeley, CA, copy to author, 1-3. Marshall wrote from "Fire Hole Basin, National Park, or Mammoth Hot Springs, Wyoming."

36. Ibid., 3-4.

37. Whittlesey, "Marshall's Hotel," 44.
38. Ibid., 45. He cites a letter to Robert E. Strahorn in *The Enchanted Land, or An October Ramble Among the Geysers, Hot Springs, Lakes, Falls, and Canons of Yellowstone National Park* (Omaha: New West Publishing Company, 1881).
39. Marshall's statement, 4-6.
40. Whittlesey, "Marshall's Hotel," 49.

The Developing Storm

1. On January 9, 1883, a U.S. Senate resolution directed Interior Secretary Teller to transmit "copies of all letters or other communications in his Department in regard to the contract made with certain parties concerning the Yellow Stone National Park, and especially any official correspondence with the Superintendent of the Park in regard to the propriety of leasing the same." This referred to documents in 1882. Teller responded, and all were published as Senate Executive Document 48 from the second session of the forty-seventh Congress of January 19, 1883 (hereafter cited as "1882 Documents").
2. Henry M. Teller to Patrick H. Conger, 28 April 1882, "1882 Documents," 1-2. Conger was appointed on April 1, 1882 by Teller's predecessor, Samuel J. Kirkwood.
3. James S. Brisbin to Henry M. Teller, 12 July 1882, "1882 Documents," 2. Born in 1838, Brisbin had a long and distinguished career in the army. According to the documents released by Teller, the secretary granted Brisbin's request to operate a steam vessel on Yellowstone Lake in a letter dated July 27, 1882.
4. William Windom to Henry M. Teller, 31 July 1882. Windom transmitted a letter from C. T. Hobart and H. F. Douglas to Teller dated July 28, 1882. Also, Bartlett, *Yellowstone*, 128. And, microfilm copy, no. 62, roll 1, National Archives, Yellowstone National Park.
5. C. T. Hobart and H. F. Douglas to Henry M. Teller, 28 July 1882, "1882 Documents," 3; and microfilm copy, no. 62, roll 1, National Archives, Yellowstone National Park.
6. "A Railroad to Yellowstone Park," *New York Times*, January 16, 1882.
7. Bartlett, *Yellowstone*, 125; and Biographical Directory of the United States Congress, "Windom, William, (1827-1891)," *http://bioguide.congress.gov/*scripts/biodisplay. pl?index=W000629. Windom retired from the Senate on March 3, 1883.
8. Philip H. Sheridan to George G. Vest, 10 December 1882, box 33, Sheridan Papers, Library of Congress.
9. Bartlett, *Yellowstone*, 139; Hampton, *U.S. Cavalry*, 56, 8n; Biographical Directory of the United States Congress, "Vest, George Graham, (1830-1904)," *http://bioguide.congress.gov/*scripts/biodisplay.pl?index=V000091.
10. Bartlett, *Yellowstone*, 139.
11. Merritt L. Joslyn to Patrick H. Conger, 10 August 1882, "Documents 1882," 3.
12. *Congressional Record*, U.S. Senate, 47th Cong., 2nd sess., 1883, 3269.
13. Attorney authorization by Henry Douglas, 1882, doc. 14; Microfilm copy, no. 62, roll 1, National Archives, Yellowstone National Park. This refers to "agreement made and executed

the first day of September 1882 by and between Merritt L. Joslyn, acting secretary of the Interior" and the parties wishing to build a hotel in the park.

14. Bartlett, *Yellowstone*, 127.

15. Patrick H. Conger to Henry M. Teller, 20 September 1882, "1882 Documents," 4.

16. C. T. Hobart, H. F. Douglas, and Rufus Hatch to Henry M. Teller, 18 November 1882, "1882 Documents," 6-7.

17. Rufus Hatch to Henry M. Teller, 1 December 1883, microfilm copy, no. 62, roll 1, National Archives, Yellowstone National Park.

18. C. T. Hobart and H. F. Douglas to Teller, 6 December 1882, "1882 Documents," 8.

19. "Death of Rufus Hatch," *New York Times*, February 24, 1893. Also, Bartlett, *Yellowstone*, 128-129.

20. Rufus Hatch to David Wear, 31 October 1985, microfilm copy, no. 62, roll 2, National Archives, Yellowstone National Park.

21. Committee on Territories, 47th Cong., 2nd sess., 1883, S. Rep. 911. This was to accompany S. 2317 from the "1883 Documents" (1-16). The bill was to amend sections 2474 and 2475 of the Revised Statutes of the United States regarding Yellowstone National Park. Also, *Congressional Record*, S. Res., 47th Cong., 2nd sess., pt. 1:193. This was to instruct the Committee on Territories to conduct an inquiry.

22. *Congressional Record*, S. Res., 47th Cong., 2nd sess., 1883, pt. 4:3268. Vest also called up the resolution on February 26 to introduce a minor change in wording.

23. S. Rep. 911, Appendix C, 12-14.

24. "Friends of the Park," *Forest and Stream*, February 8, 1883, xx, 22.

25. S. Rep. 911, Appendix D, 14-16.

26. Ibid., 2.

27. Ibid., 5. Vest joined Sheridan and Grinnell in a commitment to an extended park boundary.

28. Vest's support for Montana providing law enforcement in the park was carried through legislation proposed in 1883 and 1884 and reflects a strategic relationship with Governor Crosby.

29. Henry M. Teller to Patrick H. Conger, 15 January 1883, "1883 Documents." Newspapers in towns near the park printed Teller's letter in full (e.g., the January 22 1883 issue of *Bozeman Courier*).

30. Duane A. Smith, *Henry M. Teller: Colorado's Grand Old Man* (Boulder: University Press of Colorado, 2002), 119-120.

31. "Game in the Yellowstone," *Chicago Evening Journal*, March 10, 1883. Reprinted from the *New York Sun*. Publications that leaned heavily toward protecting the park joined Vest's crusade. They included *Nation, Harper's Weekly*, and *Century Magazine*; Bartlett, *Yellowstone*, 141.

32. "A Yellowstone Park Lease," *St. Paul Pioneer Press*, January 12, 1883.

33. Nathaniel P. Langford to George G. Vest, 15 January 1883. Vest sent a copy of the letter to Teller on January 18, 1883. Microfilm copy, no. 62, roll 1, National Archives, Yellowstone National Park.

34. Reiger, *Passing of the Great West*, 2-3.

35. "Leasing the National Park," *Forest and Stream*, December 21, 1882, xix, 1.
36. "The Park Grab," *Forest and Stream*, January 4, 1883, xix, 1.
37. "Friends of the Park," *Forest and Stream*, February 8, 1883, xx, 22.

Washington Wars

1. *Congressional Record*, U.S. Senate, 47th Cong., 2nd sess., 1883, 3268.
2. Ibid., 3269; Henry M. Teller to George G. Vest, 18 January 1883.
3. "The Yellowstone Contract," *Bozeman Courier*, February 22, 1883. Reprint of article from the *St. Paul Pioneer Press* in Washington, dated February 10. Earlier, *Forest and Stream* (February, 3 1883) had published reports of the passage of resolutions in Minnesota and Illinois thanking General Sheridan for calling attention to discussions of a lease with the improvement company.
4. Governor Crosby had joined the fight against a lease in a letter to Vest in December 1882, pushing a resolution through the territorial legislature and announcing his support of General Sheridan's idea to expand the park.
5. "Grabbing a Great Park," *New York Times*, January 20, 1883.
6. "Yellowstone Park," *New York Times*, January 23 1883.
7. *Congressional Record*, U.S. House, 47th Cong., 2nd sess., 1883, pt. 4:3193.
8. "Yellowstone Park," *New York Times*, January 23, 1883.
9. *Congressional Record*, U.S. House, 47th Cong., 2nd sess., 1883, pt. 4:3193.
10. Ibid.
11. "The Yellowstone Park," *New York Times*, February 24, 1883, microfilm copy, no. 62, roll 1, National Archives, Yellowstone National Park.
12. U.S. Senate, February 26, 1883, 3268.
13. U.S. Senate, 3269.
14. Ibid.
15. U.S. Senate, 3482.
16. U.S. Senate, 3483.
17. Ibid.
18. U.S. Senate, 3485.
19. U.S. Senate, 3488.
20. Ibid.
21. *Congressional Record*, Act of March 3, 1883, 47th Cong., 2nd sess., 1883, pt. 4:626.
22. "Mr. Vest's Victory," *Forest and Stream*, March 8, 1883, xx, 1.

The Race to Open a Hotel

1. George G. Vest to Henry M. Teller, 13 June 1883, microfilm copy, no. 62, roll 1, National Archives, Yellowstone National Park.

2. Copy of Indenture, March 9, 1883, microfilm record, no. 62, roll 1, National Archives, Yellowstone National Park. This was signed by Teller for the government, C. T. Hobart, and attorneys for Henry F. Douglas and Rufus Hatch. The record shows a letter from Hobart and the attorneys to Teller dated March 8 requesting the lease. Also, among documents of 1883 released by Teller in response to a request from Senator Vest were the Senate Executive documents of the first session of the forty-eighth Congress (January 9, 1884), transmitting copies of all papers and correspondence relating to the Yellowstone National Park since last session of Congress (hereafter cited as "1883 Documents").

3. "The National Park," *Forest and Stream*, March 22, 1883, xx, 1.

4. Letters received with requests for leases or contracts after March 9, 1883 included Henry R. Pomeroy to Teller (March 12), Edward Voigt to Teller (March 12), and W. S. Libby to Teller (March 15), "1883 Documents," 3.

5. C. T. Hobart to Henry M. Teller, 7 May 1883, submitting the plans, "1883 Documents," 5. Also, Bartlett, *Yellowstone*, 130-131; and Mary Shivers Culpin, *"For the Benefit and Enjoyment of the People": A History of Concession Development in Yellowstone National Park, 1872-1966* (National Park Service: Yellowstone Center for Resources, 2003), chap. 2, 12.

6. Thomas Hassard to Henry M. Teller, 9 May 1883, "1883 Documents," 5.

7. C. T. Hobart to Henry M. Teller, 15 May 1883, "1883 Documents." Also, Henry M. Teller to C. T. Hobart, 9 May 1883, "1883 Documents," 6.

8. Henry M. Teller to William Hale, 25 May 1883, "1883 Documents," 34. The response was from E. S. N. Morgan, secretary and acting governor, to Teller, 4 June 1883, "1883 Documents," 7.

9. Hale responded to Teller (July 31, 1883), enclosing a series of letters among Wyoming officials, concluding C. D. Clark to E. S. N. Morgan (July 25, 1883), "1883 Documents," 13-14.

10. C. T. Hobart to Henry M. Teller, 28 May 1883, "1883 Documents," 7.

11. M. L. Joslyn to Robert T. Lincoln, 7 June 1883. Robert T. Lincoln to Henry M. Teller, 19 June 1883, "1883 Documents," 7, 34.

12. John G. Parke to Robert T. Lincoln, 15 June 1883, "1883 Documents," 8.

13. Henry M. Teller to Patrick H. Conger, 14 July 1883, "1883 Documents," 35.

14. C. T. Hobart to Henry M. Teller, 13 July 1883, "1883 Documents," 10-11.

15. Rufus Hatch to Henry M. Teller, 16 July 1883, "1883 Documents," 11-12. On July 17, the letter from Teller to Hatch approved the rate schedule ("1883 Documents," 36).

A "Perfectly Safe" Presidential Expedition

1. Philip Sheridan to George G. Vest, 31 January 1883, container 42, letter books 1871-1888, Sheridan papers, Library of Congress, 7 May 1881-October 1883.

2. Thomas C. Reeves, *Gentleman Boss: The Life of Chester Alan Arthur* (New York: Knopf, 1975), 317-18; George F. Howe, *Chester A. Arthur: A Quarter-Century of Machine Politics* (New York: Frederick Ungar Publishing Company, 1935), 243-46.

3. Philip H. Sheridan to George G. Vest, 9 April 1883, container 42, Sheridan papers.

4. Ibid., 4.

5. The U.S. Senate, on March 2, 1883, appointed the Select Committee "to examine into the conditions of the Sioux and Crow Indians, to examine the feasibility and propriety of proposed reductions in the Sioux Reservation, and to examine grievances of Indian tribes in the territory of Montana." Senator Henry L. Dawes of Massachusetts was named chairman, and Vest was assigned to the committee.

6. Philip H. Sheridan to George G. Vest, 9 April 1883, 4.

7. This was the route scouted on the Sheridan expedition of 1882 by Captain Kellogg.

8. Sheridan did not say in the letter that the total journey from the train stop in Wyoming would cover about five hundred miles, more than 360 on horseback.

9. Philip H. Sheridan to F. J. Phillips, 14 June 1883, Sheridan papers, 1-6, container 42.

10. Ibid., 4.

11. President Arthur chose not to take a personal secretary on the expedition. There were occasional newspaper references to a servant, but nothing was ever found in official accounts. Phillips is mentioned as being with the president at a stop in Louisville, Kentucky, before the expedition left Chicago. He is not mentioned in any accounts after that.

12. Some published accounts said Logan did not go on the expedition because of poor health or that he wanted to avoid uncomfortable political comparisons with the president. Logan had aspirations for the Republican presidential nomination in 1884.

13. Anson Stager served in the Civil War as general superintendent of government telegraphs in all departments. He was brevetted brigadier general of volunteers. He returned to Chicago and resumed a career with Western Union and later became president of Western Edison Electric Light Company in the city. Stager made the 1882 Sheridan excursion.

14. Chittenden, *Yellowstone National Park*, 105-06.

15. Memorandum, 1927, E. A. Brown, USA, War Department, the Adjutant General's Office, as cited in Jack Ellis Haynes, "The Expedition of President Chester A. Arthur to Yellowstone National Park in 1883," *Annals of Wyoming* 14, no. 1 (January 1942): 34. Colonel Brown responded to a request from Haynes for any details of the military aspects of the expedition. Brown wrote, "The information afforded by the records of the War Department on this expedition is very meager." Copy also received by author from F. Jay Haynes Records, Montana Historical Society manuscript collection.

16. Lt. Col. Michael Sheridan to Capt. Edward M. Hayes, Fifth Cavalry, Fort Washakie, Wyoming Territory, 6 July 1883, Sheridan papers, Library of Congress. Correspondence signed by aides and clerks (September 15, 1881 to October 19, 1884, container 47).

17. Thomas C. Reeves, "President Arthur in Yellowstone National Park," *Montana the Magazine of Western History* 19, no. 3 (1969): 23.

18. Michael Sheridan to J. K. Moore, 6 July 1883, Sheridan papers, container 47.

19. Michael Sheridan to J. H. Lord, 6 July 1883, Sheridan papers, container 47.

20. Philip H. Sheridan to Robert T. Lincoln, telegram, 27 July 1883, Sheridan papers, Library of Congress; Also, field dispatches and telegrams, 1862-1883, container 59.

21. Michael Sheridan to J. T. Wheelan, 6 July 1883, Sheridan papers, container 47.

22. "Arthur's Visit," *Cheyenne Daily Leader*, July 24, 1883.

23. Bartlett, *Yellowstone*, 46.

24. "Seeing the Yellowstone Park," *Forest and Stream*, July 26, 1883, xx, 501-02.

25. As far as can be ascertained, President Arthur made no public statements in support of Sheridan's park-expansion proposal. If he attempted to influence Congress in consideration of Vest's 1884 bill on the subject, there is nothing in the public record.

The Presidential Journey

1. President Arthur was delayed a day when Postmaster General Walter Q. Gresham was detained for a funeral. When asked about his schedule in Chicago, Arthur said, "Everything is in the hands of General Sheridan." "Washington: President Arthur to Start on His Western Tour This Morning," *Chicago Tribune*, July 30, 1883.

2. Ibid.

3. *Wikipedia*, s.v. "Southern Exposition," *http://en.wikipedia.org/wiki/Southern_Exposition* (accessed October 26, 2006).

4. "President Arthur: Enthusiastically Received by Thousands—A Banquet and Reception," *Chicago Daily News*, August 1, 1883.

5. "The Exposition Opened," *Chicago Daily News* (evening edition), August 1, 1883.

6. The principal city papers of the day—*Chicago Tribune*, *Chicago Daily News*, and *Chicago Times*—sent reporters to Louisville.

7. "From Louisville: The Trip as a 'Tribune' Reporter Found It," *Chicago Tribune*, August 3, 1883.

8. "President Arthur," *Chicago Times*, August 1, 1883.

9. "En Route to Chicago," *Chicago Times*, August 3, 1883.

10. "The President: He Arrives in Chicago After a Rapid Run from Louisville," *Chicago Tribune*, August 3, 1883. Also, "Hail to the Chief!", *Chicago Times*, August 3, 1883.

11. "There Were Reporters," *Chicago Tribune*, August 3, 1883.

12. "A Chat with Chet," *Chicago Tribune*, August 3, 1883.

13. "Logan and Arthur," *Chicago Tribune*, August 3, 1883.

14. "A Chat with Chet," *Chicago Tribune*, August 3, 1883.

15. "Secretary Lincoln," *Chicago Tribune*, August 3, 1883.

16. "The President: He Arose, Breakfasted, and Received Federal and Other Officials," *Chicago Tribune*, August 4, 1883.

17. "The President," *Chicago Times*, August 4, 1883.

18. "At the Depot," *Chicago Tribune*, August 4, 1883.

19. "Come and Gone," *Chicago Daily News*, August 3, 1883; also, *Chicago Tribune*, August 4, 1883.

20. "The Great Mistake: One of the Most Distinguished Guests Mistaken for a 'Tribune' Reporter and Fired Out of the Commissary Car," *Chicago Tribune*, August 4, 1883, 1.

21. "At Clinton," *Chicago Times*, August 4, 1883.

22. "Sterling," *Chicago Tribune*, August 4, 1883.

23. "Welcome the Coming, Speed the Parting, Guest," *Chicago Tribune*, August 3, 1883.

24. "Local Comment and Criticism," *Chicago Times*, August 4, 1883.

25. Ibid.

26. Jack Ellis Haynes, "The Expedition of President Chester A. Arthur to Yellowstone National Park in 1883," *Annals of Wyoming* 14, no. 1 (January 1942): 32. Haynes quotes from the diary of his father, F. Jay Haynes, showing the miles covered from Rawlins to Fort Washakie and a description of the "outfit."

27. Tilden, *Following the Frontier*, 126-27.

28. Stephen E. Ambrose, *Nothing Like It in the World: The Men Who Built the Transcontinental Railroad, 1863-1869* (New York: Simon and Schuster, 2000), 17.

29. Merrill J. Mattes, *The Great Platte River Road: The Covered Wagon Mainline via Fort Kearny to Fort Laramie* (Lincoln: Nebraska State Historical Society, 1969), 3-21. Mattes describes historical events along the trail in Nebraska and Wyoming. Also, David Dary, *The Oregon Trail: An American Saga* (New York: Knopf, 2005), 44-81.

30. "Arthur in Cheyenne," *Daily Ledger*, August 5, 1883. This article provides an account of the brief stop by the Arthur party.

31. Vest offered one of the few political comments recorded by a newspaper on the entire expedition.

32. Tilden's *Following the Frontier* (122-24) provides background on Nye as well as an account of his appearance in Green River. Also, *Wikipedia*, s.v. "Edgar Wilson Nye," *http://en.wikipedia.org/wiki/Edgar_Wilson_Nye*.

33. All official reports sent to the Associated Press by Lieutenant Colonel Sheridan, or his helpers, from the expedition are taken from *Journey Through the Yellowstone National Park and Northwestern Wyoming. Photographs of Party and Scenery Along the Route Traveled and Copies of the Associated Press Dispatches Sent Whilst En Route* (Washington: Government Printing Office, 1883). This was published after the expedition, with just twelve copies made for special guests on the expedition by F. Jay Haynes, photographer. The book contained 105 photographs of the expedition and copies of the official Associated Press dispatches (hereafter cited as "AP Dispatch"). The copy consulted by the author is in the Robert T. Lincoln collection at the Abraham Lincoln Presidential Library, Springfield, Illinois. In a letter dated January 28, 1884, Secretary of War Lincoln thanked Haynes for the portfolio. He wrote, "I must say that I never saw such fine photographs, and they are all the more remarkable in being taken under the difficulties which you must have encountered." F. Jay Haynes Records, Montana Historical Society manuscript collection.

34. "Arthur at Green River," *Cheyenne Daily Leader*, August 7, 1883.

35. Tilden, *Following the Frontier*, 124.

36. As is the case today with dispatches from the Associated Press, member newspapers are under few restrictions when it comes to using the material. It can be used on the day it was received or can kept and used later. It can be combined with other AP material or with information gained by staff writers. It can be ignored and never used. It can be garbled and fouled by typographical errors. All of those conditions existed with AP dispatches from the expedition, and it is the reason why the original dispatches are the primary source of information for this narrative. The citations used will reference the day and dateline of the dispatch to minimize confusion.

37. AP Dispatch, Fort Washakie, Wyoming, August 7, 1883.

38. Gregory M. Franzwa, *The Oregon Trail Revisited* (Tucson: Patrice Press, 1997), 221-290.

39. Irene D. Paden, *The Wake of the Prairie Schooner* (New York: Macmillan Company, 1943), 207.

40. *Chicago Times*, September 5, 1883. Although most officials on the trip denied the existence of newspaper reporters near the expedition, Anson Stager confirmed one of reports when he arrived in Chicago at the end of the journey.

41. A. G. Clayton, "A Brief History of the Washakie National Forest and Some Experiences of a Ranger," *Annals of Wyoming* 4, no. 2 (October 1926): 279-280. Also, John C. Thompson, "In Old Wyoming," *Wyoming State Journal*, May 1943, 4-7.

42. Robert Stuart, *The Discovery of the Oregon Trail: Robert Stuart's Narratives of His Overland Trip Eastward from Astoria in 1812-1813*, ed. Philip Ashton Rollins (New York: Charles Scribner's Sons, 1935), 150-206; and Laton McCartney, *Across the Great Divide: Robert Stuart and the Discovery of the Oregon Trail* (New York: Free Press, 2003), 217-25.

43. AP Dispatch, Fort Washakie, August 7, 1883.

44. AP Dispatch, Camp Rollins, Wyoming, via Fort Washakie, Wyoming Territory, August 9.

45. Peter M. Wright, "Washakie," *American Indian Leaders: Studies in Diversity* (Lincoln: University of Nebraska Press, 1980), 147-48.

46. Prucha, *Documents of U.S. Indian Policy*, 170-73. The General Allotment Act, also known as the Dawes General Allotment Act, passed Congress on February 8, 1887 and was named for Sen. Henry L. Dawes of Massachusetts.

47. AP Dispatch, Camp Rollins.

48. Tilden, *Following the Frontier*, 119. Haynes was permitted to photograph the catch by Arthur, but he was not allowed to take pictures of him fishing.

49. Publications after the trip quoted English visitors to the park as shocked at Arthur's relaxed dress.

50. AP Dispatch, Camp Vest on Spring Creek, via Fort Washakie, Wyoming Territory, August 10.

51. "The President," *Chicago Tribune*, August 10, 1883.

52. At Fort Washakie, there were many opportunities for a reporter to pick up rumors and tidbits of information—some reliable, others not.

53. AP Dispatch, Camp Crosby on Dinwiddie Creek, Wyoming, August 11, via Fort Washakie, Wyoming, August 12.

54. Sheridan's order was consistent with those he issued on the 1881 and 1882 expeditions.

55. AP Dispatch, Camp Stager on Torrey's Lake, Wyoming Territory, August 12. The report mentioned Torrey's ownership of a cattle ranch in the vicinity.

56. George G. Vest, "Notes of the Yellowstone Trip," *Forest and Stream* 21, November 8, 1883, 282.

57. AP Dispatch, Camp Bishop, Forks of the Wind River, Wyoming, August 14, via Fort Washakie, Wyoming, August 15.

58. Jack Ellis Haynes, "Journey," 35.

59. "The President: The Party Makes a Two Days' Halt for Rest and Recuperation," *Chicago Times*, August 16, 1883.

60. In Chicago after the expedition, Stager confirmed part of this story to a *Times* reporter.

61. AP Dispatch, Camp Robert Lincoln, Wyoming, August 15, via Fort Washakie, August 16.

62. Lou Yost, telephone conversation with author, February 12, 1999; and Jody Hopkins, telephone conversation with author, February 14, 1999. At the request of the author, Lou Yost of the U.S. Geological Survey, Reston, Virginia and Jody Hopkins of the Wyoming Board of Geographic Names looked for evidence that the pass ever officially was named Lincoln Pass. They were unable to document any name other than Sheridan Pass. They concluded that in spite of the pass being named for Lincoln in 1882 or 1883, there never was any follow-through by federal officials.

63. In "Journey" by Jack Ellis Haynes, an article by Daniel W. Greenburg in *Midwest Review* 7, (June 1926) no. 6, is quoted: "The party followed the Wind River nearly to its source . . . and then commenced the ascent over what is known as [the] Sheridan Trail . . . . It was thought then to be the shortest route between the valleys of the Wind and the Snake. They camped at what is now locally known as Sheridan Pass; however, the camp was named 'Camp Robert Lincoln,' and the pass was named by President Arthur as 'Robert Lincoln Pass,' and the name should have been retained, but probably was never officially announced."

64. AP Dispatch, Camp Logan, Lewis Lake, August 23, via Livingston, August 25. Lieutenant Colonel Sheridan wrote this passage several days after actually crossing the pass.

65. Clayton, "Brief History," 289-293.

66. AP Dispatch, Camp Isham, Gros Ventre River, Wyoming, August 16, via Fort Washakie, Wyoming, August 18.

67. "The President: A Day's Incidents," *Chicago Times*, August 19, 1883.

68. AP Dispatch, Gros Ventre River, Wyoming, August 18, via Fort Washakie, Wyoming, August 19.

69. *Wikipedia*, s.v. "Gros Ventre Landslide," http://en.wikipedia.org/wiki/Gros_Ventre_landslide; and Wyoming Tales and Trails, information on the Grand Tetons and the Gros Ventre Landslide, http://www.wyomingtalesandtrails.com/tetons3.html. Also, *Wyoming: A Guide to Its History, Highways, and People*, American Guide Series (New York: Oxford University Press, 1941), 344.

70. AP Dispatch, Camp Teton, August 18, via Fort Washakie, Wyoming, August 20.

71. AP Dispatch, Camp Hampton on Snake River, August 20, via Fort Washakie, August 23.

72. "President: A Day's Incidents," *Chicago Times*, August 19, 1883.

73. AP Dispatch, Camp Hampton.

74. Haynes, "Journey," 37.

75. AP Dispatch, Camp Strong, Wyoming, August 21, via Bozeman, Montana, August 22. With this report, the courier system changed from Fort Washakie to Fort Ellis, Montana.

76. AP Dispatch, Camp Logan, Lewis Lake, August 23, via Livingston, August 25.

Inside the Park, At Last

1. AP Dispatch, Camp Logan.

2. *Congressional Record*, U.S. Senate, 47th Cong., 2nd sess., 1883, 3484. A footnote in history: The first person to enter the park that later became president was Benjamin Harrison—who, as a U.S. senator, visited Yellowstone in 1881. He was elected president in 1888.

3. Haynes, "Journey," 37.

4. AP Dispatch, Upper Geyser Basin, Yellowstone National Park, August 24, via Livingston, Montana, August 26.

5. "Kidnapping the President," *Wood River Times*, August 24, 1883. Reprinted in *Cheyenne Daily Leader*, August 26, 1883.

6. AP Dispatch, Yellowstone Lake, August 26, via Livingston, Montana, August 28.

7. AP Dispatch, Camp Campbell, Foot of Yellowstone Lake, Wyoming, August 27.

8. AP Dispatch, Camp Allison, Yellowstone Falls, August 28, via Livingston, Montana, August 30.

9. Haynes, "Journey," 37.

10. Press reports referred to in the official communiqué obviously had become more than a passing irritant. This must be considered the official pronouncement, given that Arthur and Sheridan approved all dispatches before being sent.

11. Bartlett, *Yellowstone*, 47.

12. AP Dispatch, Camp Cameron, Baronett's Bridge, via Livingston, Montana, August 31.

13. AP Dispatch, Mammoth Hot Springs, Wyoming, via Billings, Montana, September 1.

14. George Thomas, "My Recollections of the Yellowstone Park," document 19, Yellowstone National Park Reference Library, quoted in Aubrey L. Haines, *The Yellowstone Story: A History of Our First National Park*, vol. 1, (Boulder: Colorado Associated University Press, 1977), 281.

15. William Hardman, *A Trip to America* (London: T. Vickers Wood, 1884), 173-175.

16. AP Dispatch, Billings, Montana, September 1.

17. "The President: The Distinguished Party Arrives in Chicago Much Fatigued from the Long Trip," *Chicago Times*, September 5, 1883; "The Arrival," *Chicago Tribune*, September 5, 1883; "The President Arrives," *Chicago Daily News* (evening issue), September 4, 1883. All papers gave extensive coverage to the welcoming committee and arrival.

18. "The President Arrives," *Chicago Daily News.*

19. "The President," *Chicago Times.*

20. Ibid.

21. "Talks with the Pilgrims," *Chicago Times*, September 5, 1883.

22. "The President's Return," *Chicago Daily News*, September 4, 1883.

23. "Col. M. Sheridan Talks," *Chicago Daily News*, September 5, 1883.

24. "Secretary Lincoln's Say," *Chicago Daily News*, September 5, 1883.

25. "Secretary Lincoln," *Chicago Tribune*, September 6 1883.

26. "Hard-Hearted Committee," *Chicago Times*, September 6 1883.

27. Philip H. Sheridan to Robert T. Lincoln, 12 September 1883, Sheridan papers, container 47.

28. Philip H. Sheridan to O. O. Howard, 21 September 1883, Sheridan papers, container 47.

An Abundance of Chaos

1. John M. Hartman to Henry M. Teller, 20 August 1883, "1883 Documents."

2. E. S. Reddington to Chester A. Arthur, forwarded to Henry M. Teller, 14 September 1883, "1883 Documents."

3. "Hatch's Show," *Chicago Times*, August 15, 1883.

4. "The President," *Chicago Tribune*, August 21, 1883.

5. "The President: Uncle Rufus Interviewed—He Makes Some Startling Political Disclosures," *Chicago Tribune*, August 27, 1883.

6. W. Scott Smith to Henry M. Teller, report, 15 October 1883, in "1883 Documents," 16-18.

7. Henry M. Teller to H. B. Strait, 20 December 1883, in "1883 Documents," 41. Two were from New York, two from Iowa, and one each from Indiana, Maryland, New Mexico, Minnesota, Illinois, Pennsylvania, and Kansas. Originally, eleven were hired, but one was dismissed before the end of 1883.

8. Henry M. Teller to Patrick H. Conger, 23 October 1883, in "1883 Documents," 38-39.

9. Patrick H. Conger to Henry M. Teller, 4 November 1883, in "1883 Documents," 21-22.

10. Patrick H. Conger to William Chambers, 30 June 1883, in "1883 Documents," 22. Chambers was dismissed by December 20. Henry M. Teller to H. B. Strait, 20 December 1883, in "1883 Documents." The list of superintendents from Teller shows Chambers as "dismissed."

11. Patrick H. Conger to Henry M. Teller, 6 November 1883, "1883 Documents," 23. The letter was confidential.

12. Henry M. Teller to Patrick H. Conger, 12 November 1883, in "1883 Documents," 40.

13. Patrick H. Conger to Henry M. Teller, 27 November 1883, in "1883 Documents," 25.

14. C. T. Hobart to Henry M. Teller, 30 November 1883, in "1883 Documents," 1-3. Papers omitted from first release.

15. C. T. Hobart to Henry M. Teller, 21 December 1883; Patrick H. Conger to C. T. Hobart, 25 November 1883; C. T. Hobart to Patrick H. Conger, 27 November 1883; Patrick H. Conger to C. T. Hobart, 28 November 1883, "1883 Documents," 32-33. These referred Hobart to Teller for explanation.

16. "The Yellowstone Park," *Forest and Stream*, December 20, 1883, xxi, 401-02.

17. Rufus Hatch to Henry M. Teller, annual report, 1 December 1883, in "1883 Documents," 26.

18. "Death of Rufus Hatch," *New York Times*, February 24, 1893.

19. Culpin, *Benefit and Enjoyment of the People*, 25-26.

The End of Noble Deeds

1. "Yellowstone Park Matters," *Forest and Stream*, January 17, 1884, xxii, 493.

2. "Game and Forests in the Park," *Forest and Stream*, January 17, 1884, 494. In written communication with the author, Lee H. Whittlesey, park historian, says G. L. Henderson was probably Ichthus. Lee H. Whittlesey, *Storytelling in Yellowstone: Horse and Buggy Tour Guides* (Albuquerque: University of New Mexico Press, 2007).

3. Arnold Hague to George G. Vest, 28 December 1883. Printed as an article in *Forest and Stream*, 13 March 1884, xxi, 125.

4. *Congressional Record*, "The Yellowstone Park," U.S. Senate, 48th Cong., 1st sess., 1884, 1580-81, S. 221, as reported to the floor from the Committee on Territories; also, "The Yellowstone Park Bill," *Forest and Stream*, March 13, 1884, 124-25. The magazine printed the bill in full.

5. George G. Vest, U.S. Senate, S. 221, 3 March 1884, 1581.

6. Vest, U.S. Senate, S. 221, 4 March 1884, 1610.

7. Ibid., 1612.

8. George G. Vest and John J. Ingalls, U.S. Senate, S. 221, 4 March 1884, 1610-12.

9. Vest, 1610-11.

10. Henry L. Dawes, S. 221, 4 March 1884, 1611-12.

11. Vest, U.S. Senate, S. 221, 4 March 1884, 1610.

12. "Yellowstone Park Matters," *Forest and Stream*, March 13, 1884, xxii, 121.

13. *Congressional Record*, "Yellowstone Park," U.S. House, 48th Cong., 2nd sess., 1885, 1640.

14. J. Warren Keifer, U.S. House, S. 221, 13 February 1885, 1641.

15. *Congressional Record*, U.S. House, 48th Congress, 2nd Session, 1884, 1751.

16. Culpin, *Benefit and Enjoyment of the People*, chap. 2, 26.

17. Ibid., 25.

18. Ibid.

19. Ibid., 26.

20. Henry M. Teller to Patrick H. Conger, 12 July 1884, microfilm copy, no. 62, roll 2, National Archives, Yellowstone National Park.

21. "Yellowstone Park Matters," March 13, 1884, 121.

22. Hampton, *U.S. Cavalry*, chap. 4, 29.

23. "Yellowstone History: Law and Justice Come to Yellowstone," *Yellowstone Net Newspaper*, 14 November 1997, 2.

24. Hampton, *U.S. Cavalry*, chap. 4, 73.

25. Ibid., 80.

26. Bartlett, *Yellowstone*, 257.

Bibliography

Manuscript Sources

Correspondence of 1883. Philip H. Sheridan Papers. Library of Congress.

F. Jay Haynes Letters, 1883-1884. Montana Historical Society, Helena, Montana.

George Washington Marshall. Wyoming Dictations, 1885. Bancroft Library. Berkeley California.

Robert Todd Lincoln Collection. Abraham Lincoln Presidential Library and Museum, Springfield, Illinois.

Books

Ambrose, Stephen E. *Nothing Like It in the World: The Men Who Built the Transcontinental Railroad, 1863-1869.* New York: Simon and Schuster, 2000.

Athearn, Robert G. *Union Pacific Country.* Chicago: Rand McNally, 1971.

Baldwin, Kenneth H. *Enchanted Enclosure: The Army Engineers and Yellowstone National Park.* Washington: Office of the Chief of Engineers, U.S. Army, 1976. See "II: Terra Incognita: The Raynolds Expedition of 1860." "III: Through the Great Geyser Basin: The Barlow Expedition of 1871." "IV: Two-Ocean Water and Togwotee Pass: The Jones Expedition of 1873."

Barringer, Mark Daniel. *Selling Yellowstone: Capitalism and the Construction of Nature.* Lawrence: University Press of Kansas, 2002.

Bartlett, Richard A. *Great Surveys of the American West*. Norman: University of Oklahoma Press, 1962.

—. *Nature's Yellowstone: The Story of an American Wilderness That Became Yellowstone National Park in 1872*. Albuquerque: University of New Mexico Press, 1974.

—. *Yellowstone: A Wilderness Besieged*. Tucson: University of Arizona Press, 1985.

Bonney, Orrin H., and Lorraine Bonney. *Battle Drums and Geysers: The Life and Journals of Lt. Gustavus Cheyney Doane, Soldier and Explorer of the Yellowstone and Snake River Regions*. Chicago: Swallow Press, Inc., 1970.

Chittenden, Hiram Martin. *The Yellowstone National Park*. 4th ed. Cincinnati: The Robert Clarke Company, 1903.

Cook, Charles W., David E. Folsom, and William Peterson. *The Valley of the Upper Yellowstone: An Exploration of the Headwaters of the Yellowstone River in the Year 1869*. Edited and with an introduction by Aubrey L. Haines. Norman: University of Oklahoma Press, 1965.

Coutant, C. G. *History of Wyoming (The Far West)*. 2 vols. 1899. Reprint, New York: Argonaut Press Ltd., 1966.

Crook, George. *General George Crook: His Autobiography*. Edited by Martin F. Schmitt. Norman: University of Oklahoma Press, 1960.

Culpin, Mary Shivers. *"For the Benefit and Enjoyment of the People": A History of Concession Development in Yellowstone National Park, 1872-1996*. Yellowstone Center for Resources: National Park Service, 2003.

Dary, David. *The Oregon Trail: An American Saga*. New York: Knopf, 2005.

Edmunds, R. David, ed. *American Indian Leaders: Studies in Diversity*. Lincoln: University of Nebraska Press, 1980.

Ferris, Angus. *Life in the Rocky Mountains: Diary of Wanderings on the Sources of the Rivers Missouri, Columbia, and Colorado 1830-1835*. Edited by LeRoy Hafen. Denver: Old West Publishing Company, 1983.

Foster, Mike. *Strange Genius: The Life of Ferdinand Vandeveer Hayden*. Niwot, CO: Roberts, Rinehart Publishers, 1994.

Franzwa, Gregory M. *The Oregon Trail Revisited.* Tucson: The Patrice Press, 1997.

Frey, Robert L., and Lorenz P. Schrenk. *The Northern Pacific Railway: Supersteam Era, 1925-1945.* San Marino, CA: Golden West Books, 1985.

Goff, John S. *Robert Todd Lincoln: A Man in His Own Right.* Norman: University of Oklahoma Press, 1969.

Haines, Aubrey L. *Yellowstone National Park: Its Exploration and Establishment.* Washington: U.S. Department of the Interior, National Park Service, 1974.

—. *The Yellowstone Story: A History of Our First National Park.* 2 vols. Boulder: Colorado Associated University Press, 1977.

Hampton, H. Duane. *How the U.S. Cavalry Saved Our National Parks.* Bloomington: Indiana University Press, 1971.

Harris, Burton. *John Colter: His Years in the Rockies.* New York: Charles Scribner's Sons, 1952.

Hayden, Elizabeth Wied. *From Trapper to Tourist in Jackson Hole.* Moose, WY: Grand Teton Natural History Association, 1981.

Hayden, Ferdinand V. *The Yellowstone National Park, and the Mountain Regions of Portions of Idaho, Nevada, Colorado and Utah.* Boston: L. Prang and Company, 1876. Reprint Tulsa, OK: Thomas Gilcrease Museum Association, 1997.

Howe, George Frederick. *Chester A. Arthur: A Quarter-Century of Machine Politics.* New York: Frederick Ungar Publishing Company, 1935.

Hutton, Paul Andrew. *Phil Sheridan and His Army.* Norman: University of Oklahoma Press, 1999.

Jackson, Donald. *Custer's Gold: The United States Cavalry Expedition of 1874.* New Haven: Yale University Press, 1966.

Jones, James Pickett. *John A. Logan: Stalwart Republican from Illinois.* Tallahassee: University Presses of Florida, 1982.

Langford, Nathaniel Pitt. *The Discovery of Yellowstone Park: Journal of the Washburn Expedition to the Yellowstone and Firehole Rivers in the Year 1870,* with a foreword by Aubrey L. Haines. Lincoln: University of Nebraska Press, 1972.

Leech, Margaret, and Harry J. Brown. *The Garfield Orbit: The Life of President James A. Garfield.* New York: Harper and Row, 1978.

MacGregor, Greg. *Overland: The California Emigrant Trail of 1841-1870.* Albuquerque: University of New Mexico Press, 1996.

Magoc, Chris J. *Yellowstone: The Creation and Selling of an American Landscape, 1870-1903.* Albuquerque: University of New Mexico Press, 1999.

Mardock, Robert Winston. *The Reformers and the American Indian.* Columbia: University of Missouri Press, 1971.

Mattes, Merrill J. *The Great Platte River Road: The Covered Wagon Mainline via Fort Kearny to Fort Laramie.* Lincoln: Nebraska State Historical Society, 1969.

McCartney, Laton. *Across the Great Divide: Robert Stuart and the Discovery of the Oregon Trail.* New York: Free Press, 2003.

Merrill, Marlene Deahl, ed. *Yellowstone and the Great West: Journals, Letters, and Images from the 1871 Hayden Expedition.* Lincoln: University of Nebraska Press, 1999.

Morgan, Dale. *Rand McNally's Pioneer Atlas of the American West.* Chicago: Rand McNally and Company, 1969.

Moulton, Gary E., ed. *The Journals of the Lewis and Clark Expedition.* Vol. 1, *Atlas of the Lewis and Clark Expedition.* Vol. 2, *August 30, 1803-August 24, 1804.* Vol. 8, *June 10-September 26, 1806.* Lincoln: University of Nebraska Press, 1983, 1986, and 1993.

Paden, Irene D. *The Wake of the Prairie Schooner.* New York: The Macmillan Company, 1943.

Prucha, Francis P. *American Indian Policy in Crisis: Christian Reformers and the Indian, 1865-1900.* Norman: University of Oklahoma Press, 1976.

—, ed. *Documents of United States Indian Policy.* Lincoln: University of Nebraska Press, 2000.

Reeves, Thomas C. *Gentleman Boss: The Life of Chester Alan Arthur.* New York: Knopf, 1975.

Reiger, John F., ed. *The Passing of the Great West: Selected Papers of George Bird Grinnell*. New York: Winchester Press, 1972.

Russell, Osborne. *Journal of a Trapper: A Hunter's Rambles Among the Wilds of the Rocky Mountains, 1834-43*. Edited by Aubrey L. Haines. New York: MJF Books, n.d.

Saylor, David J. *Jackson Hole, Wyoming: In the Shadow of the Tetons*. Norman: University of Oklahoma Press, 1971.

Schullery, Paul. *Searching for Yellowstone: Ecology and Wonder in the Last Wilderness*. Boston: Houghton Mifflin Company, 1997.

Schullery, Paul, and Lee H. Whittlesey. *Myth and History in the Creation of Yellowstone National Park*. Lincoln: University of Nebraska Press, 2003.

Scott, Kim Allen. *Yellowstone Denied: The Life of Gustavus Cheyney Doane*. Norman: University of Oklahoma Press, 2007.

Smith, Duane A. *Henry M. Teller: Colorado's Grand Old Man*. Boulder: University Press of Colorado, 2002.

Strong, William E. *A Trip to the Yellowstone National Park in July, August, and September, 1875*, with an introduction by Richard A. Bartlett. Norman: University of Oklahoma Press, 1968.

Stuart, Robert. *The Discovery of the Oregon Trail: Robert Stuart's Narratives of His Overland Trip Eastward from Astoria in 1812-1813*. Edited by Philip Ashton Rollins. New York: Charles Scribner's Sons, 1935.

Tilden, Freeman. *Following the Frontier with F. Jay Haynes, Pioneer Photographer of the Old West*. New York: Knopf, 1964.

Walker, Paul K. Introduction to *Exploring Nature's Sanctuary: Captain William Ludlow's Report of a Reconnaissance from Carroll, Montana Territory, on the Upper Missouri, to the Yellowstone National Park, and Return, Made in the Summer of 1875*, by William Ludlow. Washington DC: Historical Division, Office of Administrative Services, Office of the Chief of Engineers, 1985.

White, David, comp. *News of the Plains and Rockies, 1803-1865*. Vol. 5, *Later Explorers, 1847-1865*. Spokane: Arthur H. Clark Company, 1998.

Whittlesey, Lee H. *Storytelling in Yellowstone: Horse and Buggy Tour Guides*. Albuquerque: University of New Mexico Press, 2007.

—. *Yellowstone Place Names*. Helena: Montana Historical Society Press, 1988.

Articles, Newspapers, Miscellany

Cactus Hill. "Yellowstone National Park: History." http://cactushill.com/travels/West/YNP_history.htm.

Clayton, A. G. "A Brief History of the Washakie National Forest and Some Experiences of a Ranger." *Annals of Wyoming* 4, no. 2 (October 1926): 277-295.

Grinnell, George Bird, ed. *Forest and Stream*. Articles from 1883 and 1884 issues.

Hartley, Robert E. "A Touch of Illinois on a Presidential Trek to Yellowstone National Park in 1883." Presented in Oct. 1999 at history conference of the Illinois Historic Preservation Agency, Springfield, Illinois. Also, *Bulletin of the Illinois Geographical Society*, Illinois State University, Spring 2000, 38-57.

Hayden, Ferdinand V. *Preliminary Report of the United States Geological Survey of Wyoming and Contiguous Territories, Conducted Under the Authority of the Secretary of the Interior*. Washington: Government Printing Office, 1871.

Haynes, Jack Ellis. "The Expedition of President Chester A. Arthur to Yellowstone National Park in 1883." *Annals of Wyoming* 14, no. 1 (January 1942): 31-38.

Hutton, Paul A. "Phil Sheridan's Crusade for Yellowstone." *American History Illustrated* 19, no. 10 (February 1985): 10-15.

—. "Phil Sheridan's Pyrrhic Victory: The Piegan Massacre, Army Politics, and the Transfer Debate." *Montana the Magazine of Western History* 32, no. 2 (Spring 1982): 32-43.

Linecamp Web site. "Northern Pacific Railroad." http://www.linecamp.com/museums/americanwest/western_clubs/northern_pacific_railroad/northern_pacific_railroad.html.

Ludlow, William. "An Army Engineer's Journal of Custer's Black Hills Expedition, July 2, 1874-August 23, 1874." *Journal of the West*, no. 13 (January 1974): 78-84.

The Magic of Yellowstone Web site. "Congressional Acts Pertaining to Yellowstone." http://www.yellowstone-online.com/history/yhfour.html.

Morgan, Dale L., ed. "Washakie and the Shoshone." *Annals of Wyoming* 28, no. 2 (October 1956): 205.

National Park Service. "Collins Jack [John H.] Baronett." *http://www.cr.nps.gov/history/ online_books/haines1/iee4.htm#baronett.*

National Park Service. "Yellowstone History: Law and Justice Come to Yellowstone." Yellowstone Net Newspaper. http://www.yellowstone.net/newspaper/ news111497.htm.

Peters, Jackson. "The Northern Pacific Railway." Puget Sound Model Railroad Engineers. http://www.psmre.org/hist-np.htm.

Raynolds, William F. "The Report of Brevet Brigadier General W. F. Raynolds on the Exploration of the Yellowstone and the Country Drained by That River." 1868. S. Doc. 77.

Reeves, Thomas C. "President Arthur in Yellowstone National Park." *Montana the Magazine of Western History* 19, no. 3 (1969): 18-29.

Sheridan, Philip H. *Report, Dated September 20, 1881, of His Expedition through the Big Horn Mountains, Yellowstone National Parks, Etc., Together with Reports of Lieut. Col. J. F. Gregory, Surg. W. H. Forwood, and Capt. S. C. Kellogg.* Washington: Government Printing Office, 1882.

—. *Report of an Exploration of Parts of Wyoming, Idaho, and Montana in August and September, 1882, with Itinerary of James F. Gregory, and a Geological and Botanical Report by W. H. Forwood.* Washington: Government Printing Office, 1882.

Thomas, George. "My Recollections of the Yellowstone Park." Yellowstone National Park Reference Library.

Thompson, John C. "In Old Wyoming." *Wyoming State Journal*, May 1943, 4-7.

U.S. Department of the Interior. "Letter from the Secretary of the Interior" (transmitting copies of all papers and correspondence relating to the leasing of the Yellowstone National Park). 47th Cong., 2nd sess., 1883, S. Doc. 48. Microfilm, no. 62, rolls 1 and 2, National Archives, Yellowstone National Park.

U.S. Department of the Interior. "Letter from the Secretary of the Interior" (transmitting copies of all letters and communications relating to the Yellowstone National Park since last session of Congress). 48th Cong., 1st sess., 1884, S. Doc. 47. Microfilm, no. 62, rolls 1 and 2, National Archives, Yellowstone National Park.

U.S. Department of the Interior. "Letter from the Secretary of the Interior" (transmitting papers omitted from communication to the Senate on [9 Jan. 1884] and printed as S. Doc. 47, relating to Yellowstone National Park, part 2). 48th Cong., 1st sess., 1884. Microfilm, no. 62, rolls 1 and 2, National Archives, Yellowstone National Park.

U.S. Geological Survey. Map for Ashton, Idaho; Montana; Idaho (revised 1972; scale 1:250,000).

U.S. S. Rep. 66, "Report of a Reconnaissance of the Basin of the Upper Yellowstone in 1871." 42nd Cong., 2nd sess., Washington: Government Printing Office, 1871.

U.S. S. Rep. 911, Committee on Territories, 47th Cong., 2nd sess., Washington: Government Printing Office, January 5, 1883.

Virtual American Biographies. S.v. "Anson Stager." http://famousamericans. net/ansonstager/.

Weimer, J. W. "The National Park: A Visit in the National Playground, or the Wonderland of America." *Winfield Courier.* November 1, 1883.

—. "Wyoming Letter." *Winfield Courier.* September 20, 1883.

—. "Yellowstone National Park Trip Continued." *Winfield Courier.* February 7, 1884.

The Western Associated Press. Dispatches from the Arthur expedition en route, August and September 1883. "Journey through the Yellowstone National Park and Northwestern Wyoming 1883," photograph portfolio by F. Jay Haynes. Washington: Government Printing Office, 1883. From the Robert Todd Lincoln Collection, Abraham Lincoln Presidential Library, Springfield, IL.

Whittlesey, Lee H. "Marshall's Hotel in the National Park." *Montana the Magazine of Western History* 30, no. 4 (October 1980): 42-51.

Wikipedia. S.v. "Chicago and North Western Railway." http://en.wikipedia.org/wiki/ Chicago_and_North_Western_Railway.

Wikipedia. S.v. "Edgar Wilson Nye." http://en.wikipedia.org/wiki/Edgar_Wilson_Nye.

Wikipedia. S.v. "Northern Pacific Railway." *http://en.wikipedia.org/wiki/Northern_Pacific_Railway.*

Wikipedia. S.v. "Southern Exposition." *http://en.wikipedia.org/wiki/Southern_Exposition.*

Wiley, H. B. "Yellowstone Park in 1883." *Montana the Magazine of Western History* 3, no. 3 (Summer 1953): 8-18. Also credited to Abraham S. Wiley.

Wright, Peter M. "Washakie." *American Indian Leaders: Studies in Diversity.* Edited by R. David Edmunds. Lincoln: University of Nebraska Press, 1980.

Publications

Cheyenne Daily Leader

Chicago Daily News

Chicago Times

Chicago Tribune

Congressional Globe

Congressional Record

Dubois Frontier

Forest and Stream

New York Times

Scribner's Monthly

Winfield Courier

Wyoming State Journal

Index

Hatch, Rufus 53
Villard, Henry 144
Northern Pacific Railway. *See* Northern Pacific Railroad (NP)
North Absaroka Wilderness 152
North Platte 93, 97
Nye, Edgar Wilson "Bill" 95, 96

O

Odell, R. R. 45
Old Faithful 26, 27, 30, 36, 37, 41, 45, 47, 55, 58, 72, 121, 126
Oregon Trail 94, 97, 100
Owl Creek 102
Owl Creek Mountains 103

P

Parke, John G. 75
Parker, Ed 45
park appropriation 20, 21, 27, 52, 56, 65, 67, 68, 70, 146
Park Branch Line 35
park superintendent salary 19, 27, 38, 66, 67, 68, 70, 149
Payson, Lewis E. 154
Perham, Josiah 34
Peterson, William 14
Phillips, F. J. 80
Piegan Indian lands 24
Platte River 93, 97
Platte River Road 94
Pleasant Valley 127
Pomeroy, Samuel Clarke 18
Popo Agie River 100
  Big Popo Agie River 93
  Little Popo Agie River 100
Powder River 25
Promontory Point, UT 93
Pullman, George M. 87, 90

Q

Queen's Laundry Bath House 36, 39
Quincey, Charles L. 48

R

Rawlins, WY 29, 79, 80, 83, 93, 97
Raynolds, William F. 14
Reddington, E. S. 133
Reeves, Thomas C. 79
Rhodes, C. D. 28
Roberts, C. A. 48
Rockies. *See* Rocky Mountains
Rocky Mountains 96, 106, 108, 113
Rock Creek Station, WY 25
Rock Island and Pacific Railroad 29
Rollins, Daniel 81, 86, 91, 103, 107
Roosevelt, Theodore 152
Rosebud River 24
Rowland, R. H. 45
Russell, E. M. 44
Russell, Fort 94
Russell, Osborne 32, 33
Russell-Topping lease application 45, 52

S

Sackett, Delos B. 24, 28, 54, 55, 56, 125
Samuel, M. 48
Schurz, Carl 40, 44
Scribner's Monthly 16, 18
Secluded Valley 32
Sentinel Meadows 36
Shattock, J. H. 91
Sheep Mountain 114
Sheldon, E. N. 24
Shenandoah 23
Sheridan, Michael V. 78, 82, 83, 90, 91, 113, 114, 115, 125, 126, 127, 128, 131
  1881 expedition 24

T